D0113866

Praise for *The Democratic Enterprise*

"In Unilever, we are determined to foster an environment that provides everyone the opportunity and support to find and harness our natural swing – so we can all deliver outstanding results within a framework of shared values, goals, and purpose. I do not believe there is shortage of great talent. There is, however, a shortage of great environments and leaders who create such environments. It is therefore encouraging to find that we are not alone in this. Professor Lynda Gratton has captured, in a very profound way, the emerging realization of what truly matters in transforming businesses: people, purpose, and participation. In a word, democracy."

Nial FitzGerald, Chairman, Unilever

"From time to time, a new idea crops up in the world of business that most managers consider to be absurd but that ends up transforming companies. Zero defect was one such idea. The democratic enterprise is another. It is an aspirational quest but, as Lynda Gratton demonstrates in this marvellously written book, there is enough that corporate leaders and human resources specialists can do today to embrace the power of democratic processes to both raise the economic performance of their companies and build delightful organizations."

Sumantra Ghoshal, Professor of Strategy and International Management,
London Business School

"Lynda Gratton has crafted a new classic. The Democratic Enterprise draws on Greek and political traditions about democracy – demo (people) and kratos (rule) – and applies them to modern organizations. By defining employees as citizens and investors, Gratton identifies six tenants and three building blocks of the democratic and delightful organization. These ideas are conceptually interesting and actionable. They will help individuals figure out how to succeed in their role in the modern corporation; human resource professionals architect individual and organizational systems; and leaders engage employees and create organizations that win. It is a masterpiece that connects individuals and their organizations with rich theory and realistic action."

Dave Ulrich, Professor of Business, University of Michigan

The Democratic Enterprise

LIBERATING YOUR BUSINESS WITH FREEDOM, FLEXIBILITY AND COMMITMENT

Lynda Gratton

 Prentice Hall
FINANCIAL TIMES

An imprint of **Pearson Education**

London • New York • Toronto • Sydney • Tokyo • Singapore
Hong Kong • Cape Town • Madrid • Paris • Amsterdam • Munich • Milan

PEARSON EDUCATION LIMITED

Head Office
Edinburgh Gate
Harlow CM20 2JE
Tel: +44 (0)1279 623623
Fax: +44 (0)1279 431059
Website: www.pearsoned.co.uk

First published in Great Britain in 2004

ISBN 0 273 67528 1

British Library Cataloguing in Publication Data
A CIP catalogue record for this book can be obtained from the British Library

10 9 8 7 6 5 4 3 2

Typeset by Northern Phototypesetting Co Ltd, Bolton
Printed and bound in Great Britain by Biddles Ltd, Guildford & King's Lynn

The Publishers' policy is to use paper manufactured from sustainable forests.

About the author

Professor Lynda Gratton is Associate Professor of Organizational Behaviour at London Business School and a global authority on the people implications of strategy. At London Business School she directs the world-renowned executive programme 'Human Resource Strategy in Transforming Organizations and was a member of the board of the American Human Resource Planning Society. Between 1992 and 2000 she directed the Leading Edge Research Consortium in partnership with companies such as HP, Kraft Foods and Citibank. Reflections on these companies formed the framework of *Strategic Human Resource Management: Corporate Rhetoric and Human Reality* published by Oxford University Press in 1999.

Her ideas about human resource strategy have profoundly influenced managers all over the world. Her book *Living Strategy: putting people at the heart of corporate purpose* published by Financial Times Prentice Hall in 2000 has become a classic for HR professionals and an important part of the toolkit for line managers.

Over the last decade Dr Gratton has created a clear agenda for how organizations can become inspiring and meaningful. How each can become a 'democratic enterprise'.

Author's website: www.lyndagratton.com

For my mother and sons… Barbara, Christian and Dominic

Contents

THREE

DEMOCRACY AT WORK

FOUR

THE DRIVERS TO DEMOCRACY

FIVE

BUILDING INDIVIDUAL AUTONOMY

SIX

CRAFTING ORGANIZATIONAL VARIETY

SEVEN

SHAPING SHARED PURPOSE

EIGHT

LEADERS AND CITIZENS AT WORK

NINE

THE FIVE GOOD REASONS TO BECOME A DEMOCRATIC ENTERPRISE

Preface

'I am tempted to believe that what we call necessary institutions are often no more than institutions to which we have grown accustomed. In matters of social constitution, the field of possibilities is much more extensive than men living in their various societies are ready to imagine,' reflected Alexis de Tocqueville, one of the great observers and philosophers of nineteenth-century America.[1]

De Tocqueville could have been reflecting on contemporary organizations. We have become accustomed to how they are structured, managed and run, but many more possibilities exist. His words came back to me with resounding power when I talked to a senior manager in the telecoms company BT. 'Can you imagine in 15 years' time trying to explain to a child that every morning lots of people used to get onto a train, have an appalling journey, and then pour out the other end? And at the end of the day they would all get on the same train and do that everyday? Can you imagine how lame that's going to sound?' said the BT manager.

The Democratic Enterprise is concerned with grasping the organizational possibilities which are now tantalizingly within our reach.

It is not a lone nor idealistic cry. Contemporary de Tocquevilles – people like Warren Bennis, Charles Handy and Peter Drucker – have all observed the vagaries of organizational life and, like their philosophical forebears, have come to their own far-reaching conclusions. One of the threads connecting their ideas is that it is within our grasp to create organizations which can flourish economically and can also be places of excitement and stimulation, fulfilment and tranquility.[2]

'It is possible that if managers and scientists continue to get their heads together in organizational revitalization, they *might* develop delightful organizations – just possibly,' says Warren Bennis.

Can we indeed develop 'delightful organizations', places where we would be pleased for our children to be members, not out of a sense of loyalty, but because they will be able to reach their full potential? For me the acid test is whether you would want your child to work for the company of which you are a member, or indeed for the company you currently lead.

If your answer is a resounding 'no' or even a thoughtful 'maybe', then the challenge you face is to make a real difference. I believe it is possible for each of us to be a part of an organization that enables and encourages us to become the best we can be.

> **For me the acid test is whether you would want your child to work for the company of which you are a member, or indeed for the company you currently lead.**

What might this organization be and by what principles might it be defined? The golden but elusive thread which runs through the words of Charles, Warren and Peter is democracy: personal involvement and participation in organizations where choice flourishes and where shared purpose is the unifying force.

Democracy has a long history but I believe we can now re-capture and re-interpret the very best of democracy – the feelings of citizenship and involvement that created the vitality and innovative spark of ancient Athens. We can now recreate the space, the feeling of time and the value of conversation and reflection which pervaded Athens as Socrates and Plato strolled through its broad boulevards.[3] Or indeed to bring to fruition the thoughts of liberal philosophers. John Stuart Mill, who profoundly understood the imperatives of individual autonomy, wrote: 'When people are engaged in the resolution of problems affecting themselves or the whole collectively, energies are unleashed which enhance the likelihood of the creation of imaginative solutions and successful strategies.'[4]

We are witnessing the emergence of a new way of looking at people and their role in organizations which takes its references from Plato and John Stuart Mills.[5] We have the opportunity to practise what philosophers and social observers have been dreaming about for centuries.

More than at any other point in time, there is now a chance to create the Democratic Enterprise. Over the last decade it has become increasingly clear that through the forces of globalization, competition and more demanding customers, the structure of many companies has become flatter, less hierarchical, more fluid and virtual. The breakdown of hierarchies provides us with fertile ground on which to create a more democratic way of working.

But beyond these forces are two that I believe will act as triggers to the concepts at the heart of this book. The first is demographics and, more specifically, the entry into the workforce and positions of power of generations X and Y. Their preference for adult-to-adult relationships with their company, their self-determination, autonomy and technical savvy will trigger many of the elements of the Democratic Enterprise.

We have the opportunity to practise what philosophers and social observers have been dreaming about for centuries.

This important force for change is now gaining velocity through rapid advances in technology. Technology has the potential to recreate some of the closeness of ancient Greece, as it shrinks space and allows people to share information and knowledge rapidly and directly. This creates the widespread opportunity for individual excellence, autonomy and self-determination.

Demographics and technology have the power to accelerate the possibility of democracy. But to create the Democratic Enterprise, to truly seize the opportunity, will require clarity, judgement, scoping and a clear pathway.

Clarity is essential. We may warm to the engagement and creativity of the Athenian citizen, but we must remember they were supported in their endeavours by thousands of slaves, and lived in a society where women's participation was sharply limited. We may find the dreams of John Stuart Mill enlightening, yet remember at that time a large part of the working population was horribly exploited. We have to create a view of democracy which springs from the very best of the long history of democracy, but frames it in a manner that is viable within the scope of an economic enterprise, and can be made operational given the reality of organizational life. So creating clarity is vital. I create this clarity by defining six tenets of democracy:

1 The relationship between the organization and the individual is adult-to-adult.

2 Individuals are seen primarily as investors actively building and deploying their human capital.

3 Individuals are able to develop their natures and express their diverse qualities.

4 Individuals are able to participate in determining the conditions of their association.

5 The liberty of some individuals is not at the expense of others.

6 Individuals have accountabilities and obligations both to themselves and to the organization.

Judgement and scoping will also be crucial. To build this delightful organization we must know how to transform the tenets of democracy into day-to-day reality. To do this I examine the six tenets of democracy at work in seven large companies. This shows that there are, indeed, companies where the tenets of the Democratic Enterprise are part of the process, culture and management. They are viable and practical. It also shows that other companies are still firmly entrenched in the command-and-control context of bureaucracy, or in the *laissez faire* context of 'adhocracy'. For many companies becoming a Democratic Enterprise requires a new organizational blueprint.

I examine the six tenets of democracy at work in seven large companies.

A democracy exists for the benefit of its citizens, while also advancing the interests of the institution or organization. My exploration of the Democratic Enterprise builds from the experiences of three citizens of companies that are adopting one or more of the tenets of democracy. It is only through the eyes of citizens that we can truly understand citizenship. Through these citizens' eyes we learn their own responsibility to citizenship, and understand the democratic practices and processes of their companies. We glimpse democracy and see how it works on a day-to-day basis. But these glimpses are not sufficient to create a blueprint, or pathway to democracy. Living the six tenets of the Democratic Enterprise requires a blueprint with three related building blocks.

The first building block addresses the role and responsibility of the citizen in the Democratic Enterprise. At the heart is the notion of *individual autonomy*: the capacity of every member of the company to understand themselves, to view themselves as investors and to actively and relentlessly build their personal human capital. The capacity for each employee to do this, to become the best he or she can be, has enormous positive implications for both the employee and the company.

The second building block considers the obligations of the enterprise, and addresses *organizational variety*: the capacity of organizations to provide space for responsive, committed people to become the best they can be and create an organization which is innovative and flexible. I identify the eight dimensions around which space and choice are created. For each of these dimensions I identify one company which is at the forefront of creating space and choice around that dimension.

Living the six tenets of the Democratic Enterprise requires a blueprint with three related building blocks.

The final building block brings together the role of the citizen with the role of the organization to create the 'container' that frames the lives of citizens. In ancient Greece the container was the city and the challenges it faced. In state democracy the container is the state, and the boundaries of the state are well articulated and understood. For a company, however, the notion of the container is a more complex issue.

In the Democratic Enterprise citizens are autonomous and self-determining, and a key role of the organization is the provision of space and choice. But this being so, what keeps the Democratic Enterprise together? What stops it from disintegrating into a band of free agents who sell their skills to the highest bidder? This issue of 'containment', the third building block, is one of the main challenges of democracy in organizations. I label it *shared purpose*: the common goals of the organization, acting as common bonds of performance; the way in which the obligations and accountabilities of individuals become part of the organizational fabric; and the trust generated within the organization, which permeates the relationships between individuals.

Individual autonomy, organizational variety and shared purpose constitute the three building blocks of the Democratic Enterprise. But what can we as individuals do, and what might be the benefits of our actions, to ourselves and the organizations of which we are members? These questions are addressed in the final part of the book. They are answered in actions you can take immediately to move your company along the path to democracy. You can begin the construction of the first building block today, by articulating and sharing the philosophy of democracy, or striving to become more autonomous yourself. You can support the autonomy of others by involving yourself in the mentoring and coaching of others. You can become involved in the construction of the second building block through your attitude to variety within the company and the manner in which you embrace choice and create space for you and others, engaging them in their own constructions. Finally, you have a role to play as an architect of shared purpose, by articulating the purpose of the firm and your role within it, by creating clear goals and accepting your obligations to yourself and others.

These are actions, and obligations, we share as citizens of democracy. The Democratic Enterprise is the meeting place for citizens committed to being the best they can be, and determined to meet their obligations to themselves and to their fellow citizens.

The journey to the Democratic Enterprise, to a company that espouses and supports the six tenets, will require focus and perseverance. It will mean truly supporting individual autonomy. It will require organizations to relentlessly build choice and create freedom. And it will place real challenges on the leadership team to craft and communicate a sense of shared purpose.

From the perspective of the organization, my argument is that democracy has three key benefits.

Why bother? What could be the benefits to individuals and to organizations? As the stories unfold in this book we build a coherent picture of the value of democracy. From the perspective of the organization, my argument is that democracy has three key benefits. First, companies like BP and McKinsey which are encouraging individuals to become autonomous and agile do themselves, collectively, become more agile. It is what Rodney Chase at BP describes as 'swallows', the capacity of individuals to rapidly 'flock' around new opportunities. Next, committed, purposeful organizations have committed and purposeful members. As BT found, the involvement and empowering nature of democracy builds strong and sustainable alignment between individual behaviour and the goals of the company. Finally, as the leadership team at the pharmaceutical company AstraZeneca discovered, the tenets of democracy create a wonderful platform to integrate diverse businesses. When the relationships are adult-to-adult, when all individuals are able to participate in the conditions of their association, there is a basis for rapid and successful integration.

But the recipients of the benefits of democracy are not simply organizations. Each one of us has the opportunity to flourish and gain renewed meaning in our working lives by becoming members of organizations that support the democratic tenets. How? First, each one of us feels more engaged, more excited, and more alive when we are in situations where we have freedom and a sense of shared purpose. These are the times when we engage our will and our energy. These are the times when we are in what has been described as 'the flow'. These are precious times for each of us, and, as we will see, in organizations which support the six tenets, we are more likely to experience these moments.

But the recipients of the benefits of democracy are not simply organizations. Each one of us has the opportunity to flourish and gain renewed meaning in our working lives by becoming members of organizations that support the democratic tenets.

Many people feel disconnected from their organization. At times they feel they have been treated unfairly and unjustly – when others receive 'side deals' to which they are not party or when they are not given the full story about a decision. Under these circumstances our relationship with the company becomes strained and potentially fractured. Companies which live by the six tenets and support individual autonomy are able to create an environment of transparency in which there is the potential for everyone to be treated in a fair and just manner.

Finally, in the Democratic Enterprise there is the possibility for the individual and organization to create a win–win relationship, where the individual benefits are not at the expense of the organization, and the organizational benefits are not at the expense of the individual.

The Democratic Enterprise can become the beacon for how organizations will develop, and the touchstone against which you decide to join and stay with a company. The choice is yours.

Welcome to citizenship!

Citizens' tales

The Democratic Enterprise can only be realistically viewed from the inside out, from the perspective of the citizen. What are the experiences of citizens? How do they go about their daily lives? How are decisions taken? How are the needs of individual citizens weighed against the needs of the group? This is how we understood ancient Athens, through the stories of citizens. For the eighteenth-century philosophers the same was true. Their dreams of autonomy and freedom were constructed from the perspective of what it would be to be a citizen.

In this description of the possibilities of the Democratic Enterprise, I have taken a similar perspective. We begin with the story of three citizens. Through their eyes we see how decisions are taken, how they view themselves as members of a wider organization, how they have attempted to create a balance between their needs and the needs of their colleagues and of the organization.

These three people have not been chosen for their heroic qualities, or indeed for the awesome deeds they have committed. They have been chosen because they are representative of many of the challenges each one of us faces in our day-to-day lives.

None of them are working in organizations that we could call truly democratic. Certainly Greg Grimshaw at BP is able to exercise his personal autonomy in BP in a way that many other employees in other organizations are not able to do. But BP is not a truly Democratic Enterprise. It has neither the range of choice or freedom that would put it into that category. And the same is true of Nina Bhatia at McKinsey and Stewart Kearney at BT.

Neither BT nor McKinsey is a truly Democratic Enterprise. However, in their aspirations and goals, and in their practices and processes they have some of the elements of the Democratic Enterprise.

Is this sufficient? Shouldn't we begin our journey into the Democratic Enterprise with employees in companies who could be truly called democratic? The problem here is two-fold. First, many of the so-called 'experiments' in democracy have been simply been short-term interventions that have dealt with a particular part of the organization and which have tended to have a very specific shelf life. They have remained at the experimental stage. These experiments never gained real traction in the organization because they did not address the whole organizational system, simply a part of it.[1]

My aim in the three building blocks is to approach the creation of the Democratic Enterprise from an organizational wide, systemic perspective. The building blocks are not an isolated programme. They address the whole organizational system; the processes, practices and culture which are the very foundations of the organization. So these three citizens have been chosen from three companies where democracy is beginning to become part of the system, to be built into the fabric of the organization, rather than tacked on to a part of it.

There is a second problem to finding a truly Democratic Enterprise. Many of the examples of democracy are small, entrepreneurial companies, often located in the heart of a metropolis like London, or in California.[2] Alternatively, they are larger companies led by a charismatic founder.[3] There is much that we can learn from these companies. However, the majority of people do not work in small democratic start-ups in London or California. Nor do they work for companies with visionary founding leaders. Most of us work for medium or large companies that may or may not believe that the six tenets of the Democratic Enterprise are necessary or indeed useful. It is to these people and to these organizations that this book is addressed. So while BP, or BT or McKinsey are not truly Democratic Enterprises, in their practices and processes they show how the first steps to democracy can be taken. By doing so they demonstrate that if large, unwieldy, often bureaucratic, companies can step towards democracy, each one of us can take similar steps.

The story of Greg Grimshaw at BP

21 June 2001: Greg Grimshaw is ready for a new challenge. A 1991 chemical engineering graduate, Greg joined BP straight from Bradford University through BP's Early Development Programme (EDP). Since then a variety of jobs have taken him from offshore rigs in the North Sea to positions as a production chemist, a reservoir engineer, a systems production engineer and then a commercial analyst. He is currently global e-HR leader, responsible for the development of BP's strategic direction in the e-HR function. In his decade at BP, this is his 13th job.

His interest now is in a job in Azerbaijan or Trinidad. He knows they will be crucial regions for BP over the coming years and is keen to build an experience base in one or both. At his desk, he notices his bi-weekly e-mail from *myAgent*. Earlier in the month he updated his online résumé, *myProfile*, to include some of his more recent experiences. He also e-mailed a number of his colleagues to seek feedback about his working style and competencies. To his surprise they rated his project skills more highly than he had, and this got him thinking about new opportunities. A set of competencies not unlike his, he had learned, were particularly in demand in the downstream business group.

Opening *myJobMarket*, the globally networked job portal, he sees ten matches between his 'dream job' profile and current job vacancies. Listed first is a chemical engineering job with a rating of 80%. While at some companies that might be the 'lower end' of their desired correlation between position and applicant, at BP Greg knows there is a much wider range of possibilities – and opportunities. In fact, that afternoon he receives a note from the team leader for one of the other positions, for which Greg's match is only 55%. She has read Greg's profile and is encouraging him to apply. Stimulated by her interest and always up for a new challenge, he carefully considers the qualifications she's seeking.

Later that week Greg takes a look at the BP homepage on the internal employee portal. Like every other employee who has logged in he sees the stock prices of BP, the various chat rooms, and the HR service portals. Then he clicks on the *myFuture* portal to continue his job search. The job with the 55% match had interested him but he has decided to opt out of the search, in part because of a lack of confidence in his team-leading skills. As he explains, 'I had led teams in the past, but they were always together in one site and never exceeded eight people. In this job over half the team are in different locations. I just did not feel I had the skills to manage such a virtual team.' Reflecting on this concern, he updates his competency profile to highlight 'managing virtual teams' as a development need. He clicks on *myLearning* to create a portfolio of relevant experiences. He also makes an online registration for a two-day workshop on managing virtual teams, and orders a couple of books recommended by the training portal.

For Greg, taking responsibility for his developmental and his career is about building capabilities and maximizing opportunities to learn, while being knowledgeable and responsive to the likely long-term needs of BP. His interest in Azerbaijan or Trinidad is a case in point.

In fact, taking responsibility for his own development began soon after he joined BP when, as a member of the EDP programme, he rotated through several jobs in his initial three years. At that time BP had an early version of an electronic internal job market portal, advertising all jobs below Business Unit Head. Employees used a simple search tool, sorting options by content, location and job level. The system was called the 'Green Screen' because it consisted essentially of a green terminal and a keyboard.

His first big opportunity, however, did not come through the Green Screen. Instead, in one of his early job rotations he was asked to work as an engineer in the downstream business. This was an internal reorganization project. While working as an engineer Greg became involved in broader organizational issues and found he enjoyed the challenge. He stayed a year before joining another project, this time as a reservoir engineer. In 1996 he tested what was by then an Internet-powered job system and ended up returning to London as a petroleum engineer, switching to offshore operations engineer for another two years.

By 1999 BP CEO, John Browne, had placed the company on a fast-track acquisition path and was determined to integrate the newly acquired AMOCO and ARCO companies as fast and efficiently as possible. Many hundreds of change managers were selected and trained and Greg was asked to be one of those leaders. 'I decided to take the challenge. It was far from my technical experiences as an engineer, but I thought the integration experience at ARCO would be challenging and fascinating.'

By 2000 Greg was in discussion about a new position, a commercial role in the BP corporate centre, Britannic House. He was finalizing the details when he saw on *myAgent* a completely different role, in the e-HR team. Greg was intrigued. 'I liked the sound of it, but I certainly did not fit the profile. I had no background in either IT or HR!'

Greg reflects on the lack of an obvious competence fit:

'It's all about BP's philosophy. We believe people can learn. Other companies look for an 80–90% match between a person's current skills and the job description. At BP, 60% would be considered a high match. My skills match in the e-HR role was probably around 20%, but I had a track record that I could learn quickly.'

Nick Starrit, who at the time was BP's Group Personnel Director, saw this as very much par for the course:

'In BP there is an ethos that jobs should be a stretch rather than simply a fit. We are prepared to take risks with technical skills, because we know they can be developed. What we cannot take risks with is learning ability and determination. Although Greg did not have the technical competence, he had learning ability and determination in spades.'

Nick knew this because he had tapped into BP's vast network of tacit knowledge about people and their skills. 'I talked to a number of people who had worked with Greg, and basically my question was, *Can I trust this person to learn?* Everyone is pretty up-front about skills and aptitudes.' Using this kind of direct feedback creates opportunities that going by the book, keeping people on narrower career tracks, might not. As Greg reflects:

'In BP we encourage people to achieve what they want, moving from one point to another. It is a zigzag rather than a straight line. In the banking profession it is a straight line – the longer you work, the bigger your bonus, and your position and status increases. But you are only an expert in one area. We, on the other hand, are zigzagging, getting broader experience with each turn. When you get to each point you are really much more enriched. There are very few things you learn in one job that you cannot apply to something else. For example, I managed to bring into the HR role all my offshore operations experience.'

At the heart of the zigzag is Greg's awareness of what excites and interests him. 'I don't do a job unless something is broken, and someone needs significant change. That's me . . . that's what I am good at.' In the recent past Greg, like many at BP, worked with a career coach to understand what motivates him. 'There was one thing that absolutely came out. I love to go in somewhere with a hugely complex challenge, and find ways to fix it.'

Greg took the e-HR job primarily because he realized that in his offshore role he was learning fast, but not developing his networks. The e-HR role, based in BP's headquarters, had a global reach and the opportunity to work closely with the senior team. Now, after three years, and with the rise of e-HR as a core expertise, Greg finds himself a platform speaker at conferences and increasingly seen as an HR expert.

'At this stage I could stay in the job for another five years or even leave and consolidate my e-HR "guru" status. But that would mean that I could not tack across; it would mean I would be sailing on a straight course.' Greg is clear about the consequences of 'tacking', or as he earlier put it 'zigzagging', rather than pursuing his career in a straight line. 'I realize that if I stayed in one place and did the same job I could get better and better.' But for him breadth is more important than depth, and he believes his breadth of experience only increases his value to the company. It's the commitment that has guided his career at BP to date, and it's why today he's looking for opportunities as far away as Azerbaijan and Trinidad.

Why Greg is important to the success of BP

Greg is just one of many tens of thousands of people who work for BP. Yet in many ways he epitomizes the people who work there, and his efforts manifest the company's commitment to democracy. Consider these three elements of Greg's behaviour, and how they are crucial to BP's continued success.

As an agent of integration

Over the past five years the senior team at BP has actively consolidated from a large, fragmented company to a more tightly integrated one. By 2000 the company consisted of three camps, divided by very different heritages: approximately 60,000 from BP, 40,000 from Amoco and 20,000 from ARCO. Management's strategy was to bring together the diverse strengths of the three different companies into a single new business. Breaking down barriers and creating synergy among the players was crucial to the success

CHAPTER ONE

....

Citizens' tales

of the enterprise. These efforts were supported by the creation of peer groups: horizontal structures that crossed the old company lines. But such structures mean nothing without a mindset of integration, and that's where Greg and others like him are so important. By having the courage and sense of personal autonomy to steer a zigzag course and cross old boundaries, they help form the 'glue' of friendship and reciprocity so critical to sharing information, learning from one another and building a new, common heritage.

As a sharer of knowledge

One of the founding concepts at BP is the sharing of knowledge. CEO, John Browne, describes its commitment:

> *'Any organization of scale could create proprietary knowledge through learning . . . so the question is how could you get independent atomic units to work together to share information, to learn and to retain that learning.'*

The creation of proprietary knowledge has both an individual element and a relational element. Greg's self-determination and autonomy, and his tendency to see himself as an investor, compel him to take responsibility for his own development and learning. At the same time, his propensity to tack, rather than steer a straight course, means he has been an active carrier of knowledge throughout the company. His experience managing large, complex and high-risk offshore engineering projects has given him the skill, courage and confidence to manage the e-HR through relatively uncharted territory. At the same time, as a carrier of knowledge he has an important influence on his HR colleagues, helping to cross-pollinate ideas from one function and business area to another. By doing so he actively contributes to John Browne's mission to 'create proprietary knowledge through learning'.

As a 'swallow'

The relationship between Greg and BP is firmly adult-to-adult. Greg takes responsibility for himself and for creating a portfolio of work and projects he finds engaging and exciting. As a consequence, he can be what Deputy CEO Rodney Chase calls a 'swallow', agile and adept at twisting and turn-

ing as the needs of the business become clear. Greg is not alone in considering opportunities in Azerbaijan. Rather, he is one of a 'flock' of swallows
now turning in a new direction, guided by their own desires and ambitions
– and by the future needs of their organization.

What Greg has done to be the best he could be

He has been prepared to take risks

One of the most striking aspects of Greg's story is that he has consistently
chosen to take risks and build his personal human capital. There was never
a time when he was content to remain static, to allow his portfolio of
skills to become stagnant. Instead he has turned calculated risks into new
opportunities. Consider, for example, his success in the e-HR role. Greg has
been a leader, on the cutting edge of his field and within reach of guru
status. Under his guidance BP has emerged as one of the world leaders in
the field. Yet he has chosen to jump to a completely different part of the
company, to a different business and a different job. It is a risky move, but
entirely consistent with his personal strategy of broadening his skills and
competencies. In his years at BP, it is a strategy that has served him, and the
company, well.

He has the investor mindset

There are two aspects to Greg's investor instincts. First, he takes a very clear
view of the composition of his portfolio. He knows he has the choice to go
for a relatively narrow, low-risk portfolio of skills and capabilities, or pursue
a higher-risk strategy and, potentially, a higher reward. Both are credible
investor strategies and Greg has always understood which best suited his
values, his personal style and his aspirations. Next, he has consistently taken
a view of the short term and the longer term. Taking the change management job was an example of this perspective. The role was experimental,
potentially peripheral and a possible career cul-de-sac. But Greg understood that despite the short-term disadvantages it could provide a set of
unique skills and experiences that might serve him well down the road.

Companies like BP that are espousing and advancing the tenets of
democracy can provide opportunities for people to become the best they
can be, creating a broad portfolio of skills and experience. It isn't a gift from

the companies, but a challenge – and it's one Greg and others like him have accepted enthusiastically.

What BP has done to help Greg become the best he could be

Within BP there is sufficient democracy that Greg and many of his colleagues have been able to exercise personal autonomy and become the best they could be.

Opening up the internal job market

Greg has repeatedly benefited from an internal job market that is transparent and information-rich. Much of his opportunity has occurred through the realignment of the practices and processes of career management at BP. Greg has been party to a career structure in which all but a very small number of senior roles are advertised on the employee portal, and where any individual is able to apply for any job at any time. This is the 'light touch' of career management: the decision of the senior team to create wide latitude of individual discretion, and to trust people to make the right choices.

Putting round pegs in square holes

How many other companies would have taken the risk of making Greg head of e-HR? In terms of obvious fit he had little to commend him. He had no experience working in the HR function, nor was he an IT expert. At most companies a 'best fit' candidate would have been identified within rigid parameters, excluding someone like Greg. So why were things different at BP? Certainly, BP had a large pool of accomplished HR professional and IT experts, and the technology to publicize the job and profile the candidates. Instead, hiring Greg in the e-HR role was consistent with BP's deliberate policy, reflected throughout the company, to stretch people through job challenge and create roles with sufficient 'latitude of discretion' that they can be moulded to the individual. So for Greg, the project management role and the impact of working on a high-risk, fast-paced project – his forte – came to the fore, while the e-learning and employee portal roles were integrated with other member of the team. In essence, what Greg experienced at BP was team selection, not just individual selection: by putting a team together as a cohesive whole, Nick Starrit offset the potential weaknesses in Greg's experience with the strengths of others, while effectively leveraging Greg's abilities and experience.

The story of Nina Bhatia at McKinsey

Summer 2001: Nina Bhatia is pregnant with her second child, who will be born in the spring of 2002. In her 15 years since joining McKinsey as a young associate, Nina has worked on projects which have taken her to South Korea and the US, in sectors from chocolate to steel, media to oil. At 34, she was selected to become a partner. Now, with some satisfaction she reflects on her past, and considers the path she expects to bring her and her family fulfilment and joy in the coming years. She also realizes that this could be a transitional time as she faces some tough personal and professional choices.

Should she work part-time, perhaps three days a week? Should she stay home with her new child for an extended period of time? If she does, how will she continue to support the development of her team? How will she integrate once she returns to work? She recalls the return after her first child as a 'hard landing', and wonders how she can prevent this happening again:

> *'When I come back to McKinsey after this baby is born, I will have to make some decisions. What will be my unique proposition? I know I have lots of choices. In the next two weeks I have to work through the "Nina Bhatia strategy project" and then syndicate it with my colleagues and say "this is what I plan to do, and this is the help I need, what do you think?" Self-governance pervades the way we think about ourselves.'*

She knows the options at McKinsey are broad, and that variety is tolerated. At the same time, she knows she alone will have to figure out what will work for her and what will allow her to meet commitments to her clients and team.

Nina has spent a lifetime relentlessly building her human capital. She first considered law before joining McKinsey straight out of Cambridge University, after learning about the firm from a friend. She left to get her

MBA at Harvard, then returned and has been at McKinsey ever since. 'I review my career decision every 18 to 24 months. I am committed to McKinsey, but open to exploring other options.'

Nina's was not a coherent, set piece of serial experiences. 'I am opportunistic, instinctive about what I do. If it is enjoyable and stretching I continue with it.' The focus is always on what she calls – using the language of a consultant – building my skills and creating 'my unique proposition', a portfolio of experiences and knowledge which is distinct and coherent, building a story about her and what she values and engages with. Today, considering her future and her possible transitions, she also looks back on a life of ebbs and flows, times when she has been engaged and excited, times when she has felt, as she puts it, 'bored and rudderless'.

Her career at McKinsey first really leapt forward when, at 29 and with her new Harvard MBA, she was asked to advise a European chocolate manufacturer on building a strategy for expansion into Asia. She was a young woman leading a team of Americans and Koreans, many of them older than her. She did not speak a word of Korean and was one of a few professional women in the office. Best of all, she did not know anything about chocolate manufacturing or marketing. 'The only thing I knew about chocolate was that it tastes good', she remembers.

It was a rapid, up-hill learning experience. 'This was my shaping assignment, a real catalyst event. Technically the project was simple, but very interpersonally challenging.' At the same time she learned something that would become central to her ethos: the management of boundaries. Reflecting on her experience in Korea she recalls:

> 'I had no local knowledge, only my training and experience. I had nothing else to fall back on. I had to live on my wits. I had to learn to stand up for myself. The work culture appeared hard working, but was not necessary. Everyone was in the office until 10:00 or 11:00 at night. I said I would only be there until 7:00 in the evening. I was drawing a line . . . this is how I am going to work. I learned to draw boundaries.'

Since then Nina has worked on a range of successful assignments, creating strong relationships with clients and colleagues and actively supporting and developing her team. These projects have been important to McKinsey, and vital to Nina's own development. 'I have been exposed to people who are really good at what they do. They are the examples from whom I set my own standards. They helped me understand, you need to know what it is you want to do and work from this.'

At the same time, some of her deepest learning and character shaping has come when faced with hard decisions. She recalls a time a couple of years back:

'It was a year of extremes. I was really overdoing it. At the same time I was working on a really difficult project, I did not know the industry, and I did not hit it off with the client. I became ill and tired. When I went to the doctor they diagnosed chronic anaemia. I was just worn out.'

At the same time, Nina's team was giving her ambivalent feedback. Over the years she had always received positive feedback and was seen as committed and sharp. Now for the first time her feedback was less than positive, and she was devastated. 'I took great offence at this, it really bothered me. Why didn't people understand the pressure I was under?'

Within two weeks of this low point, however, a conversation with her director opened up a new assignment with a large, multinational client – and gave her an opportunity to redeem herself, in her own eyes and in the eyes of others. The new challenge gave her space, and coaching from others build up her confidence and strength again. Looking back she understands how important the feedback was to her. 'I really felt under pressure. But through thinking about it and talking to others I began to discover aspects of myself that are strengths and I learned the power of tough messages.'

She also learned to make hard choices about colleagues. She recalls a catalyst assignment: 'The project was poorly scoped and within a week we were working all night and day to meet our deadlines. I learned there are some people you won't work well with, and that making the choice about who to work with has a big impact. I learned you have to decide who you want to work with.'

Nina has also been clear about the decisions she has made to balance her family and work and the consequences of these decisions:

'I have had to make some real trade-offs. I do much less informal chitchat with my team because I am committed to getting home in the evening. And I try to have client meetings only one evening a week. The trade-off is that people some times see me as brusque and abrupt, that I don't have time for them.'

There is much we can learn from Nina's story. As a successful woman she has always thought that creating a family would be an important aspect of her life. So balancing work and life was always at the forefront. This entailed taking a very clear-sighted view of herself and of the opportunities she faced. Over the years she has done much to become autonomous and manage the boundaries of her life. She has developed a clear view of what is important to her and what she is prepared to do to meet her aspirations and manage the expectations of others.

What is also striking about Nina's story is that although she is an intelligent and gifted women, she has experienced many swamplands in her life: times when she pushed herself too far, times when she lost her compass and belief in herself. Learning from these low points spurred Nina to honestly confront aspects of herself of which she was less proud. A recurring theme at such times is the encouragement and support she received from the other partners at McKinsey – people who let her communicate openly, gave her frank feedback and helped her to meet all her personal and professional challenges.

Why Nina is important to the success of McKinsey

Serving 1,700 clients

McKinsey serves upwards of 1,700 clients located around the globe, in a range of business sectors and facing diverse functional issues. The sheer complexity is immense. Unlike other large consulting companies, McKinsey does not place hundreds of associates with a single client for a period of years. Instead, associates work in relatively small groups, on projects of fixed duration, even as short as a couple of weeks. Agility and a broad range of skills are imperative to delivering in this business model. Breadth on the part of individual associates and partners helps enable rapid reconfiguration of skills. At the same time, the continual broadening and deepening of their experience, intellect and acumen has helped keep McKinsey on the forefront of ideas and knowledge-creation in the field of business strategy. By investing in Nina's human capital, the firm has made substantial investment in attaining and maintaining the pinnacle of industry knowledge and strategic consultation.

Creating networks of knowledge

Nina is part of a network of friendships and close professional relationships throughout McKinsey. By investing in Nina and her network of peers the firm has increased the potential knowledge base of the whole organization. The emphasis at McKinsey is on the creation and sustainability of 'social capital': the depth and extent of social ties that connect employees across the organization, and to others outside the company. This social capital is an essential element of the intangible asset value of the firm. It is the conduit by which ideas and knowledge traverse the company; more importantly, it is the space within which new ideas are generated. Simply put, the disparate teams of people McKinsey puts together, with their individual ways of looking at the world and their unique ideas, are more likely to create new knowledge and cross-pollinate their ideas than static groups. Nina, like other partners at McKinsey, play a crucial role in the creation and nurturing of new knowledge through the depth and breadth of social ties.

What Nina has done to become the best she could be

She has engaged in active self-reflection

One striking aspect of Nina's story is her voracious appetite to reflect on her own experiences and to actively learn from them. There is never a time when she is not learning from her experiences, and from her attitudes to these experiences. As a consequence, her cycle of learning has a complement of skill acquisition and a component of self-awareness. Clearly, the processes at McKinsey in which all partners and associates of the firm are asked to describe their accomplishments and plans for the future play a strong role in her own propensity for reflection. But in a sense it does no more than provide context and legitimization. What Nina brings to this process, crucially, is candour: her ability and her willingness to cast a strong and sometimes uncomfortable light on her behaviour and values; to illuminate not only what she is proud of, but also to look clearly at her failures and sources of anxiety and displeasure – then to strive to improve.

She has 'protected' her intentions

Nina continuously creates and recreates a picture of who she is and what she wants to become. Her active self-insight and reflection help ensure this picture is actively grounded in reality, based on her perceptions of herself and supported by those of her colleagues. Many people have ideas about what they want to become, but lose the ideal, becoming distracted from their journey, making choices that take them off the pathway, creating lives so fragmented that the notion of the whole self ends up lost in the maze.

Nina has been able to keep to her view of herself in part because she has deliberately and consistently protected her intentions. She has created mechanisms and processes that have enabled her embryonic view of herself to be developed and protected from distractions and fragmentation. She has continuously worked on keeping intact what she holds dear about herself, and maintaining a clear view of what she wants to become.

Three strategies have been central to her approach. First, her active boundary management has helped protect her from distractions and fragmentation. She has been clear about what she wants to achieve and what is outside the boundaries. As she has noted, this rigorous boundary management has costs associated with it – in her case, costs of sociability and perceived conviviality. But these are costs she has accepted to protect her intentions.

Second, she has protected her intentions by periodically reviewing where she is, the experiences she's had and her reactions to them. By doing so she has been able to privately gauge whether she was on-track in her aspirations. Finally, through mechanisms, such as her annual review and her personal statement, she has made public declarations of who she is and why this is important to her. Each of these mechanisms has enabled her to protect her intentions and to ensure that her choices and decisions remain a true reflection of what's important.

What McKinsey has done to support Nina to be the best she could be

Providing continuous, challenging feedback

Earlier we discussed the networks of which Nina is a member and how they contribute to the currency of the social capital of McKinsey. From an individual perspective, we know that social capital develops most readily in those who are authentic to themselves and who are perceived by others to be trustworthy. Nina benefits from the sheer scale of directed, performance-related feedback she receives from her team leaders, colleagues and clients. (Of course, she also provides valuable feedback to others.) She benefits too from the way in which feedback is given and the context in which it takes place. As we learned, her colleagues do not shy away from giving both positive, supportive feedback, and feedback that is specific and critical. This approach helps to minimize blind spots – areas in which she might otherwise fail to understand information about herself that others share. Meanwhile, self-insight is maximized. Through her authenticity Nina is in a stronger position to create network ties, and as a consequence to help build the social capital of the firm.

Clarifying obligations and accountabilities

At McKinsey there is a strong ethos to create and maintain obligations and accountabilities. For Nina these deeply felt obligations to herself, the firm and her clients create a sense of direction when she is deciding on courses of action. The obligations to herself include becoming the best she can be by accepting stretching, challenging projects and living by the ethos of self-development. The obligations to McKinsey include delivering to the very best of her ability and continuously creating and supporting high performing projects. In careful balance they help keep McKinsey profitable, its clients satisfied, and members like Nina challenged and fulfilled.

The story of Stewart Kearney at BT

As Nina ponders her past and future, Stewart Kearney rises from bed and walks to his desk in his bright, spacious home office. He begins his day talking with colleagues on the phone and working on an important strategy document for the next BT (British Telecom) board meeting. After a few hours, satisfied with his draft for the time being, Stewart takes a quick break and reviews his calendar. He has a telephone conference booked in for the afternoon, and then plans to catch up with some reading and online research.

Stewart's home is in the green rolling hills of middle England, and living in a beautiful place is one of the most important aspects of his life. Until recently, however, he often doubted whether what was best for his soul and his spirit, was best for his career. He liked the jobs he had worked for BT, all within ten miles of his home, but he also knew they were limited in scope and opportunity. Most of the interesting strategic jobs, he realized, were located in central London.

In April 2000, however, Stewart considered the details of a new position at BT, one that wouldn't include a 'work close to home, or close to the action' compromise. 'It sounded really intriguing, an HR strategy role with some important challenges. What really caught my eye, though, was it was described as "location negotiable". That means that it can be done almost anywhere.' As it turns out, the HR job was one of a large number of positions being transitioned from fixed locations to negotiated locations. In fact, once Stewart joined the team he realized that out of six people, only one was working from an office in London. 'The team leader, for example, was working from his house in the New Forest.'

Stewart's initial months of home-working were tough. 'No one really understood about what it was to work at home, and there was not much in terms of support, no advice. It took over six weeks to get the computer equipment delivered to my home office, and there was no one to help with the software installation. It was three months before my computer worked well, and during that time I was ready to quit a couple of times.' And as challenging an issue as technology was, for Stewart there was an even bigger issue to tackle:

'The idea of home-working is saving the time on commuting, which is an absolute delight. But the downside is you do not get the sociability of the office-working environment. Also, when I wanted to get a cup of coffee, although it might take only 15 minutes I'd feel guilty that I had left my desk; I felt if someone tried to contact me I should respond immediately. On the other hand, when I was in an office, I would go up seven floors to get a coffee, maybe meet someone in the corridor on the way, and so on, and there was no sense of guilt about being away from my desk.

In the end, though, I realized I was trusted, and this gave me a greater sense of responsibility. I came to realize the permission was being given, but nobody was saying it out loud, as a set of rules. Instead, you have to learn the tacit rules by talking to other people. Sharing your concerns and seeing their reaction.'

Over the next year the team settled into a way of working. 'We are basically results orientated. If you are not at your desk at 11:00 because you are in the supermarket, that's fine, because you choose to work in the evening or over lunch.' The team also began to adjust to each other. 'I know that one of my colleagues has young children and will not be available from 3:00 to 3:45 when she picks them up from school. But I know when I check my e-mails there will be one from her from the previous evening. She obviously spreads her work over the course of the day and around her family.'

Stewart is clear about the implications of the choice he has made. 'Working from home may not provide enough visibility if you are career-orientated. But it is all about personal preferences. For me the freedom to work at home is enormously important, and I would not have taken this job if it were located in central London. I would certainly earn more money working in central London, but the luxury of working from home and having freedom and flexibility overrides a greater pay package.'

Interestingly, Stewart says he would not have asked to be located at home. It was only when BT offered this option that he could take it. 'Back then, neither the culture nor the technology was in place for the decision. Home-working was not the convenient and natural choice it is now. Before it felt like a paternalistic environment, and now it is more of a professional, adult environment. I feel greater responsibility and make sure I take care of my own development.'

Why Stewart is important to the success of BT

By being engaged and committed

Engaged and committed employees are crucial to the performance and longevity of organizations. These employees are prepared to deliver performance that is above the norm. Stewart and other BT employees like him are more likely to be innovative and take the risks necessary to push their ideas forward.

Through his resilience

Much of the underperformance in organizations occurs because people are stressed, and as such are operating below their potential level of performance. People who are under stress are more likely to be absent from work and less likely to really engage in their work. Stewart has created a way of working which fits with his perception of himself and enables him to work on difficult projects while remaining emotionally resilient, capable of dealing with the stresses and strains of complicated projects. His self-knowledge and understanding have made him important to the success of BT as the company deals with complex issues requiring resilience and thoughtfulness.

What Stewart has done to be the best he could be

He has been prepared to acknowledge his needs

Each of us has unique needs and aspirations, which describe who we are and what we wish to become. There are occasions when these needs and aspirations run counter to the expectations of others, or are outside the norms of traditional work arrangements. The gap between aspirations and realities is the terrain of sacrifice. The sacrifices within this terrain can be mapped with some precision. Some are sacrifices that can severely impact our well-being and capacity to work in a high performing manner. Other sacrifices may have limited impact on our well-being, and may be more than justified in their benefits to ourselves and our organizations.

Much of the terrain of sacrifice occurs because people are caught within industry norms and do not know any other way. Stewart had known for some time that the daily commute into London would impact on his well-being and enjoyment of life. As a prisoner of industry norms, he self-limited his job opportunities. At that time few senior managers would expect to work from home in any company, so Stewart bore his dissatisfaction with as much grace as he could muster. However, he always understood himself sufficiently to know the extent of his sacrifice. As a consequence, when BT began to trial home-working Stewart was one of the first to sign up. He had enough insight to understand himself and know what would make him content and high performing.

He understands the consequences of his choices

Stewart has behaved as an adult in his relationship with BT. He has understood what is important to him and been prepared to shape his expectations to fit into what's important. Perhaps most importantly, he has understood the consequences of the choices he's made. Stewart realized that if he chose to work at home his network within the senior team at BT might deteriorate. He also understood that if he continued to use home-working as a criterion to select roles, there would be other senior roles that would not be available to him. And as an early adopter of BT's home-working model, he opted in at a time when the risk and rewards were not all clear. So, not only has Stewart been prepared to make choices and take risks based on what's important to him, he has also been sufficiently accountable to acknowledge the consequences of his choices and indeed to live with them.

What BT has done to support Stewart to be the best he could be

Creating variety

Over the last decade there has been a growing awareness at BT that the needs and aspirations of employees are widely varied: what brings contentment and the capacity to perform to one may not be shared by another. BT's response has been to widen the latitude of discretion as much as possible. To create sufficient organizational variety and freedom for people to exercise choices. As a consequence, employees are able to configure and reconfigure their options on an ongoing basis to meet their changing aspirations and needs. By balancing variety with the needs of the business BT has helped ensure that choices made by individuals are not made at the expense of their colleagues or the performance of the company.

Treating employees as autonomous

One of the interesting aspects of the attitude of BT's senior team has been its lack of paternalism. Stewart and his colleagues have simply been asked to build a business case which showed the positive impact of their decisions on the performance of BT, and how they believed their arrangements would work on a day-to-day basis. The decision to support Stewart's home-working was rational and based on data. What was not brought into the equation were the reasons Stewart wanted to work from home. The fact he enjoyed working at home was no more or less important than if he had an elderly relation to support or small children to look after. In a parent–child relationship the temptation is always to use power to make judgements on behalf of the individual. At BT the senior team resisted this temptation and created a small number of business-based rules which specify the conditions – instead of the reasons – under which home-working is a viable option.

The value of the Democratic Enterprise

So what unites these three different people at three different companies? What are the threads, if any, that connect these people and the companies of which they are members?

While each is certainly strong and autonomous, none is heroic. Rather, they reflect the choices and dilemmas faced in day-to-day working lives. What job should I take next? What is important to me now and in the future? What will excite me? How can I meet my obligations as a parent with my obligations to my company and my own professional development? These are ordinary, autonomous people who have made choices and faced dilemmas many of us are faced with. By observing them and the companies in which they work we are witnesses to the ebbs and flows of the contemporary enterprise.

The trio are citizens rather than employees. The distinction is vital. They are adopting some of the conditions of citizenship and are all members of companies adopting some of the tenets of democracy. All three work in organizations in which they have had opportunities to become autonomous, choice-making people. All have made substantial choices about how they work and their relationship with the companies of which they are members.

For Greg autonomy has included zigzagging to create a working life of variety and surprise; for Nina it's meant building expertise while managing her boundaries; for Stewart it's been about making choices and being absolutely clear about the consequences of those choices. Each has developed a relationship with his or her company that is at its core adult-to-adult, with all the will and responsibility that this entails.

Liberating your business with freedom, flexibility and commitment

Much of this has come from their individual propensity to take responsibility. But their organizations have also played roles: supporting their needs for autonomy, creating information-rich environments to help them to make thoughtful and informed choices, and providing meaningful alternatives in location and work style. Crucially, they have also ensured that in the midst of this variety and choice there is still an understanding of the purpose of the company and of the individual's role within it.

Each company's path to democracy has been different. At McKinsey many of the basic tenets of democracy were inscribed in the beliefs and aspirations of its founding fathers. Their fundamental belief was in personal autonomy and freedom partnered with a profound sense of citizenship. This was reinforced by successive managing partners and is as strong today as ever. At BP, the journey towards democracy has come from values and aspirations over time, culminating in the belief that democracy has a positive and lasting effect on the performance of the company. That conviction has been the driving principle for CEO John Browne who has professed that bringing choice to development will enable a more rapid alignment of the talents of all BP's employees.

At BT the journey towards the six tenets began with a belief that to differentiate itself in the marketplace BT would have to understand and implement the elements necessary to becoming an 'employer of choice'. Theirs was a journey driven by rationality and data. The initial studies showed that talented people felt dissatisfied and left BT because they experienced it as inflexible and bureaucratic. For this talented group, bringing choice in time and location would make a significant difference to the 'employee proportion' at BT. Hence the journey began.

For each of these companies the journey toward democracy started in a different place. But each has continued the journey gathering momentum in recent years. Their shared pursuit begs the question: What has been the value of supporting individual autonomy and crafting organizational variety?

Perhaps most obviously, a company of self-determining employees behaving like adults is infinitely more flexible and responsive than a company of followers. BP Deputy CEO, Rodney Chase, puts it this way: 'It is incredible how quickly the organization moves to meet new opportunities. It is like watching a flock of swallows in terms of speed and agility.' Swallow employees are responsive to the first signs of change in the environment and capable of rapidly reconfiguring their skills and abilities to make best use of the opportunities these changes create. This mindset can also be crucial during mergers and acquisitions. It is no secret that many M&As endeavour fail because the hoped-for synergies are not realized. At BP, the successful integration of four major oil and gas companies was in part a consequence of the self-determination of BP employees like Greg and their ability to zigzag across the heritage companies, taking with them their contacts and knowledge.

Organizations moving toward democracy are building a context in which their employees are engaged and collaborative. Employees stay with a company in part to be the best person they can be and, in part, to craft lives that bring them fulfilment. At BT, for example, studies have shown that employees like Stewart who exercise choice in time and location are significantly more committed to the organization, and more likely to stay than those with no ability to exercise choice. At BT there is a 'working out' of the conditions of employment. The senior team understands that much employee disengagement and lack of performance results from feeling cheated, of feeling they have not been actively involved and consulted in decisions, such as those relating to benefits, that they believe are crucial to them. By engaging employees BT is building a committed and flexible workforce.

Employee engagement is one benefit of the democratic relationship to the organization, but beneath this lies other, deeper advantages. The benefits Greg, Nina and Stewart experience in the democratic relationship are crafted in the minutia of their everyday lives, as individual as they are. There is no one unitary benefit of the democratic relationship that is expressed equally for every employee. Instead, there are individually expressed benefits and individual responsibilities of citizenship. Knowing these responsibilities, on an individual level, requires self-awareness; keeping to them over time requires accountability. That's what we ask for in adult relationships and that's what democracy demands.

CHAPTER TWO

What democracy means

T o understand the beginnings of the democratic journey, we have to cast our imagination back many thousands of years. It was on the wide promenades of ancient Greece 2,500 years ago that the debates took place that formed the central source of inspiration for political ideals that have continued until this day. The aim of Greek democracy was a community in which citizens could, and indeed should, participate in the creation and nurture of common life. The citizenship as a whole formed the Assembly, the key sovereign body of Athens. The Assembly met over 40 times a year and had a quorum of 6,000 citizens, all of whom could be accommodated in the Parthenon. All major issues such as the legal framework, finance, taxation, war and more, came before the assembled citizens for deliberation and declaration.[1]

It is impossible to replicate Athenian democracy in contemporary life, or indeed in contemporary organizations. The basic *polis* of Athens was, as many organizations would aspire to be, marked by unity, solidarity and participation. But the *polis* of Athens was an exclusive group, the rights of women were strictly limited, and many thousands of slaves, between 80,000 and 100,000 at any time, had neither rights nor privileges.

Yet in this imperfect society democracy first took root. The word is derived from the Greek word *demokratia*, built from *demos* (people) and *kratos* (rule). In essence, democracy means a form of government in which the people rule. That is not to say that the meaning of what constitutes democracy has remained stable through the centuries, or indeed that the original notion is without ambiguity. Historically there has been much criticism of both the theory and practice of state democracy, especially in terms of what constitutes '*people*' and what is a '*rule*'. Despite these ambiguities, democracy has become a political ideal for people around the world. As the political philosopher David Held observes: 'Democracy has become the fundamental standard of political legitimacy in the current era.'[2]

As citizens we live in the age of democracy. We have become familiar with the trappings of democracy and take for granted democratic principles of involvement in legislation and crucial decision making. We assume that our rulers will be accountable to the rules, that they should be chosen by the ruled, and that the rulers should act in the interests of the ruled.[3] We also enjoy the democratic principle of being treated as individuals, with the role of the state to provide the necessary conditions to enable citizens to pursue their own interests. The notion of democracy implies that citizens are sufficiently self-reflective and self-determining to take those actions that best serve both their own interests and the interests of the communities of which they are members. It would be naive to assume that these principles automatically fall under the banner of 'democracy'. Or indeed that democracy is a reality for all citizens at all times in the increasing number of states in which it has been proclaimed.

Democratization of the state has brought substantial benefits to citizens. It has provided a means of containing the powers of the state, of mediating among competing individuals and projects, and of making political decisions accountable. Modern democratic states have the fundamental common goals to enable citizens to pursue their own interests and to uphold the rule of law to protect and nurture individual liberties. By doing so states have the potential to enable each individual to benefit from the common good; to become, in the words of the one time GE CEO, Jack Welch, 'the best they can be'.

To understand the journey into the future we need to understand more about the past. What is the legacy and what are the issues that lead us to state democracy in the form it now takes, and what are the issues and paradoxes that encompass our notions of democracy? By better understanding state democracy, we are in a stronger position to create an agenda, or a set of tenets, to frame enterprise democracy.

A short history of democracy

Classical democracy

The ancient Greeks taught us equality among citizens, liberty, and respect for the law and justice. The modern liberal notions that human beings are 'individuals' with 'rights' can be traced back to Athens. Commentators at that time described a community in which all citizens could and should participate in creating and nurturing the common life. The Athenian concept of citizenship included taking a share in these functions, participating directly in the affairs of state. As Pericles wrote at the time, 'We do not say that a man who takes no interest in the politics is a man who minds his own business; we say that he has no business here at all.'[4]

Athenians on the whole prided themselves on their free and open political life in which citizens could develop and realize their capacities and skills. Pericles described a form of life in which:[5]

> 'Each single one of our citizens, in all the manifold aspects of life, is able to show himself the rightful lord and owner of his person, and do this, moreover, with exceptional grace and exceptional versatility.'
>
> Thucydides, *The Peloponnesian War*, pp. 147–8

One of the most remarkable descriptions of ancient democracy can be found in Aristotle's *The Politics,* written between AD 323 and 335, in which he described one of the basic principles as 'live as you like. For this, they say, is a function of being free, since the opposite, living not as you like, is the function of one enslaved.' Aristotle highlighted a tenet inscribed in the constitutions of many contemporary democracies: that people shall be free to be themselves, to express their diverse qualities. In the same work Aristotle described another tenet of the Athenian state:

> 'A basic principle of the democratic constitution is liberty. People constantly make this statement, implying that only in this constitution do men share liberty; for every democracy, they say, has liberty as its aim. "Ruling and being ruled in turn" is one element in liberty, and the democratic ideal of justice is in fact numerical equality, not equality based on merit; and when this idea of what is just prevails, the multitude must be sovereign, and whatever the majority decides is final and constitutes justice.'
>
> Aristotle, *The Politics*

These ideals are enshrined in the notion that all shall have equal influence, that the liberty of some individuals is not at the expense of others. The classical democracy that flourished in Athens had the central principle that citizens should enjoy political equality in order that they be free to rule and be ruled in turn. Citizens participated directly in legislative and judicial functions and there was no distinction of privilege to differentiate ordinary citizens from public officials.

What flourished in ancient Athens remains meaningful and fresh. First, the very concept of the individual 'citizen', with a bounty of talent and potential, capable of will and judgement, and prepared to embrace freedom and equality. Next, the belief that citizens are capable of and obligated to active participation in the workings of the state, with a high level of personal accountability. As many commentators of the time remarked, when the quorum of citizens met within the soaring columns of the Parthenon, they were capable of extraordinary agility, speed and courage in their decision making, harnessing the power of collective action. This 'inside' agility was bred outside, nurtured along Athens' boulevards, through conversations that took place and social networks that formed among the citizens.

But perhaps the most enduring lesson from ancient Greece is the possibility of aligning the power of the individual with the needs of the community through a sense of common purpose: the notion of 'moral reciprocity'. 'The conviction that the organization serves a vital mission as an educator of each of its individual members, who in return offer their own best efforts.' As the classicists Brook Manville and Josiah Ober remarked of the Athenian citizen:[6]

> 'The core lesson he taught and learned as he participated in the business of his city were consistent: the value of collaboration, learning and open debate to solve problems and making continuously better and actionable decisions; the importance of shared values in fostering that kind of collaboration; and an ever-deepening understanding of how the goals and aspirations of individual and community were mutually and continuously aligned.'
>
> Brook Manville and Josiah Ober, *A Company of Citizens*, p. 96

This lesson for contemporary organizations and their employees is clear. When the whole company fares well, individual worker-citizens will flourish too, through loyalty both to self and organization.

Liberal democracy

From the fifteenth to the eighteenth century two different forms of political regime were dominant in Europe: the 'absolute' monarchies of France, Prussia, Austria, Spain and Russia, and the 'constitutional' monarchies and republics of England and Holland. To keep sight of our journey of democracy we need next to encounter another group of political philosophers. The traditional political thought that emerged during this time included the republican tradition and the liberal tradition of which Thomas Hobbes (1588–1679), John Locke (1632–1704) and Jean Jacques Rousseau (1712–78) were among the first exponents. John Stuart Mill (1806–73) continued building on these ideals in the nineteenth century. Notions of liberal democracy built on the earlier ideals of Athenian citizenship through representative government and citizen involvement in government. In liberal democracy, participation in political life was not only necessary for the protection of individual interests, but also for the creation of an informed, committed and developed citizenship. These political philosophers saw involvement as essential to the 'highest and harmonious' expansion of individual capacities. We begin to see echoes of the classical democracy tenets of the development of individual nature and expression of diverse qualities, with a clearer view of the impact involvement in the decision making would have on the capacity of the individual to actively develop themselves.[7]

> *'When people are engaged in the resolution of problems affecting themselves and the whole collectively, energies are unleashed which enhance the likelihood of the creation of imaginative solutions and successful strategies. In short, participation in social and public life undercuts passivity and enhances general prosperity.'*
>
> John Stuart Mill, *Considerations,* pp. 207–8

Until the seventeenth century, democracy was largely associated with the gathering of citizens in assemblies and public spaces. By the late eighteenth century it was beginning to be thought of as the right of citizens to participate in the determination of the collective will through the medium of elected representatives. However, it was only with the achievement of citizenship for all adult men and women that liberal democracy took on its contemporary form. The consolidation of representative democracy has thus been a twentieth-century phenomenon in the West, and is now widely adopted in principle as a suitable model of government beyond the West.

Direct democracy

With industrialization the new reality of the 'common man' was apparent to anyone prepared to witness the poverty and abject squalor of their daily lives. It was this reality that shaped the next phase of the journey of democracy when commentators were forced to confront the role of the state. Karl Marx (1818–83) and Friedrich Engels (1820–95) argued that the promise of the liberal democratic state of John Stuart Mill could never be realized in practice as the 'security of person' is contradicted by the reality of the class structure. Most aspects of an individual's life, they felt – the nature of opportunities, work, health, lifespan – are determined by his or her location in the class structure. What could the liberal promise of 'equal justice' mean when there are massive social, economic and political inequalities? They believed the conception of politics and democracy could only be grasped within the overall assessment of the place of the individual in society, the role of property ownership and the nature of production – and, therefore, of capitalism. As a consequence, Marx believed it was necessary to transform the very basis of society in order to create democracy. In *The Communist Manifesto* they argued for five general goals: the end of exploitation of labour in all forms through the social ownership of property, consensus on all public questions, satisfaction of all material needs, collectively shared duties and work, and self-government.[8] This would require the dissolution or what they termed the 'withering away', of the state, the elimination of markets and the creation of co-operation extending to all public affairs.

As history unfolded it became clear that Marx and Engels had not produced an adequate theory of socialism and communism or, above all, an adequate theory of their institutional structures. As was clear in the emerging communist states, when political institutions are reduced to a complex of organizations not clearly separated or differentiated, power can congeal in the hierarchical form. As the political commentator A.J. Polan noted:[9]

> '*It is . . . a gigantic gamble; the gamble that it will be possible to set about constructing the state "in the best of all possible worlds." The odds against the gamble are enormous. It does not simply demand the absence of*

peculiarly unhelpful conditions . . . It also demands a situation devoid of political conflicts, of all economic problems, of all social contradictions, of all inadequate, selfish or simply human emotions and motivations, of all singularity, of all negatively.'

Polan, *Lenin and the End of Politics*, pp. 129–30

Direct democracy has taught us the importance of placing the philosophy of the citizen in the contemporary context of industrialized society. But the contemporary society of Marx and Engels was a society of labour and brawn. The mill workers they observed were selling their labour, whereas in many contemporary societies workers trade on brain, not brawn. In the knowledge economy the relationship of the worker to the organization is less of 'asset', and more of 'investor', where the employee freely invests his or her talents and potential in the organization. In a sense it is this dynamic that allows us to now consider a return to the involved and reciprocal 'citizenship' of ancient Greece, in a way never possible when Marx and Engels observed the northern mill workers.

Competitive, elitist democracy

John Stuart Mill and Karl Marx each had an essentially optimistic and progressive view of human history. They saw humans as being able to create a life of meaning, to expand their capacities, to co-operate in their forms of self-regulation. By contrast, many of those who examined democracy in the late nineteenth and early twentieth centuries had a bleaker, more sober view about living in technically developed civilizations. Max Weber (1864–1920) and Joseph Schumpeter (1883–1950) shared a concept of political life in which there was little scope for democratic participation, and whatever scope existed was subject to the threat of erosion by powerful social forces. Theirs was a restrictive definition of democracy with the central democratic principles of choosing decision-makers and curbing their excesses. Weber saw increasingly larger bureaucratic organizations as playing a key role in the individual's sphere of influence. As Schumpeter writes:[10]

'Democracy does not mean and cannot mean that the people actually rule in any obvious sense of the terms "people" and "rule". Democracy means only that the people have the opportunity of accepting or refusing the men

who are to rule them . . . Now one aspect of this may be expressed by saying that democracy is the rule of the politician.'

Schumpeter, *Capitalism, Socialism and Democracy*, pp. 284–5

His was a view of 'leadership democracy' or 'competitive elitism' in which democracy could only function when the calibre of the politicians was high, political competition took place within a restricted range of questions, and a well-trained independent bureaucracy would aid politicians in all aspects of political formulation. His vision was essentially a technocratic vision, an attack on the idea of the individual human agent, such as had been at the heart of liberal thought from the late sixteenth century. Central to the Athens democracy and to the whole liberal tradition had been the notion of human beings as individuals capable of knowledgeable action. Schumpeter's low estimation of people's capacity paints a world in which the bulk of the population is only minimally engaged with the worlds and institutions around them. In Schumpeter's democratic system, the only full participants are the members of political elites in parties and public offices. The role of the ordinary citizen is not delineated, but is frequently portrayed as an unmantled infringement on the smooth running of 'public' decision making.

In modern managerial lexicon, we consider these as Theory X and Theory Y.[11] Espousing Theory Y are the purposeful, participating Athenian citizens and the liberal views of seventeenth-century thinkers like Locke and Hobbes: human beings are essentially good and capable of growth and active participation. Espousing Theory X are Schumpeter and Weber: human beings are essentially uninvolved and uninterested and need to be 'saved' from their indolence by a clear regime of bureaucratic command and control. It was the assumptions of Theory X that formed the underlying foundation of early automobile factories, with clear supervisory structures and workers as 'interchangeable parts'.[12] The hierarchy and bureaucracy which continue to frame many contemporary companies have their roots firmly in this view of democracy.

Legal democracy

The decade and a half following the Second World War has been characterized by many as a period of consent, faith in authority and legitimacy. In the USA, the patriotic allegiance of citizens seemed to be well established.

'The boundaries of the "new politics" were set by a commitment to social and economic reforms, by respect for the constitutional state, and representative government, and by the decision to encourage individuals' pursuit of their interests while maintain policies in the national or public interest.'

Held, *Models of Democracy*, p. 234

In legal democracy the majority principle is an effective and desirable way of protecting individuals from arbitrary government and maintaining liberty. But for political life, like economic life, to be a matter of individual freedom and initiative, majority rule must be circumscribed by the rule of the law.

In many democratic countries power has been fragmented; it is shared and bartered by numerous groups representing diverse and competing interests. Hence, political outcomes are often the result of numerous processes and pressures, with governments trying to mediate and adjudicate among demands.

This legal democracy is far from the agility and participation of ancient Athens, yet it has been capable of creating a forum in which the voice of the minority can be heard. The issue is the mechanisms by which the liberty of some individuals is not at the expense of others. The general prosperity found in the developed countries of the world has been coupled, some would say reinforced, by a decline in deference or a decline in respect for authority. During this period the neo-liberalists have committed to the view that political life, like economic life, is a matter of individual freedom and initiative. Accordingly a *laissez-faire* or free-market society is their key objective, along with a minimal state. In the 1970s and 1980s the governments of Margaret Thatcher and Ronald Reagan advocated the rolling back of the state, both to stimulate their economies and to increase individual freedom.

In the early twenty-first century many of the issues of the democratic state are played out on a day-to-day basis. What is the role and what are the responsibilities of the citizen in contemporary society, and where in this dynamic is the notion of 'moral reciprocity'? How can the state ensure that the needs and aspirations of the more powerful members of society are not realized at the expense of the weaker and less vocal? What are the mechanisms of participation?

The long journey of democracy has brought many ways of looking at the institutions of which we are members and of contemplating our role as citizens.[13] Perhaps now is the time to re-embrace some of the basic principles of Athenian democracy that have been lost in the morass of industrialization. As I shall argue later, there are a number of contemporary forces that could provide the force and momentum to re-awaken some of the lost tenets of democracy. But before considering these forces, let us first create a framework for the Democratic Enterprise.

The tenets of the Democratic Enterprise

As this short history suggests there has been an extraordinary diversity of democratic models and no treatise on the Democratic Enterprise can claim to represent the definitive set of ideas. Rather such a treatise can only amount to a set of suggestions, or what I have called tenets. I have constructed these tenets by looking at both the richness and depth of historic thinking, and at the present-day experience of democracy of our three citizens.

I have also applied three litmus tests to each tenet:

Coherence. The first is the condition of coherence, the capacity of the tenets to be mutually reinforcing, and to create a consistent system of thinking about an organization. The tenets are not intended to end debate, but rather to stimulate it, by presenting a set of unified, and unifying, principles to help frame and inform the ongoing decisions with which organizations are faced.

Viability. The tenets have been selected on the basis of economic viability. By this I mean they are within the economic structure and goals of both commercial and not-for-profit organizations.[14] The reason for this criterion is simple: citizens can only exercise their rights if they are members of an economically viable business. For this to occur there must be an expansion of economic opportunity to maximize the availability of resources to individuals. If the exercise of citizen rights jeopardizes the long-term health of the company, these rights should not be upheld. The tenets of the Democratic Enterprise have been constructed to create value for the organization while maximizing human potential.

Practicality. The third condition is 'practicality', that the tenet is capable of being operationalized in a company through a set of supporting practices and processes. In devising the tenets I have taken this notion further by specifying that they can be put to work in most companies within a relatively short period of time. This is essentially the stance of the pragmatist, and I make no apologies for it. The long-term democratization of organizations is a legitimate conversation.[15] But my concern is the realistic steps that can be taken now. My agenda is not entirely short term; rather, my expectation is that steps taken now will clear the way for discussions to follow, as democracy proves out both in benefits *and* practicality. In this way enterprise democracy is both a destination, and a journey.

With these selection criteria in mind, what do we mean when we talk of the Democratic Enterprise? There are many forms the democratization of work could take.

In its most structural form, the democratization would mirror the workings of the *demos* in ancient Athens, with the full participation of every citizen in decisions about general policy.[16] This would involve the senior team being accountable to the employees, obliged to justify their actions to the employees and, like leaders of ancient Athens, able to be removed by the employees. Further, the senior team would be chosen by the employees and would act in the interests of the employees. This form of democratization is the principle underpinning works councils in many continental European companies and will increasingly be contained within future legislation of the European Union. However, it has not been a dominant structure in Anglo-American companies, where rights of involvement are held primarily by the financial stakeholders of the company, not by employees without a financial stake. While the structural form of democracy is a legitimate form of democracy in organizations, it is not the form to which this book is addressed, as it fails to meet the third condition of selection: that is it can be made practical within a relatively short period of time.

The form of democracy which I believe has potentially the most impact on the working lives of individual employees, at least in the short term, is what David Held terms 'Democratic Autonomy'.[17] In this form the modern Democratic Enterprise would, like ancient Athens, provide the necessary conditions to enable citizens to pursue their own interests, and where the free development of all would be a common goal.

With this in mind, and drawing heavily on the discussion about state democracy, I have identified the tenets that form the basis of the Democratic Enterprise. I believe these six tenets, realistic rather than aspirational, could stand at the centre of successful organizations.

The six tenets of the Democratic Enterprise

1 The relationship between the organization and the individual is adult-to-adult.

2 Individuals are seen primarily as investors actively building and deploying their human capital.

3 Individuals are able to develop their natures and express their diverse qualities.

4 Individuals are able to participate in determining the conditions of their association.

5 The liberty of some individuals is not at the expense of others.

6 Individuals have accountabilities and obligations both to themselves and the organization.

The first two tenets have as a common framework the principle of autonomy. This principle provides the anchor point for both conceiving and building a robust model of the Democratic Enterprise. In Held's words:

> *What is the status of the principle of autonomy? This principle ought to be regarded as an essential premise of all traditions of modern democratic thought . . . the capability of persons to choose freely, to determine and justify their own action, to enter into self-chosen obligations.*
>
> Held, *Models of Democracy*, p. 303

Looking back at the stories of Greg, Nina and Stewart, it is striking the way they consider themselves and their organizations within the framework of autonomy. Think of Greg as he zigzags across BP: he understands himself, he knows what is important to him, and he is prepared to take action. Or Nina as she describes her plans for herself and for the life she wants to create at McKinsey. Pericles could have been describing Greg or Nina when he said:

> *Each single one of our citizens, in all the manifold aspects of life, is able to show himself the rightful lord and owner of his person, and do this, moreover, with exceptional grace and exceptional versatility.*
>
> Thucydides, *The Peloponnesian War*, pp. 147–8

In attempting to capture the democratic ideal of autonomy within the day-to-day experiences of citizens such as Nina, Greg and Stewart, I have used two related constructs. The first is the idea of the adult-to-adult relationship, and the second is the metaphor of the individual as an investor. By using these concepts I am attempting to capture the reality of contemporary organizational life and to create clear boundaries in which to frame the tenets.

First tenet: an adult-to-adult relationship

At the heart of democracy is the nature of the relationship between the individual and the state. In classical democracy this relationship was manifest among members of the *polis*, each capable, and each believing the other capable, of entering decisions in a fair and thoughtful manner. This was echoed in John Stuart Mill's ideal of the educated, insightful citizen capable of entering into the day-to-day activity of the state.[18] This is an adult-to-adult relationship between citizen and state. With Marx and later Weber, however, we see the role of citizens diminished to the extent that they have to be protected by the state, while the role of active citizen is taken by the elected government. Here the metaphor for the relationship would be more parent–child, with the parent protecting the rights and needs of a child incapable of self-knowledge, or indeed action and volition.

The basis of the Democratic Enterprise is a relationship between the individual and the organization that is adult-to-adult.[19] It is firmly 'Theory Y' rather than 'Theory X'. Greg, Nina and Stewart all view themselves as being in control of their lives, whatever that may mean. Think of Greg as he takes the helm of his career and tacks across the functions, businesses and countries of the BP organization. Or Nina as she reflects, 'Self-governing pervades the way we think about ourselves.' Or Nina again, taking accountability for times when she pushed too far, times when she lost her compass and belief in herself.

In the adult-to-adult relationship, responsibility for behaviour and changes in behaviour are shared by both parties; the needs of both parties are openly debated and considered, and there is freedom on the parts of both parties to act. The emphasis is on the autonomous employee, one capable of assuming both the self-insight and self-direction the role of adult entails.

Second tenet: individuals as investors

In the second tenet I address the question of where ownership of a resource resides. To Marx and Engels, industrialization had created a system in which the capitalists owned the factories and technologies and the wage-labourers were without property. Under this scenario the position of the worker is incomparably weaker than that of his or her employer, who can not only sack the worker but can fall back on employing any number of other, undifferentiated workers in the event of a sustained conflict. Workers soon discover that the individual pursuit of interests is ineffective, and it is only through collective action that they can establish the conditions for a fulfilling life. Here the picture is of the employee as commodity, manipulated by the organization and required to enter into a confrontational mode to ensure remuneration for their labours.[20]

In the majority of contemporary organizations the human asset is not mere muscle, however, but brain, and the dominant activity is not the operation of machines but the generation of knowledge. And in the world of knowledge, ownership of resources is more complex.[21] In the factories where Marx made his observations, the withholding of labour could be actively observed, and indeed the role of the supervisor was to govern this process and maximize output.

But in the knowledge economy each of us can choose to give or withhold our knowledge and it is virtually impossible to detect when we are doing so. Hence the role of the supervisor becomes obsolete, and is taken by the creation of an organizational culture of trust and reciprocity in which employees *actively choose* to share their knowledge. This notion of active choice fundamentally changes the relationship between the organization and the individual. And, as the nature of the relationship changes, so does the transaction. In Marx's world the employee is the *asset* to be controlled and manipulated. In the knowledge economy the employee is an *investor*, actively choosing to invest (or withhold) ideas, inspirations and skills.[22] Ownership of the talents and resources of the individual rests firmly with the individual.

In the words of Andy Grove, Chairman of Intel:

> 'No matter where you work, you are not an employee. You are in business with one employer – yourself – in competition with millions of similar businesses world-wide. Nobody owns your career. You own it as a sole proprietor.'

The investor mindset is perhaps most clearly seen in Nina. Recall her words:

> 'I will have to make some decisions. What will be my unique proposition? I know I have lots of choices. In the next two weeks I have to work through the "Nina Bhatia strategy project" and then syndicate it with my colleagues and say "this is what I plan to do, and this is the help I need, what do you think?"'

Nina places herself firmly into the investor mindset. Investors are individuals who take primary responsibility for both the creation of their talents and resources and the deployment and leverage of these resources. We can actively manage our personal and career resources just as we might manage our financial resources. Again, the emphasis is on personal autonomy, the capacity to be self-directed.[23]

For the condition of investor to be met, two tenets of the democratic relationship must be in place: that individuals are able to determine their conditions of association, and, by doing so, that they are able to develop and express their diverse qualities.

Third tenet: the expression of diverse qualities

Autonomy requires what Carl Jung called *individuation*, the capacity of each person to become themselves. Not what their parents want them to be, not what their teachers want them to be, not what their partners want them to be – but what they want to be, and indeed what they can be.[24] What Nina wants to be, of course, is not the same as what Stewart wants to be, or indeed what Greg wants to be. Implicit in this freedom is the individual expression of diverse qualities.

John Stuart Mill described the expression of diverse qualities as a central aspect of liberty:

> 'Liberty of thought, feeling, discussion and publication (unburdening "the inward domain of consciousness"); second, liberty of tastes and pursuits ("framing the plan of our life to suit our own character"); and third, liberty of association or combination so long as, of course, it causes no harm to others.'

John Stuart Mills *On Liberty*, pp. 71–2

To Marx and Schumpeter, expression of individual variety was lost beneath the heavy hand of mechanization and automation. In Marx's view 'individuals' have limited choice; instead they are prisoners of their past, particularly of the social class and economic circumstances to which they are born. Similarly, Schumpeter viewed people as vulnerable to what he called 'extra-rational' forces, capable of denying their capacity for growth and ensnaring their freedom to make choices about themselves.[25]

In contemporary democracy we have an opportunity to return to the spirit of Aristotle and John Stuart Mill in our embrace of *individuation*. We can re-cast democracy as a basis for tolerating and negotiating difference. After all, what makes for joy and meaning for one individual is not true for all individuals at all times. This speaks to both the individual, in his or her propensity for autonomous behaviour, and to the organization, in its capacity to deliver sufficient variety for diverse qualities to be expressed.

In these first three tenets we have set an agenda for the Democratic Enterprise. It specifies the relationship between the individual and the organization, speaks to the ownership of the resources held by the individual, and calls for the free expression of the diverse qualities of the individual. Each of these tenets has as its underlying expectation that each individual can become the best he or she can be. Thus, these tenets form an important base to creating the autonomy and inspiration which rests at the heart of the Democratic Enterprise, and which we observed in the stories of our three citizens.

But, while Nina, Stewart and Greg are individual citizens, they are also colleagues, active participants in the performance of the companies in which they are members. John Stuart Mill captured the possible tension in his third element of liberty, '. . . liberty of association or combination so long as, of course, *it causes no harm to others*' (my italics). The emphasis here is on 'no harm to others'. But for Nina, Stewart and Greg, their objective is not simply to create no harm; it is to actively and relentlessly contribute to the success of their work teams and their organizations. It is to the contribution of the individual to the organization that the final three tenets are addressed.

Fourth tenet: participation in the determination of conditions of association

Participation in determining the conditions of association specifies the rights of individuals, the entitlement to pursue action and activity. Rights define spheres of independent action, enabling the creation of *space* for action. Without active determination of the conditions of association it is impossible for any employee to truly enter into an adult-to-adult relationship, or behave as an active investor. Within true participation, the individual is an active maker of choices.

We see participation running through the stories of our three citizens. How Nina has actively participated in finding roles and job experiences that would stretch her, yet still enable her to meet her obligations as a mother. How Stewart has actively participated in creating the boundaries of his job to manage his personal needs while still delivering on the BT's business goals. But active participation in the conditions of association was never an end in itself for any of our citizens; rather, participation was one of the life forces that kept them engaged in the company. These are the words of John Stuart Mill:[26]

> '*When people are engaged in the resolution of problems affecting themselves or the whole collectively, energies are unleashed which enhance the likelihood of the creation of imaginative solutions and successful strategies. In short, participation in social and public life undercuts passivity and enhances general prosperity.*'
>
> John Stuart Mill, *Considerations*, pp. 207–8

What do 'conditions of association' actually refer to within an organizational context? We return to these conditions in more detail when we look at the three building blocks of the Democratic Enterprise. But even now we can see these conditions at work in the stories of the citizens. For Nina participation is key to the allocation of projects and jobs and her allocation of time. Her ability to be the best she could be depends on her opportunity to participate in deciding the stretching roles she will take, and her participation in determining the hours she works. Participation in determining the hours of work is also important to Stewart at BT, along with the opportunity to participate in determining the location of his work.

In this fourth tenet the point of negotiation is primarily between the organization and the individual, but in the fifth tenet the arena is broadened

to also include the relationship between the individual and his or her colleagues.

Fifth tenet: the liberty of some individuals is not at the expense of others

This is one of the fundamental tenets of the Democratic Enterprise, that
choices made by some individuals are not at the expense of others. The
determination of the conditions of association is based in part on 'rights', of
the space for action. But rights also constrain: they specify the limits on
independent action so it does not curtail or infringe others. As we have discussed, autonomous individuals have different wants and values. And, as
investors, they have differing amounts, and types, of resources to leverage.
Democracy cannot be about dumbing down to the lowest common denom-
inator. Nor can it be about the more powerful appropriating resources at the
expense of the less powerful.

Within the Democratic Enterprise there are individual wishes and
desires. But they do not occur in isolation from colleagues or company. For
example, Nina's wish to spend less time in the evenings with clients has an
impact on her immediate colleagues. Stewart's desire to work from home
has a similar effect on his co-workers. In Greg's case, his capacity to build a
broad portfolio of skills puts him in a very powerful position in remuneration negotiations: what stops him from exploiting his position to obtain a
package that is unjust in comparison with others? (And what of senior executives with still more power than Greg?) This aspect of the relationship
between citizens has always been a central dilemma for political theory:
finding a balance between might and rights, powers and law, duties and
rights[27] – and achieving fairness, if not equality, in compensation.

For Marx the issue was clear: the powerful would always exploit the weak
and only through solidarity and action would the weak assume sufficient
power to have their needs met and avert exploitation. The role of the state
was to act in the interests of the majority, rather than in the interests of the
most powerful. In contemporary democracy the balance between might and
right is assumed by the government as the creator of laws that specify the
distribution of opportunity and resources.

In a democratic state there will be areas of dispute, and opportunities for
the choices made by the strong to be at the expense of those with less power

and access to resources. The same is true of the Democratic Enterprise, and as a consequence the Democratic Enterprise must offer a just means of negotiating value differences that provides protection for the employee from the arbitrary use of authority and coercive power. Historically organizations have created mechanisms to negotiate differences and, in my account of the Democratic Enterprise that follows, I describe some of the ways this can occur. Central to this provision is the sixth tenet, the accountabilities and obligations of individuals to themselves, their colleagues and their organizations.

Sixth tenet: accountabilities and obligations

The obligations of the citizen have always been central to democracy. In the classic democracy of Athens, each citizen had clear obligations to participate in the creation and nurturing of the common life. Athenian citizenship entailed taking a share in the functions of the state by participating directly in the affairs of the state. Athenian democracy was marked by a general commitment to principles of civic virtue: dedication to the republican city-state and subordination of private life to public affairs and common good. The public and private were intertwined, and individuals could only fulfill themselves and live honorably as citizens through the *polis*.

In the Democratic Enterprise, accountabilities and obligations are crucial aspects of the relationship between the individual and the organization.[28] Nina at McKinsey, for example, is part of a complex web of obligations. She has obligations to herself (to be the best she can be, to develop breadth and depth). She has obligations to her clients (to deliver world-class expertise and advice) and to her team (to mentor, coach and support). At the same time, McKinsey has obligations to Nina: to support her desire to participate in a challenging range of roles and ensure she does not become too specialized. Nina has rights (for personal development, for market-based remuneration) but also responsibilities. It is the implicit contract of obligations that binds rights and responsibilities. Much of this contract is implicit, rich in assumptions rather than facts, uncertainties rather than predictability. One striking aspect of Nina's story is how adept her organization is at 'contracting capability': the ability to make and keep strategically appropriate psychological contracts based on voluntary participation rather than control. The concept of obligations and accountabilities is particularly pertinent to the Democratic Enterprise, and forms a key aspect to the third building block.[29]

Democracy at work

H ow common are the experiences of Greg, Nina and Stewart? To what extent are contemporary companies adopting the tenets of the Democratic Enterprise to enable their citizens to have some of the choices Greg, Nina and Stewart have? Understanding the practices of contemporary organizations will help bring an understanding of gaps between the tenets of the Democratic Enterprise and everyday experiences of employees.

The Democracy Study, begun in 1993 was designed to answer these questions. In it we observed employee attitudes and people management processes in the UK businesses of seven large organizations. These organizations are not in the same sector or business. Rather they were chosen to be representative of organizations in general. The sample includes a global bank, a pharmaceutical company, a computer company, a food manufacturing and a national retail bank. We also studied two organizations that either had been, or still are, in the public sector. A government-owned services company, and a large public hospital in London. We studied (with the exception of Parcelforce) the organizations at three points of time, in 1993–4, in 1996–7 and again in 2000–01. At each of these times we went back to the same part of the organization and surveyed a representative sample of employees. In the first year study we surveyed 1,764 employees, in the second study, 1,592 employees and in the final study, 1,248 employees. In addition to collecting employee survey data, in each of the three studies we interviewed about 30 managers and employees in each organization and ran focus groups with the members of the HR department. We also collected extensive policy and process documentation.[1]

The Democracy Study

Citibank:
Multinational diversified financial services company. Merged with Travelers in 1992.

GlaxoSmithKline:
Multinational pharmaceutical company formed from the merger of a number of significant companies.

Hewlett-Packard:
Computer company grown organically until the recent Compaq merger.

Kraft Foods:
Multinational food manufacturer, marketing and sales company. Created from a merger of a number of significant brands.

Lloyds TSB:
UK-based retail bank and financial company formed from the merger of Lloyds and TSB.

Parcelforce:
UK government-owned distribution company.

Chelsea and Westminster Hospital:
Large, highly sophisticated NHS hospital in the centre of London.

We explored each of the six tenets of the Democratic Enterprise by designing a number of individual survey items pertaining to each tenet. These are described for each tenet and shown in the following six figures. The figures present the percentage of employees in each of the seven organizations who agreed or strongly agreed with the survey item.

First tenet: an adult-to-adult relationship

The adult-to-adult relationship is played out in contemporary organizations in many complex and subtle ways. At its heart is the quality and openness of the communication between the individual and his or her boss, which in the democracy study was operationalized through two survey items: (*I get a great deal/quite a lot of informal feedback from my boss,* and *I have a formal dis-*

cussion about my work performance twice or more than twice a year). In the Democratic Enterprise the adult nature of the relationship is also demonstrated by the involvement the individual feels in the everyday workings of the enterprise, operationalized through two items: (*It is acceptable to question others about why things are done in a certain way*, and *In my organization not just management are expected to solve problems and offer solution*). Finally, in the Democratic Enterprise individual autonomy is developed (or indeed destroyed) by the supportiveness of this relationship: (*In my company people are criticized more readily than praised*).

As Fig. 3.1 shows, with regard to the first element of the tenet, the openness and quality of communication, over 50% of employees in Kraft Foods, HP and GlaxoSmithKline believe this to be so. When we look at the second element, the involvement in everyday working then we can see that this is an element that is being played out across many of the organizations. Again, Kraft Foods, HP and GlaxoSmithKline employees describe themselves as the most involved. In the final element, the nature of the support of the autonomous relationship (which is a reversed scale) people are least likely to believe they are criticized at HP and Kraft Foods, while over 50% of the employees we sampled at Lloyds TSB and Parcelforce believed they were more likely to be criticized rather than praised. We are beginning to see clear differences between these organizations in the employee experience of democracy. Let us now turn to the second tenet to consider whether the adult-to-adult relationship is played out in beliefs about the individual as investor.

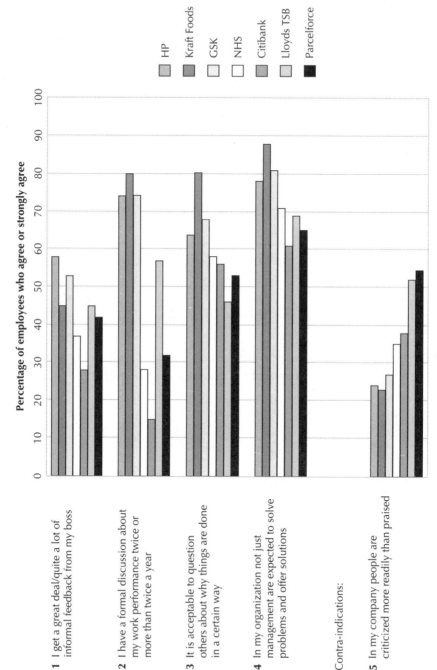

Percentage of employees who agree or strongly agree

Legend:
- HP
- Kraft Foods
- GSK
- NHS
- Citibank
- Lloyds TSB
- Parcelforce

1 I get a great deal/quite a lot of informal feedback from my boss

2 I have a formal discussion about my work performance twice or more than twice a year

3 It is acceptable to question others about why things are done in a certain way

4 In my organization not just management are expected to solve problems and offer solutions

Contra-indications:

5 In my company people are criticized more readily than praised

FIGURE 3.1 ◆ First tenet: an adult-to-adult relationship

Second tenet: individuals as investors

This tenet addresses the question of where ownership of resources resides in the Democratic Enterprise. To Marx and Engels industrialization had created a system in which the 'capitalists' owned the factories and technologies and the wage-labourers were without influence and property. Under this scenario the position of the worker was incomparably weaker than that of his or her employer, who could not only sack the worker, but could also fall back on employing any number of others in the event of sustained conflict. Marx argued that under such circumstance workers soon discover that the individual pursuit of interests is ineffective, and it is only through collective action that they can establish the conditions for a fulfilling life. He described the employee as viewed as mere commodity, an asset to be controlled and manipulated by the organization.[2] Contemporary views of democracy have replaced the unskilled worker which was at the centre of Marx's description, with the knowledge workers who pervade many organizations. Rather than an asset to be manipulated, the employee becomes the investor, actively choosing to invest (or withhold) their ideas, inspirations and skills.

The capacity of employees to actively build and invest in themselves is an individual characteristic, but is also mediated by the organization of which they are a member. In the Democratic Enterprise the employee 'investor' is able to build their personal human capital in order to become the very best they can be. They do this by constantly building their skills for the present and the future. At the same time, they are members of organizations in which their skills and ideas are valued.

The first part of this tenet was operationalized in two survey items. For individuals to be investors they need to develop for the present, but also for the future (*I am able to choose training which relates to my future development*), to have a choice about the direction of their development (*In my career development I have a choice of different career paths*). We have also included two items which would indicate a lack of belief about the individual as an investor. The belief that many will not have access to development (*Career development is only offered to high flyers*), and that the investor mentality is not encouraged (*The organization does not encourage me to develop new skills*). The second element of the individual as an investor is the notion that investing and developing is valued within the context of the organization. This was operationalized with two questions (*New ideas are highly valued in my organization* and *Successful people in my organization continue to try new things*).

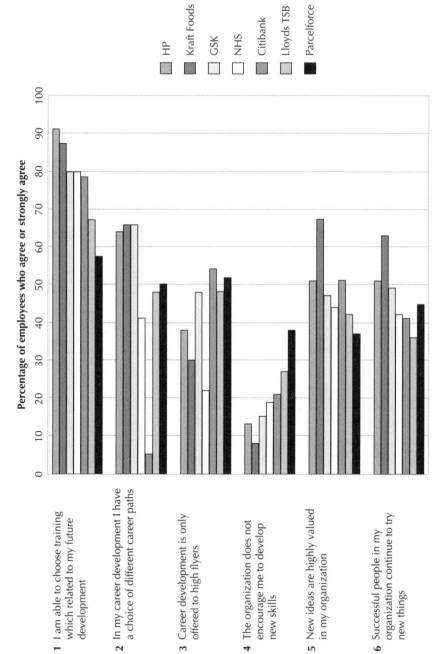

Percentage of employees who agree or strongly agree

Legend:
- HP
- Kraft Foods
- GSK
- NHS
- Citibank
- Lloyds TSB
- Parcelforce

1 I am able to choose training which related to my future development

2 In my career development I have a choice of different career paths

3 Career development is only offered to high flyers

4 The organization does not encourage me to develop new skills

5 New ideas are highly valued in my organization

6 Successful people in my organization continue to try new things

FIGURE 3.2 ◆ Second tenet: individuals as investors

As Fig. 3.2 shows, in many of the organizations in this study over 50% of employees believe they can indeed invest in their future development. However, only in HP, Kraft Foods and GlaxoSmithKline do they believe they have access to broadening their development options. As Items 3 and 4 show, this is particularly the case in Citibank, Lloyds TSB and Parcelforce. With regard to leveraging from development through ideas, it is only in Kraft Foods and HP that over 50% of employees believe new ideas and new ways of doing things are valued.

For the conditions of the investor to be met, two tenets of the democratic relationship must be in place: that individuals are able to determine the conditions of association, and by doing so, to develop and express their diverse qualities.

Third tenet: the expression of diverse qualities

In ancient Athens and again in the words of nineteenth-century philosophers such as John Stewart Mill, the basis of democracy is that each individual citizen has the opportunity to become the best they can be.[3] By the time Marx and Engels viewed industrialization in the mid-nineteenth century, their observation was not that each individual could express their diverse qualities, but rather that people had limited choice. They described employees as being prisoners of their past, particularly of the social class and economic circumstances to which they were born. Similarly Schumpeter, writing in the early twentieth century, viewed people as vulnerable to what he called extra-rational forces, capable of denying their capacity for growth and ensnaring their freedom to make choices about themselves.[4] In the contemporary Democratic Enterprise, where the emphasis is on knowledge, we have the opportunity to re-cast democracy as a basis for tolerating and negotiating differences. After all, that makes for joy and meaning for one individual is not true for all individuals at all times.

This tenet is operationalized with a series of items about the individuals attitude to their career development. The first expresses the idea that in building their future they are indeed able to express their wishes and interests and as a consequence their diverse qualities (*My career opportunities are affected a great deal by my own wishes and interest*). The final three items all operationalize the lack of opportunity to express diverse qualities over time (*My career opportunities are affected a great deal by how much I am liked by my boss; by internal politics* and finally, by individual characteristics, *gender, ethnicity, age and an inability to work flexible hours*).

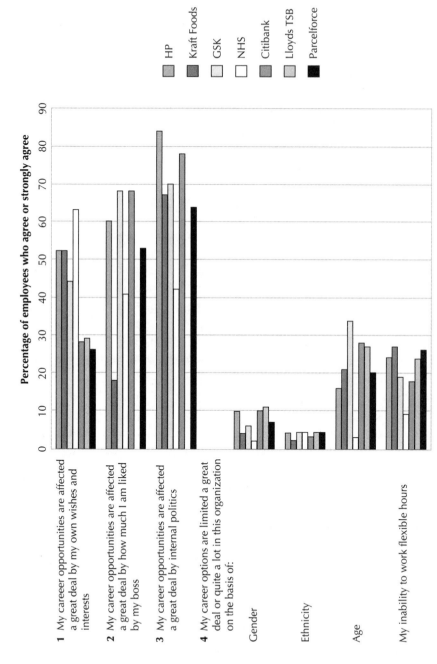

Percentage of employees who agree or strongly agree

Legend:
- HP
- Kraft Foods
- GSK
- NHS
- Citibank
- Lloyds TSB
- Parcelforce

1 My careeer opportunities are affected a great deal by my own wishes and interests

2 My career opportunities are affected a great deal by how much I am liked by my boss

3 My career opportunities are affected a great deal by internal politics

4 My career options are limited a great deal or quite a lot in this organization on the basis of:

Gender

Ethnicity

Age

My inability to work flexible hours

FIGURE 3.3 ◆ Third tenet: the expression of diverse qualities

The Chelsea and Westminster Hospital provides the strongest context for the wishes and interests of people to be reflected in their development, while the retail bank Lloyds TSB and the employees of Parcelforce are least able to create this context.

Fourth tenet: participation in the conditions of association

In the tenets of the Democratic Enterprise, the individual is able to actively engage in the determination of what it is they do, and how they do it. There is a 'latitude of discretion' which provides the space within which choice can be exercised. Without this space there is no opportunity for individuals to take action. Participation in the conditions of association specifies the rights of the individuals, and their entitlement to pursue action and activity. As a consequence, it defines the spheres of independent action, in a sense, the creation of space for action. Without this space for action it is impossible for the individual to establish an adult-to-adult relationship or indeed to view themselves as investors.

Within the context of work there are four elements of association. The first, which we have considered in both the first and the second tenets, is the opportunity to bring ideas into the workplace and to know that these ideas will be valued (*It is acceptable to question others about why things are done in a certain way. In my organization not just management are expected to solve problems and offer solutions. New ideas are highly valued in my organization. Successful people in my organization continue to try new things*). The second element of association is the capacity to determine the framing of work, the goals and targets of work (*I am solely responsible for setting my own work targets*, and *I determine my work targets together with my boss*). The third element is the capacity to influence how remuneration is structured and whether performance influences rewards (*An element of my reward is performance related*) and the extent of choice (*I have a choice over the composition of my pay and benefit arrangements, and have a choice over the balance between my pay and having more convenient work arrangements*). The final element is the capacity of employees to determine where they work and when they work and as a consequence, to balance their work and their life (*When I was offered this job I was able to choose different work hours. When I was offered this job I was able to choose a different work place. This organization does all it can to help its employees maintain a healthy work/life balance*).

As we can see, over 50% of employees from HP, Kraft Foods, Glaxo-SmithKline and the Chelsea and Westminster Hospital determine their work targets with their boss. There is no company where over 50% of employees are solely responsible for setting their own work targets. The highest percentage is at the Chelsea and Westminster Hospital, where 22% of employees are solely responsible for setting their own work targets. With regard to pay decisions, with the exception of HP, less that 28% of employees in all of the companies report that they have any active involvement. The two banks (Lloyds TSB and Citibank) have the highest percentage and Kraft Foods the lowest percentage. There are also clear differences between the companies in their capacity to enable employees to become actively involved in determining the conditions of their association with regard to working hours and location. Only at HP are more than 50% of employees given an opportunity to determine their place of work, and for hours of work the highest is the Chelsea and Westminster Hospital with 28% of employees. The companies that are least likely to engage their employees in decisions about hours or location is Kraft Foods and Lloyds TSB. In the final item (*The organization does all it can to help its employees maintain a healthy work/life balance*), the implications of this lack of involvement are clearly shown, with HP employees most likely to believe the company does help them, and those at Citibank and Lloyds TSB least likely.

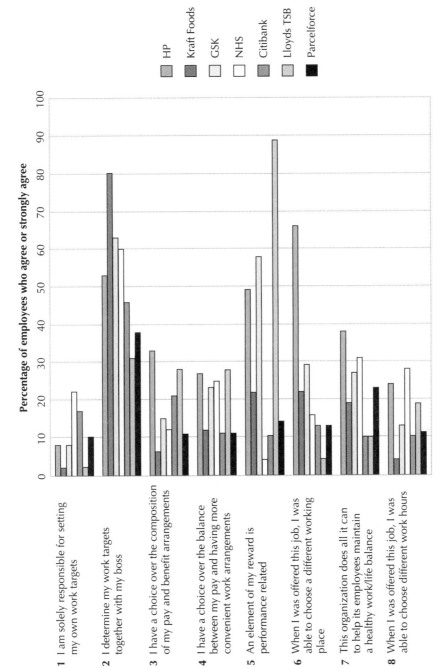

Percentage of employees who agree or strongly agree

Legend:
- HP
- Kraft Foods
- GSK
- NHS
- Citibank
- Lloyds TSB
- Parcelforce

1 I am solely responsible for setting my own work targets

2 I determine my work targets together with my boss

3 I have a choice over the composition of my pay and benefit arrangements

4 I have a choice over the balance between my pay and having more convenient work arrangements

5 An element of my reward is performance related

6 When I was offered this job, I was able to choose a different working place

7 This organization does all it can to help its employees maintain a healthy work/life balance

8 When I was offered this job, I was able to choose different work hours

FIGURE 3.4 ◆ **Fourth tenet: participation in conditions of association**

Fifth tenet: the liberty of some individuals is not at the expense of others

As the earlier tenets have described, within the Democratic Enterprise individuals are able to exercise choice within the context of an adult-to-adult relationship and in the spirit of an investor. As contemporary commentators on democracy have argued, the determinations of these conditions of association are based in part on the 'rights' of the individual.[5] As we have seen in the fourth tenet, these are the rights to have ideas valued, to be involved in determining work targets, to be involved the composition of remuneration, and to choose where and when they work.

But as the ancient Athenians demonstrated, the rights of citizenship also invoke constraint. Specifically, as the writers on liberal democracy concluded, the rights of citizenship also specify the limits on independent action, specifically that the action of one does not curtail or infringe others.

This aspect of the relationship between individuals has always been a dilemma for political theorists, and is also one for organizational theorists. Finding a balance between might and right, power and law, and achieving fairness if not equality. In the state there will be areas of dispute, and opportunities for the choices made by the strongest to be at the expense of those with less power and access to resources. In the Democratic Enterprise there must be a means for negotiating value differences that provides protection from the arbitrary use of authority and coercive power and which enables a fair and just environment to be created.

This tenet has been operationalized in three elements. The first element is the individual's perception of the distribution of their own pay compared to the pay of others (*My pay is fair compared with others doing a similar job in my organization*). The second element is employee's general perception of the environment of fairness and justice, operationalized with three items (*Overall I think the personnel policies of this organization are fair*, and *I can expect my employer to treat me in a consistent and predictable manner*, and *I believe my employer has high integrity*). The final element is a counter-indicator and captures the antithesis of the fifth tenet, that the liberty of some individuals is not at the expense of others (*People compete against each other in a harmful manner*).

As the data in Fig. 3.5 show, only at the Chelsea and Westminster Hospital do more than 50% of employees believe their pay is fair. For most com-

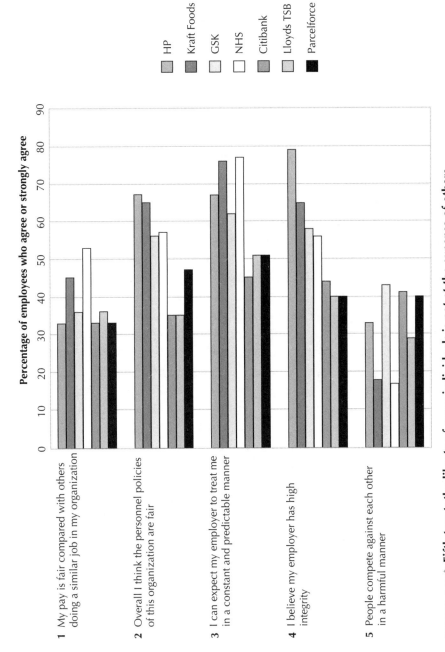

Percentage of employees who agree or strongly agree

Legend:
- HP
- Kraft Foods
- GSK
- NHS
- Citibank
- Lloyds TSB
- Parcelforce

1 My pay is fair compared with others doing a similar job in my organization

2 Overall I think the personnel policies of this organization are fair

3 I can expect my employer to treat me in a constant and predictable manner

4 I believe my employer has high integrity

5 People compete against each other in a harmful manner

FIGURE 3.5 ◆ **Fifth tenet: the liberty of some individuals is not at the expense of others** panies in the sample, less than 35% of people believed this to be the case. We can also see that the general perceptions of fairness and integrity differ markedly across the companies. HP and Kraft Foods are described by their employees as the most fair with the highest integrity, while Citibank and Lloyds TSB are described by their employee as the least fair. In the final element, employees in Chelsea and Westminster Hospital and in Kraft Foods are least likely to describe that they compete against each other in a harmful manner and those in GlaxoSmithKline, Citibank and Parcelforce are most likely to describe that they do so.

Sixth tenet: accountabilities and obligations

The accountabilities and obligations of the citizen have always been central to the concept of a democracy. In ancient Athens, each citizen had clear obligations to participate in the creation and nurturing of the common life. The writers of Liberal Democracy emphasized the positive role of individuals understanding what was expected of them. Moreover, there is evidence that many of the earlier experiments in worker participation floundered because of this tenet. Workers did indeed have a wide latitude of discretion, but they did not know what it was they where supposed to do. Faced with this lack of direction they became anxious and less creative.[6] Much has been recently made of the nature of the contract of obligations that binds individuals to organizations and specifies their rights and responsibilities. Much of this contracting will be implicit rather than explicit, rich in assumptions rather than facts, uncertainties rather than predictability.

In ancient Athens it was the space of the city and the notion of the citizen and the *polis* which held the community together. In the contemporary organization there are no opportunities for the whole community to stand together, it has to be different from, and more than this. As contemporary commentators on democracy have argued, what holds the Democratic Enterprise together is not the rules and power of the bureaucracy, but rather the feelings of shared purpose and reciprocity created through accountabilities and obligations.

We examined accountability and obligations in these seven companies through four elements. The first element is the sense of a shared purpose, that people understand what the organization is trying to achieve and their role within it (*There is a common sense of purpose among the employees*, and

Percentage of employees who agree or strongly agree

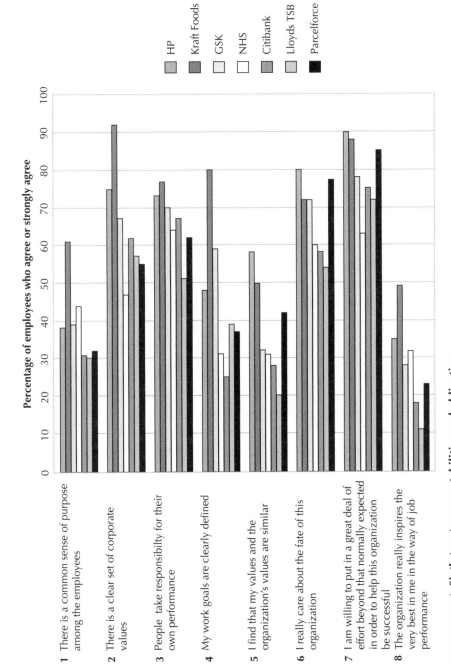

Legend:
- HP
- Kraft Foods
- GSK
- NHS
- Citibank
- Lloyds TSB
- Parcelforce

1 There is a common sense of purpose among the employees

2 There is a clear set of corporate values

3 People take responsibilty for their own performance

4 My work goals are clearly defined

5 I find that my values and the organization's values are similar

6 I really care about the fate of this organization

7 I am willing to put in a great deal of effort beyond that normally expected in order to help this organization be successful

8 The organization really inspires the very best in me in the way of job performance

FIGURE 3.6 ◆ **Sixth tenet: accountabilities and obligations**

Liberating your business with freedom, flexibility and commitment

There is a clear set of corporate values, People take responsibility for their own performance, My work goals are clearly defined). The second element is the belief the employee has about their personal connection with the organization (*I find that my values and the organization's values are similar).* The third element is the feelings of obligations and accountabilities the individual has to the organization (*I really care about the fate of this organization, I am willing to put in a great deal of effort beyond that normally expected in order to help this organization be successful).* Finally, we capture the element of involvement and excitement which many commentators reported in ancient Athens and which the Liberal Democratic writers often referred to (*The organization really inspires the very best of me in terms of work performance).*

In terms of the 'containment' of the potential autonomy of the Democratic Enterprise, the container of a sense of purpose and values is strongest in Kraft Foods where people clearly understand their accountabilities and obligations. The second element is particularly fascinating. Generally, employees across all seven companies care about the fate of the organization and are willing to put in effort to help it become successful. This is particularly marked at Parcelforce. But as we can see, none of the organizations in this study have been able to create working environments in which more than 50% of people feel inspired, and for some this is less than 25%.

The state of enterprise democracy

We began this study of democracy by asking whether the experiences of Greg, Nina and Stewart are indeed shared by people across other companies. We answered this question in part by surveying many thousands of employees across seven large and complex companies. The data for each of the six tenets create what one might call a profile of democracy, a map of current practice. What can we learn from this map of current practice? Faced with this data each one of us will draw our own conclusions and interpret the data in our own way with reference to our own organization.

The issue of differences between companies is fascinating as indeed the question of why some companies are more democratic than others. But before turning to this comparative question let us first consider the experience of the total sample of employees.

Democracy at work

As the data show, there are tenets of democracy which are strongly embedded in companies and elements were the embedding is significantly weaker. The most embedded tenet is the sixth tenet, that of accountabilities and obligations. In many of the companies we studied people understand what it is they are accountable for and their obligations. A majority of employees say they are willing to put in a great deal of effort beyond that normally expected in order to help their organization succeed. This is good news for a Democratic Enterprise and is far removed from the uninvolved, uninterested employee of whom Schumpeter wrote.

There are also tenets that appear to be only weakly operationalized across all the companies. This is particularly the case for the fourth tenet, the opportunity people have to participate in the conditions of their association. This democracy study shows that in many companies less than 25% of employees are able to influence the composition of their pay and benefit arrangements, to choose their working hours or to choose their working location.

The contrast between the strongly embedded sixth tenet and weakly embedded fourth tenet is perhaps most clearly illustrated in the case of Kraft Foods. Here is a company in which people believe they are engaging in an adult-to-adult relationship, see themselves clearly as investors, have a strong sense of justice and fairness and a keenly felt sense of obligations and accountabilities. Yet at the same time around some crucial aspects of discretion, particularly location and hours, their choice is severely limited.

The six tenets can be viewed separately, as they have been in this Democracy Study. However, it is also possible to view them collectively. A potential classification is shown Fig. 3.7.

The six tenets have been collapsed into axes along two dimensions: Autonomy and variety and Shared purpose. While clearly the first axis is not completely unitary (in the sense that a company could have high autonomy and low variety) as a dimension it has the advantage of simplicity. Placing these two dimensions into the model yields four potential configurations.

Clearly *democracy* refers to the capacity to operationalize all six tenets: people are autonomous, they have variety to create the space for action, and a strong sense of shared purpose. There is also a possible organizational context when there is a strong sense of shared purpose, but employees have very little space in which to make actionable choices, and limited understanding of their own potential autonomy. This is a *bureaucracy*, the organizational

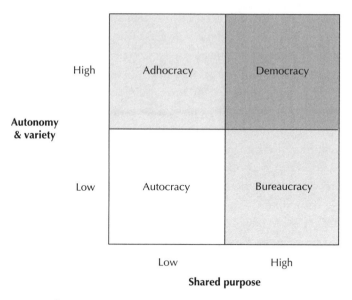

FIGURE 3.7 ◆ **The Democracy Matrix**

form that is most suited to relatively stable environments in which a command and control approach ensures clarity of purpose within tight boundaries. An *adhocracy* emerges when employees view themselves as active investors and continuously build their own personal human capital. However, there is little keeping this band of 'investors' together. There is a limited sense of shared purpose and when the opportunities arise the most skilled will leave to join another loose collective. Typically professional teams such as lawyers, investment bankers and academics create these adhocracies. In a sense the mirror image of the democracy is the *autocracy*. Where the democracy creates space and a sense of purpose, the autocracy has neither space nor purpose. It is essentially a task-driven organizational form where people follow direction with limited engagement or shared meaning.[7]

Each of these organizational forms is to some extent represented in the seven companies in the democracy study.

Autocracy. In an autocracy, employees have limited choice or discretion in their day-to-day work, tasks are clearly defined and results closely monitored. What keeps the autocracy together is the controlling of tasks rather than the sense of shared purpose. Autocracies have historically flourished in stable environments with semi-skilled workers who are operating in a task focused environment. The employee data show that of the seven companies Citibank and Lloyds TSB are autocracies with regard to the first and second tenets; there is very limited autonomy or choice. And as the data from the final tenets highlight, there is a relatively limited sense of shared purpose.

The analysis of the longitudinal data from our research shows that their paths to autocracy are rather different.

As a UK-based retail bank, Lloyds TSB historically developed in a highly regulated financial environment. For decades it operated in what can be likened to a semi-cartel with the other major national retail banks. Under these non-competitor conditions, the bank flourished as a bureaucracy. The exercise of personal will was minimized, and the bank attracted and retained people who were comfortable in the parent–child relationship. A decade ago the sense of shared purpose in this organization was high. Employees understood their roles, and in particular the role they played in the local community in which their branch of the bank operated. The bank functioned primarily on the basis of a parent–child relationship and employees saw themselves as assets, or resources in a benign and positive bureaucracy. Roles and responsibilities were clear; people understood what was expected of them, and, as Weber might have put it, the organization ran like a well-engineered machine.

All that has changed with the liberalization of the financial markets and the entry of new Internet and retail-based banking. The resulting cost competition has seen a dramatic reduction in the banking network and the closure of many local community branches. As a consequence of these competitive pressures, the sense of purpose and shared destiny, which was once so clear, has been replaced by confusion among many employees about their role and long-term viability of the retail banking network. Our interviews highlighted the concerns employees felt about the future of the bank, and therefore about their own future. For many employees, particularly those who joined the organization on the assumption of a 'parent–child' relationship, this new reality is potentially devastating. As the sense of shared purpose faded, the retail bank began to look less like a well-engineered bureaucracy, and more like an autocracy, with employees, who were unclear of their destination, simply taking orders. A shared sense of purpose has been replaced by day-to-day supervision of tasks.

Our longitudinal Democracy Study suggests that the journey to autocracy for Citibank was the result of a loss of a shared sense of purpose and also of autonomy and variety. The earlier democracy studies indicate that the sense of purpose was significantly greater in the early 1990s.

The employees in the survey and those we interviewed felt relatively well aligned with the purpose and goals of the organization. They understood the longer-term goals of the company and the role they could play to help it achieve these goals. During this period the HR team at Citibank continued to develop a whole portfolio of practices and processes such as 360° feedback and personal development workshops which supported employees' sense of autonomy.

The snapshot of the employee data we collected in 2000, and which is shown earlier, caught the organization shortly after the Travelers merger. In the period of our study we observed the clash of cultures and operating practices between these two giants. Travelers had historically been seen as a sharply focused, results-driven, relatively macho organization. So at the time of the study what was probably an autocracy/bureaucracy was merging with a budding democracy in the shape of Citibank. The collision of these two cultures and structures destroyed the sense of purpose that the Citibank people had previously experienced (see the sixth tenet) and also began to dismantle the practices and processes which had historically supported the adult-to-adult relationship that had been nurtured at Citibank (see the first tenet). In the midst of every merger inevitably much is 'unfrozen' and much of the sense of shared purpose is fragmented and dissipated. We know this to be the nature of mergers.

But as the data clearly show, the challenge for the senior teams of both Lloyds TSB and Citibank is to both retrace their steps in building a shared sense of the new purpose, and to continue to build practices and processes which support and acknowledge personal autonomy and choice.

Bureaucracy. Bureaucracy flourishes when there is a strong sense of shared purpose, when people understand the goals of the organization and what they have to do to achieve these goals. However, with regard to autonomy and variety, there is limited discretion about how the goals are met or indeed around the freedom of the individual. Bureaucracies flourish at times of relative stability but become overly static and inflexible if the environment of the organization becomes more competitive and unpredictable. The classic bureaucracy in this study is Parcelforce. Government ownership has until recently created a protective wall between the company and the competitive

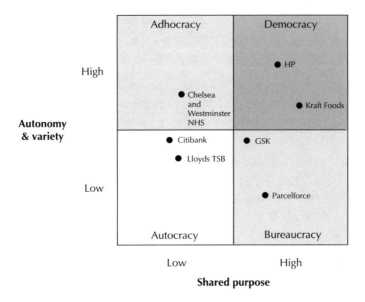

FIGURE 3.8 ◆ **Pathways to democracy**

forces in the distribution industry. However, as government intervention recedes, so too the forces of competition will hit the company with full force and there may well be a need to create a stronger sense of the new purpose while building more employee choice around location and time.

Kraft Foods is on the cusp between a bureaucracy and a fully fledged democracy. It has many of the characteristics of a democracy. As the employee survey data shows, there is a strong and unifying sense of purpose and a clear alignment between the goals and values of individual employees and the goals of the company. With regard to the autonomy/variety axis there is a strong sense of an adult-to-adult relationship. Of all the employees in the study, those at Kraft Foods (as tenet one and tenet two show) are most likely to believe that they can question how things are done, and actively engage in problem solving, in the belief that their ideas will be listened to and valued. The issue for the senior team at Kraft Foods is illustrated in the fourth tenet. Compared to both HP and GlaxoSmithKline, the company has done little to create space for employees to make choices around pay and benefit arrangements, working different hours, and at different locations. Perhaps it is no surprise that less than 20% of employees believe the company does all it can to help them maintain a healthy work/life balance. The current challenge to the senior team (and one of which they are well aware) is to create the space and choice of a true democracy.

Adhocracy. In an adhocracy individuals are relatively 'free agents' with a strong sense of personal autonomy, but a diffused sense of the purpose of the organization. This was the primarily categorization for many employees at the Chelsea and Westminster Hospital. Many employees, particularly those who are medical professionals, have a strong sense of personal autonomy. However, the hospital for many of these people, failed to act as a 'container' for their skills. Managers and professionals described to us that for them patient care is at the centre of their purpose. This is essentially an individual purpose. More diffuse organizational goals such as cost or efficiency had very limited meaning for them.

Democracy. The study shows that in the year of the study (2000), HP was the most democratic of the companies we studied. We will take a closer look at some of the practices at HP when we consider the pioneers of democracy in Chapter Six. Essentially, as each of the tenets show, the HP employees we surveyed had a relatively clear sense of purpose and alignment with their own values and they believed their employee had high integrity. While at Kraft Foods the sense of shared purpose is generally stronger, it is in the question of choice that HP differs. Employees at HP believe they are able to choose training that relates to their future development, they are able to make a choice about the composition of their pay and benefit arrangements, to choose different work hours, and working place. This combination of a strong sense of purpose and autonomy makes for a very agile company. The data was taken prior to the Compaq merger so it is fascinating to speculate on whether these attributes remain intact, or whether, as in the case of Citibank, they have been diluted with the shock of the merger.

At GlaxoSmithKline the context rests somewhat between a bureaucracy and a democracy. The sense of shared purpose (tenets five and six) is less strong than HP and Kraft Foods, but stronger than the other companies. Many employees believe they are engaged in an adult-to-adult relationship and there is some exercise of choice, particularly around location.

Why are some companies more democratic than others?

The Democracy Study shows that there are some companies, notably HP and Kraft Foods which are significantly more able to operationalize the six tenets of democracy. The signature at HP was remarkably stable across the three studies. With the exception of the responses to the sixth tenet, where some items were significantly lower in the 2000 study than in the two previous studies. Our extensive interviews with line managers and employees alike reinforced the data presented here. For HP, the HP Way, which in its own language spoke of many of the aspects of democracy, continued to act as a guiding light to management thinking and decision making.

Many of the tenets of democracy were also reflected in the employee experiences of Kraft Foods. Again, this company has remained remarkably stable over the three studies. During that period the percentage of employees agreeing to the items in the fifth and sixth tenets significantly increased. Over the period of the study we observed a strong sense of individual autonomy combined with a clear sense of citizenship, of an exciting and shared sense of purpose. The democratic tenets were supported not by inspirational founders, as in the case of HP, but rather by a management team relentlessly driving for managerial excellence. It was this drive for excellence that supported the longer-term development of employees and which created and communicated a clear sense of organizational purpose and will. Many of the tenets of democracy are simply characteristics of well-managed companies, companies like Kraft Foods. The challenge for the management team at Kraft Foods is to really capitalize on the asset base of people by linking this professionalism with the creation of greater space for personal choice to be exercised.

The companies with the least democratic signatures were the retail bank, Lloyds TSB and Parcelforce. Why might that be so? Our detailed research reveals that there are a number of interrelated explanations that reveal some of the possible challenges to the Democratic Enterprise.

The first challenge is employee and management mindset. At Lloyds TSB, our detailed interviews revealed that many of the people who joined retail banking over the last decade did so because they saw the retail banking sector as a safe haven of predictability. The parent–child relationship, predictability and lack of space for individual action taking was a potential source of benefit. As a consequence, many of the employees at Lloyds TSB lacked the personal autonomy that underlies the first two tenets of the Democratic Enterprise. At the same time, the bureaucratic, command and control environment this created worked well for the bank during the time it operated in a relatively stable and predictable economic environment. We observe the employees at Lloyds TSB at a time when the retail banking sector is increasingly competitive and the parent–child relationship is increasingly undeliverable.

The second possible challenge to the Democratic Enterprise is employee education. One could argue that perhaps democracy could never flourish with an employee group such as those at Parcelforce who in the main left school at 16 and have limited educational experience. This has been one of the long debates of democracy in ancient Athens. Some argued that for the citizenry to be active decision-makers, there needs to be a relatively highly educated *polis*. There is certainly some support of this question, but we should note that there is a proportion of the workforce at Kraft Foods who also finished formal education at a relatively young age. Whether the individual takes responsibility for their formal education, or, as in the case of Kraft, the company plays an active role – we can see that democracy is more likely to flourish when the citizens are educated.

The final possible constraint to the Democratic Enterprise is traumatic upheaval. Ancient Athens was to eventually fall to rival empires and powers. The citizen democracy that had been created over 250 years was fragile. We saw a similar fragility in Citibank. The data on Citibank collected in 2000 show an employee group which is not sustained by the six tenets, particularly the fifth tenet. However, these data simply represent a snapshot in time. When we look more carefully at the data from the 1994 and 1997 studies, we can see that the number of employees who believed the tenets were upheld reduced significantly in the final study.

Why was this so? Our extensive interviews conducted during that time revealed that the merger between Citibank and Travelers that took place during that period severely ruptured many of the democratic tenets. Some of the effects of the merger fractured the beliefs employees had about the capacity of the company to behave in a fair and just manner and reduced their understanding of accountabilities and obligations. That is not to say that all the mergers we studied had the same effect. During the period of the study both Kraft Foods and GlaxoSmithKline acquired companies. But there appears to be something about the trauma and scale of the

Citibank and Travelers merger that severely impacted on the democratic tenets.

Our Democracy Study shows that it is possible for companies such as HP and Kraft Foods to be democratic and also financially viable. Democracy and Enterprise is not an oxymoron. The study also reveals the extent of the challenge and shows how fragile enterprise democracy can be. But it is possible to build a path to democracy. Particularly, as we shall see, when the forces for democracy are becoming overwhelming.

The drivers to democracy

C reating organizations that are built from the inside out, which have people at their heart, and which encourage individual action taking, makes sense in the knowledge economy. Engaging people in adult-to-adult relationships, supporting their autonomy, and creating a clear sense of obligations and accountabilities, is crucial when the most important resource is what people know and how they are able to develop and leverage this knowledge. As we saw in the behaviour of the three citizens, the Democratic Enterprise supports agility and fast action taking. The processes of choice and initiative create bridges of integration between disparate business units. People who are supported and able to make decisions are also more confident, committed and aligned.

As organizations become ever more reliant on the knowledge and trust of employees, the basic tenets of the Democratic Enterprise will assume a more central role in corporate philosophy. In this scenario we can expect a gradual and continual adoption of democracy. The Democratic Enterprise will not be created overnight, however. Rather, it will emerge through a series of small, tactical steps. In the companies of the three citizens, for example, the democratic tenets have evolved over time as a result of a number of primary drivers.

In some cases a new CEO with a new vision profoundly influences the philosophy of the corporation and, by doing so, the form and structure of the company. So, for example, the aspirations and expectations of BP's CEO, John Browne, profoundly influenced Greg's experience. Nina's experience at McKinsey, on the other hand, was shaped by the ideals of founding partner Marvin Bower, whose ideals have been kept alive by successive partners. Sometimes the sources of pressure are external. At BT, for instance, the shaping of the organization occurred in response to pressing external threats. Stewart's experience at BT, and the capacity of the company to adopt the democratic tenets, was shaped by the company's economic circumstances. For BP, McKinsey and BT, the shaping conditions were specific to each company. At BP and McKinsey the democratization process was caused by a gradual evolution. At BT it reflects an external shock to the system. This raises an important question. Can the rate of change be increased by organization-wide shocks to the system? To answer we need to look for possible shocks which could either accelerate or decelerate the degree of adoption.[1]

Beyond the ever-increasing flexibility of organizations, there are two sources of potential shocks. Both are outside the control of any organization, and both will assume greater prominence and momentum over the next decade.

The first is the shift in our experiences of life, and what people want from life and work. Young people, generations X and Y, are more likely to demand the six tenets, particularly the adult-to-adult relationship and their capacity for self-determination. At the same time, those currently in senior positions, the baby boomers born in the 1940s and 1950s, are ever-more determined to create a variety of associations with the companies of which they are members. The second force of democratization is clearly demonstrated in the stories of the three citizens. The opportunity to live the tenets of democracy is greatly supported by recent technological developments in the interface between the individual and organization. This interface is likely to become increasingly technologically enabled over the next decade.

The first force of democracy: the shift in individuals

There is a plethora of subtle shifts taking place in companies which will create some of the conditions under which democracy will flourish. At the same time, individuals of all ages are becoming more receptive to the ideas of autonomy and as a consequence, more demanding of organizational variety. Those currently in senior positions are now looking for autonomy in the latter stages of their career. At the same time, generations X and Y, who are playing increasingly pivotal roles in organizations, have enhanced expectations of individual autonomy and organizational choice.

The baby boomers want a life

Some of the baby boomers now lead large companies. They are an important generational cohort in the life of many organizations, and also play a role as parents, mentors, sponsors and role models to the current working cohort. The baby boomers are the parents of those currently joining companies, generation X (born between 1962 and 1977) and generation Y (born after 1977).

For many baby boomers their work experience was firmly parent–child. Their generation was brought up to accept the formalization and rigidity of corporate life. Many grew up in intact nuclear families with a working father and an at-home mother. Their own parents had vivid childhood memories of the anxiety and poverty of the Second World War, and their early teens were spent searching for jobs during the post-war depression. This generation heard their parents' stories about their childhood experiences and understood war rations, shortages, sacrifices and heroism. Like their parents, they aspired to join large companies as safe havens in difficult times. They competed hard for the right to join these companies and entered with the expectation that they would spend much of their working life in their employment.

The baby boomers inherited and subsequently shaped and evolved the rigidity and predictability of corporate life. They formalized processes around pay and development, and felt most comfortable within the clear structures of working in offices at predetermined regular times. Many of the vestiges of standardized processes and practices in contemporary organizations arose from their implicit needs. The tenets of democracy do not come naturally to them.

This generation worked longer hours than ever before. Much of this work was emotionally and intellectually taxing with significant and negative carry-over from working lives to personal lives.[2] For some baby boomers the long hours and their dedication to work, had a detrimental impact on their opportunity to build fulfilled lives. Nowhere is this more apparent than in the lives of female executive baby boomers. In the US over 40% of senior corporate women aged 41 to 55 don't have children. Within this group many regret that they did not have children earlier in their careers.[3] They, perhaps more than any other segment of the baby boomers, understand with complete clarity the sacrifices they made. The tragedy is that it is not clear that these sacrifices were necessary. Too often these executive women failed to have children not because they did not believe they would be capable of multi-tasking, but rather because of 'presenteeism'. In many companies long hours were encouraged as a surrogate for meaningful measures of performance. The double tragedy is that as the BT study on time flexibility which supported Stewart's choice shows,[4] people who are able to exercise a choice about their working hours are more productive not less. But it is not just women without children who may have sacrificed in this generation. Robert Reich, former US Secretary of Labor, in his chronicle of the dissolution of the American family asks the provocative question of those who failed to craft a working life that was capable of bringing joy:[5]

> *'Given the new economy the choices people are making about families are entirely rational. But the more fundamental choice has never been posed, and the more basic question never asked: Would we choose every aspect of this new reality if we fully appreciated its consequences for the family life we may otherwise have? In other words, as with other aspects of our personal lives, is the new economy worth what it costs us?'*
>
> Robert Reich, *The Future of Success: Working and Living in the New Economy*, p. 175

It is likely that many baby boomers made decisions about their working lives without fully appreciating the consequences. So what we know of the baby boomers is that they crafted organizations with limited choice. The sacrifices they made as a consequence are plain to see by successive generations who are now more likely to demand an adult-to-adult relationship.

One impact the boomer generation has on contemporary organizations is as role models for younger people. They are role models in the sense that their children may actively make choices so that they are not like their parents, rather than model themselves on their parents. In particular, they will be more demanding of a negotiated relationship with their employer in a way in which their parents never were.

Yet, as they move towards the latter phase of their career many of the boomers are taking a more meaningful view of their lives. In their late 40s and

50s, they want to exercise the autonomy and choice which was never available to them earlier in their working lives. A recent survey of Stewart's colleagues at BT, for example, shows that the vast majority do not want to take any more responsibility and are prepared to accept reduced pay and promotion in order to build more fulfilling lives. The generation that did much to shape the current reality of working lives is now looking for something different. They want more choice and more variety. And members of this generation are not simply taking early retirement and leaving organizations. As the demography of the Western world swings towards a greying, ageing workforce, so the needs of this generation are becoming more important.

Generations X and Y want autonomy and choice

One could argue that the impact of the boomers on organizational life is likely to be a slow burning one rather than a shock to the system. This may be the case, but their children who are now entering companies could well create the shock that makes a significant difference.

A major impact of the baby boomers on contemporary organizations is as the parents of generation X and generation Y. The burnout of the baby boomers was witnessed in full technicolour by generation X. Now in their late 20s and 30s, generation X witnessed the dissolution of the nuclear family and the influence of television and mass media.[6] They also increasingly saw their parents as the innocent victims of the corporate redundancies in the 1970s and 1980s. They also felt the impact of downsizing and rightsizing in the early 1990s as they watched their parents struggle with job loss. They saw their parents' love affair with the corporation beginning to tarnish and the parent–child relationship becoming less attractive and viable.

What replaced this for generations X and Y was a growing scepticism and indeed a growing realism about what companies could actually provide for their workers. Perhaps more importantly, they understood the obligations, duties and responsibilities that they personally had to shoulder. They had seen their parents sacrifice their personal needs to the company requirements. Many had vicariously experienced the tragedies of the 'organizational man', and became increasingly determined not to fall victim to the forces of de-personalization in the traditional model of work. As a consequence, they are beginning to take a more upfront approach.

The drivers to democracy

In 2001 I listened to Candice Carpenter, the co-founder and chairman of iVillage.com, address MBA students:

'What you are going to be when you grow up is a meaningless question; keep your life on a track you respect; make every five years count, the 30-year gold watch model is dead, get the most out of a three- to five-year relationship; identify your dream job and choose jobs for mastery, not glamour; seek feedback voraciously; keep fluid, make real choices.'

Her framing was absolutely within the second tenet of the Democratic Enterprise, the investor mindset. Even with the bursting of the dot.com bubble which marked the entrance of this cohort to the labour market, much of her message is still relevant. These students saw themselves less as 'assets' to be managed, and more as 'investors' to build a working life capable of bringing meaning.

However, while these generations may have witnessed the reality of corporate life vicariously through their parents, they are also the recipients of the wealth their parents generated. Generation Y, who entered the workforce in the early years of this century, have grown up in an atmosphere of greater economic prosperity than any previous generation. They are optimistic and confident. Of course, it is impossible at this stage to know how this cohort will develop as they age and their context evolves. However, early signs suggest that their optimism and confidence translates into a more upfront attitude to negotiating an adult-to-adult relationship and a greater push for the variety which would enable them to express their diverse qualities and build work–life balance.[7] This generation is certainly ambitious, and having experienced prosperity, is ambitious to maintain their lifestyle. However, they want this delivered in a flexible way, particularly in terms of working hours and personal development. It is the variety of the democratic organization that appeals to them.

People from this generation are self-reliant, clearer about what they want, more upfront in their interactions with institutions and more pragmatic in their approach to the deal. They want to be involved in decisions and see their ideas and contributions actively solicited. They have lived in a context of rapid acceleration of technology. This is the first generation to grow up online. We might expect technologies which will power choice to be accelerated as this generation assumes positions of influence within organizations. And not only is this generation technologically savvy, it is more diverse and more familiar with working and living in a flexible way.[8] Generation Y grew up with their parents filling their day with activities. They are used to being on the move and expect to be constantly stimulated by activities. In 1981 parents programmed 60% of an American child's weekday time; by 1999 this had risen to 75%. As a result, generation Y grew up multitasking. They know how to make the most of every minute. The democratic tenet of variety and self-expression is central to them.

Much of the structure and many of the processes that create rigidity and inflexibility in contemporary corporations were either created, or stewarded by the baby boomers. Contextual changes have destroyed much of this, as career ladders broke and job levels compressed.[9] Nevertheless, as the earlier analysis indicates, the vestiges of many aspects of this rigidity remain and can still be seen. They are evident in the inflexibility around working hours; in the ways in which the internal market for jobs and projects is controlled; in the 'one size fits all' attitude to training and development; in a culture of 'presenteeism'; and in the tight definition of roles and the diminishing of the 'latitude of discretion'. The entry of generation Y into organizations will do much to destroy these vestiges of rigidity and build democracy. They have the technical savvy, the flexible mindset and a belief in a balanced life. And most importantly, they are prepared and able to negotiate for this deal – to assume an adult-to-adult relationship. They want to be treated as individuals; and to have knowledge about their choices. They want to be given the tools to manage themselves and their careers. The entry of generation Y to roles of corporate responsibility could well be the shock which transforms the system.

The second force of democracy: the shift in technology

The societal forces that underlie democracy are ever-increasing. Across generations, both young and old are looking for a different way. Those currently leading large corporations are burning out and are increasingly clear about the sacrifices they made. At the same time, generations X and Y are more familiar with choice and variety, more able to work in a context of ambiguity and multi-tasking, more able indeed to embrace the tenets of democracy.

If this was the only wave of change –the only shock to the system – it could simply remain that . . . a wave crashing against an immobile object. But there is more happening which has the potential to fundamentally change the nature of practices and processes within organizations. This is the wave of technology and it is to this that we now turn. If the generational mindset is the 'soft wiring' of democracy, space and choice; then technology will increasingly become the 'hard wiring' of the Democratic Enterprise.

The primary impact technology will have on hard wiring democracy is in software technology and the creation of platforms and networks. Software technologies have the capacity to make an enormous amount of previously restricted information available to individuals. This will ultimately support their capacity to be autonomous and insightful. Platforms and networks will support this. They will enable aspirations to be tied to specific outcomes.[10] Take the example of Greg Grimshaw at BP as he zigzags around the corporation. Before the technological developments that supported the creation of the employee portal, the internal labour market at BP was supported manually. Imagine photocopying by hand and circulating to the 100 worldwide locations of BP the many hundreds of job and project vacancies that occur every week. Or encouraging 100,000 people to fill in and keep up to date a profile of their current skills and competencies, development needs and preferred work locations. Then imagine trying to manually match the hundreds of jobs with the 100,000 profiles, while all the time updating the jobs and the individual career plans on a weekly basis. The sheer logistical complexity of the task meant the vision of a worldwide job market was simply not feasible. What it meant in practice for BP, as for other multinational companies, was that choice was given to a small proportion of people who were perceived to be of high potential. But that opportunity was effectively denied to the majority of employees. What ever the management philosophy or the desire to broaden choice and democracy, the technology was simply not available to support this desire. It was only with the network and software developments of the mid-1990s that it became possible to support the creation of employee portals and make choice available outside the high potential population.

Or consider the decision Stewart at BT made to work from home. Even in the mid-1990s this would have been technologically impossible. Certainly BT was trialing mobile working from the early 1990s, but the technology to support this was both expensive and unreliable. These early trials were important in creating knowledge about the support necessary to home-workers. But they were not sufficiently successful to be rolled out across a wider community. It was only with the developments in broadband technology from 2000 onwards, which brought both efficiency and reliability, that people like Stewart could have the choice to work from home while keeping in constant touch with their peers and colleagues.

For BT and BP – and the pioneering companies described in Chapter Six – recent technological developments have been instrumental in providing bundled information to employees and to linking them together to create and deliver organizational variety. These technologies have been adopted by these companies to facilitate employee choice and create fairer and more democratic ways of working. Yet at the same time, many of these technologies create a level of employee involvement and choice which can potentially go way beyond the initial strategic intent of the senior executive team. In a sense these technologies which link and create choice have the characteristics of disruptive technologies.[11] This is the term given to those technologies which fundamentally change some crucial aspect of the value creation chain or disrupt the conventions of the sector.

If we can view these technologies as disruptive, what exactly is it they are disrupting? At BT, BP and McKinsey technology has disrupted two important conventional elements. First, it has disrupted the parent-to-child relationship between the company and the individual by bringing an enormous amount of information into the sphere of individual employees. This has fundamentally shifted the balance of power towards an adult-to-adult relationship, and ultimately to a more democratic social order. Second, technology has created a platform for the delivery of variety, which has made one size fits all, seem like ancient history. In all these pioneering companies these technologies were embraced as a support to the managerial philosophy of autonomy and choice. In other companies the philosophies may not directly support democracy, but nevertheless, these technologies, once introduced will inevitably push for democracy as information flows throughout the organization and variety flourishes. It would take a very powerful management team with a clear set of rules and procedures to stop the inevitability of the technology. And once the genie is out of the bottle it will be enormously difficult to push it back in again.[12]

The technologies that underpinned the choices which Nina, Stewart and Greg made are just the embryonic form of what is to come. Over the next

The drivers to democracy

decade the predicted technological advances have the capacity to support the tenets of autonomy and self-expression. Figure 4.1 shows the predicted expansion of information over the next decade.

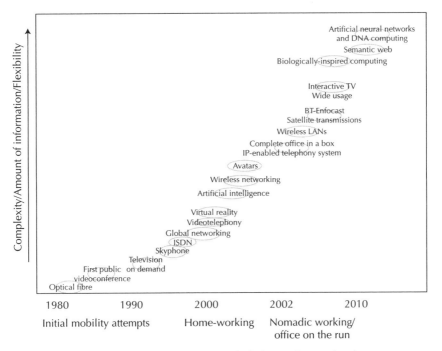

FIGURE 4.1 ◆ **Technological advancement in information technology**

We can anticipate that over the next decade technology will enable even greater opportunities for employees to exercise autonomy and express their diverse qualities through the assimilation of meaningful information. Advances in areas such as artificial intelligence, neural networks and mobile-enabled wireless will build global connectivity. Full voice interaction with machines will create a more natural interface between man and machines, while *avatars* – 3-D representations of people that allow interaction in cyberspace – will support the creation of virtual relationships.

Technological advances will support the six tenets of the Democratic Enterprise in many different ways. As we shall see, technology will support the individual autonomy so crucial to the adult-to-adult relationship and the investor mindset. Technological advances also have the potential to create the variety and choice which underpin organizational flexibility.

Support for individual autonomy

Information will increasingly be tailored to meet the needs and development aspirations of individuals. In this way technology will support their autonomy. This is how the representatives of the American government's Advanced Distributed Learning initiative saw this development:[13]

> *'We envision a future in which everyone will have an electronic personal learning associate. This device will be able to assemble learning or mentor presentations on demand and in real time – any time, anywhere. The presentations will be tailored to the needs, capabilities, intentions and learning state of each individual or group of individuals. The device will be portable, perhaps small enough to be carried in a shirt pocket.'*

These fully portable electronic performance portfolios will be carried wherever an individual goes and will be used by them, their teams and their organization for a variety of purposes, including credentialling, building knowledge and skill inventories, accessing performance, and matching individuals to learning content. The competencies in each role will be mapped by their value to the organization and also their uniqueness as a source of competitive advantage. This mapping will enable organizations to focus on developing those competencies that are high value and unique.

Rapid advances in intelligent tutoring systems will largely remove the need for formal, event-based learning in the workplace. Sheep dip training will be a thing of the past. Instead intelligent tutoring software will look over their shoulder as an individual performs tasks, it will anticipate what they will need next, and offer suggestions for their next move. The intelligent tutor will help an individual see patterns of behaviour that affect their performance and identify the alternatives to replace these patterns. This will have a significant impact on the choice individuals have in the way that work is performed. Increasingly these technologies will support learning by doing as just-in-time learning becomes the norm. Learning will be dissolved into working and doing. Training will be chunked into micro doses; learning will be embedded in task performance. Technology will recede from our consciousness as advances in voice and handwriting recognition smooth the interface.

For people like Greg, who enjoy moving across roles and responsibilities, the possibilities of customization which will increase dramatically over the next decade. They will enable him to plug into knowledge as and when he needs it. Aided by neural networks, capable of pattern matching, his personal computer will identify his working patterns and configure the e-learning modules most appropriate for him at that moment. At the same time, streaming video technology will enable a custom made set of learning objects to be selected and configured to meet his skill needs on a day-by-day basis. Some of these learning objects will be short videos, others will be graphics, while others will be text. These learning objects will then be assembled and sequenced into the pattern most likely to suit Greg's learning style and presented to him when and where he needs them.

Support for flexibility and variety

Many of the technology advances over the coming decade will have a profound influence on the expression of individuality through choice, and ultimately the flexibility with which work is done. Choice and flexibility will be increased in three key ways. First, through technology which supports mobility, allowing people like Stewart at BT to work virtually. Second, through technologies such as 'avatars' which will support communality in virtual work. And third, through developments in artificial intelligence and neural networks which will enable multi-tasking within and across companies to occur with greater ease.

Over the coming decade we can expect to see a proliferation of the global networks which will support virtual working. Wireless connectivity will revolutionize mobility by freeing people from wired connections and enabling secure links to be created between mobile computers, mobile phones, portable handheld devices and the Internet.[14] Initially workers in much of the developed world will have public access to wireless local area networks (WLAN) which will enable them to access data from their laptop in any location. For people like Stewart virtual working will become ubiquitous as voice recognition enables access to web-based information without the need for fixed PCs. These new wave voice technologies will enable 'voice portals' to be created and by doing so broaden and simplify the user interface. Wireless connectivity will support virtual working by creating location and time flexibility. At the same time, it may well be that the potential inhumanity of virtual working will be made more human through advances in *avatar* technologies. These 'photo-realistic 3-D models' are graphic representations of a human being in a computer-generated world. So your personal avatar will be stand in for you at meetings and engage in conversations. For Greg at BP in 2003 the search engine termed '*myAgent*' searches jobs and projects for him across the internal labour market of BP. By the middle of the century, his avatar will represent Greg in his search for interesting jobs both within BP and with the communities and companies to which BP is linked.

As we have more choice about the projects and tasks we work on, so the scheduling and monitoring of these tasks will become ever more complex. And remember generation Y is particularly adapt at multi-skilling. By the end of the decade, artificial intelligence and neural networks will act as the links between people and tasks as more work is achieved through virtual companies.[15] These technologies will also enable advanced work scheduling to take place, where the preferred working patterns for every individual employee can be linked to the ebbs and flows of the working day.

Together the 'soft wiring' of changes in mindset of the generational cohorts, and the 'hardwiring' of technological developments will do much to make the six tenets of the Democratic Enterprise a reality for many people. Over the next decade the experiences of people like Greg and Stewart and Nina will not be restricted to the lucky few.

In this chapter we have examined how demographics and technology are driving organizations towards the model of the Democratic Enterprise. In particular, we have seen that technology has the potential to provide the *hard wiring*, while shifting generational attitudes provide the *soft wiring*. The convergence of these factors mean that the foundations have now been laid to built the Democratic Enterprise. But as we saw many companies are struggling to deliver on the six tenets.

The question is how can companies best harness the power of these two drivers of democracy to construct a Democratic Enterprise. The answer, I believe, lies with three important building blocks. It is to these that we now turn.

Building individual autonomy

T he route to the Democratic Enterprise is not some off-the-shelf organizational change programme. True, long lasting change is more subtle, sophisticated, sensitive and democratic.

It begins with the acknowledgement and living of the six tenets of the Democratic Enterprise. The six tenets of the Democratic Enterprise are brought to reality through three building blocks.

The tenets

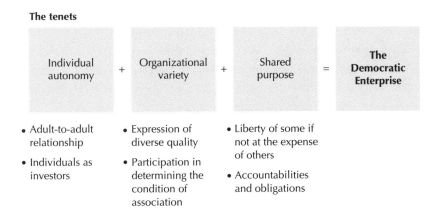

FIGURE 5.1 ◆ **The building blocks**

The first building block is the relationship individual employees have with themselves. It addresses the first set of the democracy tenets: the capacity of employees to behave as adults, and their capacity for self-awareness. This is termed 'individual autonomy', and it relates to individuals as citizens who choose to invest their talents in the organization. The second building block is more focused on the practices and processes within the organization to deliver on the democracy tenets of the expression of diverse qualities, and the determination of the conditions of association. The second building block is the capacity of the processes and practices within the organization to enable employees to exercise choice through the creation of variety, hence, this is termed 'organizational variety'. The third building block is the establishment of a 'shared purpose' through the creation of accountabilities and obligations capable of balancing the needs of the organization with the needs of the individual.

The citizen investor

In the Democratic Enterprise the basis of ownership of an individual's personal human capital shifts from an asset to be managed by the company, to that of an investor, where individuals build, deploy and invest their own personal human capital. The analogy here is with the way in which personal financial capital is invested and deployed. These differences between the notions of asset and investor are profound. They highlight differences in ownership, but also in the feelings individuals have about themselves, their self-determination, their self-awareness and their capacity to make choices based on this self-awareness. An asset has no freedom to act; it is simply a resource to be assigned and re-assigned. But an investor has both the autonomy to choose and the freedom to act.

If individual employees are to be viewed as investors rather than 'assets', then what is it they are investing? In this first building block I believe there are three aspects of personal human capital which are crucial to the individual and to the organization. The first of these is intellectual capital, which is the capacity to learn and to accumulate explicit and implicit knowledge. The second is the individuals' emotional capital – their capacity for self-awareness and to behave with self-understanding and integrity. The third aspect is the individuals' social capital, their personal authenticity and trustworthiness, and the network of friendships and relationships they have created.

These three aspects of personal human capital are the engine for individual autonomy. Without them individuals have neither the resources nor the capacity to exercise their will, In his description of the forms which democracy can take, the political philosopher David Held describes the autonomy of the citizen in this way:

> 'The capacity each individual has to reason self-consciously, to be self-reflective, and to be self-determining. It involves the ability to deliberate, judge, choose and act upon different possible courses of action in private as well as in public life.'
>
> David Held, *Models of Democracy*, p. 300

Held was referring to the role of the citizen in the democratic state, but the same could be said of the employee in the Democratic Enterprise. The notion of the autonomous individual underpins the adult-to-adult relationship. It is at the heart of the search for each individual to become 'the best they can be'. Individual autonomy is a prerequisite for the expression of diverse qualities, or what Jung termed 'individuation'. The first building block of the Democratic Enterprise is the capacity of individual employees to become self-determining, and the propensity of the organization to support this autonomy.

The investor mindset is focused on developing and leveraging personal human capital to get the best return. In other words, citizen investors invest their talents and commitment in the organization in the expectation of realizing their own potential. But in becoming the 'best one can be' as Jung pointed out, the emphasis is on the individual. In other words, what each one of us can become is unique to each of us. The challenge for the Democratic Enterprise is to nurture each individual to become the best *they* can be. So the organizational challenge is to create a context of practices and processes in which there is sufficient space, freedom and latitude for each individual to realize their personal potential.

The elements of human capital

Our three citizens, Greg, Nina and Stewart, are seeking to build and leverage three elements of human capital which have implications for themselves and for their organizations. First, they want to build *intellectual capital* by creating knowledge. This is the basis for success in most organizations, and it is at the heart of their individual development and the creation of a personal asset base which creates their personal value. This in turn enables them to exercise choice. Second, they maintain energy and emotional stability by building *emotional capital*. This enables the continual growth and fulfilment of ambition. For organizations, energy is crucial to the momentum that drives performance, innovation and flexibility. When energy lapses in organizations the inertia that takes its place has a detrimental impact. We maintain emotional capital and energy through self-awareness and insight, and making choices that ensure we do not become overly stressed or dissipated. Third, they seek to forge relationships which create *social capital*. For the organization this is crucial as traditional hierarchical roles and responsibilities are now being replaced by integrated structures held together by relationships of trust and reciprocity. It is within these relationships that ideas are generated, and insights created. And indeed for each one of us, the formation of relationships is crucial to our well-being. Human beings have a natural desire to build their human capital, which is good for the individual and the organization.

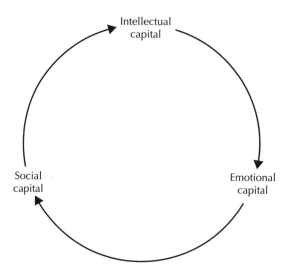

FIGURE 5.2 ◆ **The elements of human capital**

These three elements, or personal assets, are highly interrelated. It is through their combination, the feedback-loops and the connectivity, that they bring advantage to the organization and to the individual. Social capital in the form of extensive, fluid and reciprocal relationships with others helps individuals develop intellectual capital by accessing the knowledge and skills that other people possess. Emotional capital brings the integrity and self-awareness to build open and trusting relationships, which underpin the creation of relationships. The learning propensity of intellectual capital can be a driver for self-development, resulting in the self-awareness of emotional capital. And with this reinforcing feedback-loop, the self-knowledge built through open and meaningful relationships further enhances self-awareness and self-esteem.

Together, emotional, social and intellectual capital forms the basis for strong and supportive relationships and for developing the courage and grit necessary for entrepreneurship and taking action. In turn, action leads to knowledge – people learn by doing, by experimentation, by testing ideas. The reverse is also true – knowledge and skills are a prerequisite for effective action. A similar kind of symbiotic relationship exists among all the elements of personal human capital.[1]

These are the three elements that, from the individual's perspective, constitute *personal human capital*; and from an organizational perspective *organizational human capital*. The notion of human capital refers to what each of us has. Collectively, it refers to the resource base of the organization. But we are more than the sum of our human capital. As individuals, we do many things that have nothing to do with our personal human capital. The key word here is capital – i.e. productive resources, and the adjective is human. It refers to our personal productive resources. What is it about people that translate into value for themselves and the organizations of which they are part? To understand the autonomy we need to understand what it is that organizations and individuals seek to achieve. We now turn to a deeper view of these three areas of human capital.

Intellectual capital

Intellectual capital is central to the individual and the organization.[2] For the individual, intellectual capital has three aspects. The first is the capacity and propensity to be a continuous learner. This was crucial to Greg; it enabled him to be considered for roles that were substantially outside his current competency profile. The second element, cognitive complexity, is the capacity to understand and interpret complex data and establish trends. Much of this attribute, which underpins much of intellectual capital, is likely to be predetermined; it is hard-wired into the structure and connections of the brain. At McKinsey, for example, Nina was chosen by an initial selection phase, based on her results in tests such as GMAT. This is an attempt to use cognitive complexity as an initial screen into the company. From learning capacity and cognitive complexity comes the final and most obvious measure of intellectual capital – the development and accumulation of specialized knowledge. This can be held as wither tacit or explicit knowledge.[3] Tacit knowledge is the knowledge that is difficult to explain to others. As Chris Argyris describes[4] it:

> *'Tacit knowledge is what we display when we recognize one face from thousands without being able to say how we do so, when we demonstrate a skill for which we cannot state an explicit program, or when we experience the intimation of a discovery we cannot put into words.'*

Chris Argyris and Don Schon: Theory in Practice

In some industry sectors tacit knowledge: of immense importance to the individual and much organizational emphasis, particularly with mentoring and coaching, is focused on enabling others to learn from the tacit knowledge held by one person.

In the Democratic Enterprise, much of the capability of individuals to become autonomous and reach their full potential relies on the value of their asset base. Greg's capacity to exercise choice to move across functions and to direct his job moves was predicated by his personal skill set and knowledge, and his excitement and capacity to learn. Without this, he could still exercise his choice to apply for these jobs, but he would not have the skills to be judged competent to do the job. The same is true for Stewart at BT. Working from home was made possible by the business case he constructed in which he demonstrated that he had the knowledge and skills to perform the role from his own home.

It is a continual cycle of development of the greater an individual's personal value, the more access he or she has to variety, and the more possibility he or she has to make choices and operate as a citizen. An essential part of this personal value is knowledge. People acquire knowledge by being continuously exposed to the latest ideas and concepts and by applying these ideas and insights. Part of an individual's investment in developing intellectual capital will be in the form of time and money to participate in ongoing educational activities. But more of it is likely to take the form of the trade-offs they make between appropriating the returns from existing knowledge, and committing resources to develop new knowledge. So, for example, reading, taking sabbatical leaves, retraining, and becoming part of the networks in which relevant new knowledge is created, are all activities that support learning. Important as it is, however, this is likely to contribute a relatively small part of total learning unless there is the capacity to obtain greater leverage through induction and reflection. Intellectual curiosity is a key asset.

Intellectual curiosity requires the courage and personal sense of autonomy to form one's own 'theories'. The quality and usefulness of such theories depend, to some extent, on individual attributes such as creativity, the capacity for pattern recognition and personal cognitive complexity. However, the courage to engage in such theory-building endeavours can be enhanced through both practice and reinforcement from mentors who become 'thinking and talking partners', and stimulating colleagues who help create an intellectually challenging environment that facilitates action learning. For the determined developer the freedom to choose feedback-rich work, a stimulating environment and knowledgeable mentors and sponsors will be crucial to building their intellectual capital.

Intellectual capital is held at both the individual and organizational level.[5] As individuals build their personal intellectual capital so, too, it accumulates at the organizational level. The intellectual capital of the organization is expressed as both the depth and breadth of explicit knowledge. That is the knowledge that has moved from the domain of individual and tacit, to the domain of organizational and explicit. This occurs through mentoring and coaching and with practices and processes that store knowledge and enable it to be retrieved in a meaningful manner.[6] So for Nina at McKinsey, the corporate knowledge portal is an attempt to collect, assimilate and store the intellectual capital of the members of the firm in a form which makes it available across the company.

It is the capacity of the organization to access the collective knowledge of the individual employees which is at the core of the second aspect of organizational intellectual capital – that is the propensity of the organization to learn and to do so at speed. At the individual level, learning capacity is expressed as the ability to synthesize, to reflect and to create and test theories in use. The same is true at the organizational level where the collective propensity for learning is the basis of organizational learning.

What role can organizations play in developing intellectual capital? Clearly much of the development of knowledge and therefore intellectual capital is self-driven. Individuals each take personal responsibility for the books they read and the time they set aside to study and reflect. Yet while this personal determination is crucial, much can be facilitated, and indeed blocked, by the context in which they operate.[7] In order to make wise choices which optimized intellectual development, it was important for Greg, for example, to be a member of a company with both open and transparent internal markets for jobs, projects and task forces. Similarly, for Nina to develop her intellectual capital she needed to be in a company that was rich in information. An information rich environment was also important for Greg; his decision to build experience in Azerbaijan or Trinidad was based on information about the oil scenarios he received from the regional briefings.

For organizations the four key elements for building intellectual capital are:

- the capacity to build explicit knowledge by accessing training opportunities which are most appropriate to building knowledge and skills at any point in time;

- the capacity to build tacit knowledge by establishing developmental relationships with a more experienced individual who acts as a mentor or coach;

- the capacity to build firm specific and transferable knowledge by accessing rich developmental opportunities and significant and diverse jobs and projects;

- the capacity to create time and space for personal reflection and reading.

Emotional capital

The Democratic Enterprise is one in which people are sufficiently self-aware and emotionally resilient to develop autonomy and become the best they can be. The notions of self-awareness and self-insight are ones that we return to many times as we consider the democratic journey. They are the basis for individual resilience, and also of integrity. Unless we understand ourselves, we cannot be true to ourselves, and we cannot act with integrity.[8]

Individuals who have developed emotional capital and are capable of acting with self-insight and integrity also bring important benefits for the organization. First, the skills and propensity of the creation of individual self-insight, with all the questioning this entails, makes for a more insightful organization. People who are insightful about themselves are also likely to be insightful about the organization. The capacity and courage to ask the tough questions of oneself creates the intellectual muscle to ask the tough questions of the organization. Second, emotional resilience provides the capacity to face adversity and to make tough decisions. People who are emotionally robust and capable of exercising their will create organizational energy.[9] The alternative is that individuals who are emotionally underdeveloped with limited self-awareness and resilience collectively create communities in organizations where energy is rapidly dissipated.[10]

In our three citizens we saw that energy was the powerhouse of their endeavours. Energy builds the momentum to make choices and become autonomous. To lose energy is to atrophy and become inflexible. In part their energy came from emotional well-being, from an understanding of themselves and what is important to them at the present time.[11] In building energy and creating insight they have to make some important choices. Self-insight comes partly through introspection and partly by acknowledging how we are seen by others. So, as Nina found, the choice of mentor and coach is key. Nina's mentors were able to provide a realistic reflection of her personal strengths and development needs, and to build a partnership in which they play a key role. Remember how tough it was for Nina to receive negative feedback and evaluation from the members of her team? As she remembers:

'I really felt under pressure. But through thinking about it and talking to others I began to discover aspects of myself which are strengths and I learned the power of tough messages.'

Mentors and coaches played an important role in Nina's personal development. By providing timely feedback and advice, they helped her to access and reflect on her 'blind spots'. This revealed aspects of herself that were apparent to others, but about which she had limited awareness.[12] For Nina this self-insight was crucial as it enabled her to learn from her mistakes.

Executives who 'derail' later in their career rarely do so because they do not have the necessary knowledge or job related skills. In the vast majority of cases, their derailment is caused by their inability to understand themselves and to adapt their behaviour to the situation.

We have discussed the importance of self-insight and knowledge in creating emotional resilience. But sustaining self-insight also requires a personal strategy to maintain long-term well-being and energy. These strategies are essentially individualistic, reflecting personal characteristics and needs. To build these energy strategies requires an understanding of the choices and consequences faced in creating a balanced life, particularly the choices around where and when we work. For Stewart at BT, for example, the choice he made to work from home was taken because he began to understand the corrosive effect the long commute was having on his own energy. The same is true for Nina at McKinsey, who has taken time out at various stages in her career to build up her badly depleted energy resources.

For organizations the four key elements for building emotional capital are:

◆ the capacity to choose to access and seek personal feedback from colleagues within and outside the working team;

◆ the capacity to build developmental relationships with mentors and coaches;

◆ the capacity to choose to take time for personal reflection;

◆ the capacity to build energy by making choices about the parameters of work – in particular where and when work occurs.

Social capital

Social capital binds together the knowledge of individuals and creates one of the corner-stones to the creation of emotional capital.[13] At the individual level social capital involves relationship-building skills and the ability to engage in deep and meaningful relationships. The depth and breadth of these relationships is influenced by two personal characteristics; authenticity and trustworthiness. Those who are not authentic are unlikely to build strong social ties. Here the link with emotional capital is strong; authenticity, being true to ourselves, is an expression of self-awareness and insight.

But there is another aspect to relationship building capabilities – the propensity to be trustworthy. This involves behaving in ways that encourage trust and minimizing actions seen as untrustworthy by others.[14]

At the organizational level, social capital equates to the depth and extent of social ties that connect employees within the organization, and also those that connect members of the organization to the world outside. Some of these relationship ties will be strong, based on frequent and in-depth interactions; others will be weak, based on infrequent interactions. As we shall see, both play important roles in the development and value of social capital to both individuals and the organizations of which they are members.[15]

Relationships with others play a central role in the creation of knowledge and insight, support and counsel to self-knowledge, and provide a social infrastructure where trust can flourish. Many of the decisions faced by our three citizens concern the extent to which they build and maintain relationships, and the time and resources they choose to invest in that process. Some of these relationship choices are made for them. They come as part of their personalities. For example, they may be more or less sociable, and have preferences for the number of people they prefer to interact with and the amount of time they like to spend with others. The 'self-monitoring' aspect of personality explains why some people prefer to build broad, loose, complex and diverse networks, while others choose to focus on tight networks of people with whom they spend much of their time.[16]

Yet even within these personality parameters, each of the three citizens had relationship choices. Nina places much emphasis on creating deep and long-term relationships with a relatively small number of people. Typically, these are people she works with, or is in close physical proximity to. These *strong relationship ties* are crucial to her emotional well-being and the maintenance of her emotional capital.[17] This is where her self-insight was built and where she relaxed and became herself. It is also where she learned tacit knowledge from others. She feels comfortable and at ease within these tight circles of friends.

But, while these tight networks may be crucial to an individual's well-being, to choose to build them to the exclusion of other types of relationships can, in the long term, be counter-productive. It may reduce insight and ultimately the value of personal human capital. Much of what takes place in these networks of close friends is duplication from earlier conversations. In fact, research suggests that as much as 60% of the information received in these networks is redundant; it has all been said and heard before. Of course, this repetition is one of the great joys of close relationships as it builds continuity and shared experience. But to live exclusively within these close ties will inevitably diminish knowledge[18] over time. An over-reliance on close network ties reduces intellectual capital because tight networks of people are usually very similar to each other. Often they are of the same age or gender, or have the same knowledge background, or indeed are from the same part of the organization. To build her intellectual capital, Nina therefore has to create both strong relationship ties, and weak relationship ties.

About half a century ago the Austrian economist Joseph Schumpeter had a profound insight. Progress, he realized, comes from combinations. New combinations of existing knowledge create new knowledge. Combination of biology, physics and chemistry created the knowledge of molecular biology, for example. Combinations of technical and marketing knowledge are at the heart of many new products. This has important implications for social capital. The really new and insightful ideas come not from within tight networks of friends and relationships, but rather from people who come together from across very different areas and disciplines. These wider networks of relationships are termed *weak relationship ties* and they are important to both individuals and organizations.[19]

When Greg took the job on the ARCO integration and then chose to move to the HR project he was in position to combine the knowledge he had built from the two. As a consequence, he was in a much stronger position to bring new ideas to subsequent jobs. In fact, he would not necessarily have to work full-time in both of these roles. It could be that simply being part of a task force or project team within each group would bring the same benefits. By providing a bridge between the ARCO integration group and the HR group he was exploiting the value of combinations or what have been termed 'structural holes' – the gaps in the relationships across the organization that can yield productive combining opportunities.[20] He was able to arbitrage across these weak relationship ties, creating value by bringing ideas and knowledge from one to the other. Developing multiple weak networks gave Greg the opportunity to access a wider diversity of knowledge and therefore increase the possibility of connecting these networks to create value through new combinations. By doing so he is able to build his own personal asset base, which ultimately contributes to the asset base of BP.

But bridging across groups and functions, and within and outside the company is not easy. For many people it is easier and more comfortable to stay within the bounds of relationships with people who do similar things and behave in similar ways. Memberships of multiple networks involve a great deal of effort. As Greg found, bridging across diverse knowledge domains is more complex than maintaining one's specialization within a single domain. The starting point for bridging and combining is the courage to work in novel situations. Finding this courage is also the most difficult step. Novel situations inevitably mean moving outside our comfort zones. We leave behind the comforts of known surroundings, familiar systems and old associations. But it is also by stepping outside 'life as usual' that all bridging begins. For Nina at the age of 28, moving to Korea to work in a team on a project in which she did not have knowledge of either the sector or the product was an enormous 'bridging' challenge. But, looking back she still describes this as a 'shaping experience'. It was here she learned about herself, built her skills and began to understand about the management of boundaries.

Each individual needs the freedom to build the tight and loose networks that together constitute social capital. This involves making active choices about the groups they work with. These include both immediate work groups and access to cross-functional and geographically diverse project groups and task forces. The first builds the intimacy of tight networks while the second is the framework for the development of the looser, more diverse networks so crucial to the development of knowledge.

For organizations the four key elements for building relationships as social capital are:

◆ access to networking opportunities through the provision of knowledge of current vacancies in project teams, task forces and jobs;

◆ access to knowledge about the skills and knowledge required in roles and their developmental opportunities;

◆ the ability to apply to be considered for membership of projects teams, task forces and jobs in functions, business and geographies outside the current role;

◆ the capacity to meet people from outside the immediate work area, and with people from outside the organization.

Behaving as an investor rather than as an asset is all about the active and continuous building of personal human capital – expressed as intellectual capital, social capital and emotional capital. For each of our three citizens there was much value to be gained by this. But, for their organizations there are also real advantages to the accumulation of personal human capital.

Employing and developing people with strong intellectual capital builds the explicit and implicit knowledge base of the company. Strong relationship ties ensure that ideas are swiftly shared across the company, and new ideas and innovation are generated occurs across disparate groups. Employing and developing people with strong emotional capital begins the process of creating an organization which has insight and where there is sufficient energy for the company to overcome the forces of inertia.[21]

	Intellectual capital	Emotional capital	Social capital
Personal human capital	• Learning capacity • Cognitive complexity • Specialized tacit and explicit knowledge	• Self-awareness • Integrity • Resilience	• Sociability • Authenticity • Trustworthiness
Organizational human capital	• Explicit knowledge • Learning potential	• Organizational insight • Organizational energy	• Strong relationship ties • Weak relationship ties

FIGURE 5.3 ◆ **Building human capital**

Leveraging human capital

What are the mechanisms by which active investors can capitalize on their personal human capital? And what are the organizational processes and practices that support this leveraging of investment?

In business, people make hard decisions about the allocation of scarce resources all the time. They make deals, negotiate and bargain for what they believe is right. With our citizens we saw that actively building and leveraging their personal human capital required the same up-front attitude. This involves keeping their options open and developing general, portable skills rather than narrow, company-specific skills. It means having the courage to make personal investments in knowledge acquisition; and negotiating hard for the opportunity to build social networks.

In the Democratic Enterprise the term investor implies a greater degree of personal freedom. Assets are manipulated and controlled. Investors take a view. They decide when to invest and when to disinvest; when to take the value that has been created and when to leave that value to grow. They also balance short-term needs with the desire for longer-term stability; to manage risks and rewards. Each of these citizens is an investor who chooses to actively invest their personal human capital. In doing so they face three key questions: What should be my broad goals and investment priorities? How can I identify opportunities to increase my assets? How can I best balance the equation between investment and return on assets?

Clearly the opportunity to leverage and realize personal human capital is influenced by the opportunity to choose between options of remuneration and bonus structures. Those who have the opportunity to actively leverage can make choices about their total remuneration package at any one time. So, they may want to take a high-risk strategy and take much of the value they have created in shares or options or they may choose to balance a lower current cash component with a greater pension allocation. And these decisions are likely to change over time. Yet while the choice of remuneration portfolio is a major lever there are more subtle levers – such as the decision to substitute time for money, or money for time. Working flexibly, part-time, or taking a career break are all choices individuals have made to trade time for money. In order to leverage their personal human capital, individuals have to be free to make the following choices:

◆ control about the long-term/short-term package which constitutes the total remuneration package;

◆ the opportunity to be rewarded for skill accumulation and knowledge transfer;

◆ the opportunity to share in the success of the endeavour in which personal human capital has been invested;

◆ the opportunity to make trade-offs between remuneration and time allocation (job-share, working part-time, sabbaticals).

Each of our three citizens builds and leverages their personal human capital in the form of intellectual, social and emotional capital. At the same time, their own ability to develop their personal human capital makes a contribution to the learning potential of their company. They contribute to the insight and energy of the company, and to the relationship ties within the company. By becoming the best they could be, they play their part in ensuring the organization could become the best it could be. We also saw that the creation of the three elements of personal human capital took place through the exercise of choice. For each of these people to realize their potential required a context in which they were able to actively build and leverage their assets. We can see in Figure 5.4 a summary of these key contextual organizational factors.

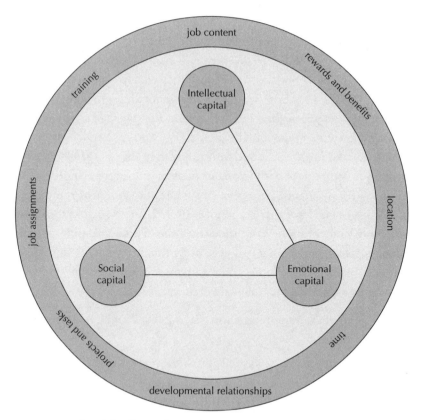

FIGURE 5.4 ◆ **The eight dimensions of variety**

How individuals become autonomous

For our three citizens, personal autonomy came from a sense of who they are and a notion of what it is they want to be. As each of them journeyed through the terrain of their personal and work lives they strove to build their knowledge and understanding, to create deep and meaningful relationships with those around them, and to engage the courage of choice and action.[22]

Having the courage to truly become an investor rather than an asset, an adult rather than a child, demands a reflective, conscious process of self-development and learning. In each of the stories of the three citizens we saw how they actively navigated – sometimes making tough decisions – to learn and to build a life that had meaning for them. In the old corporate paradigm much of this role of learning and development was assumed by the company. Employees simply followed the well trodden skills-development paths of their predecessors. But as organizations embark on the pathways toward democracy, the old paternalism is no longer valid. Democracy requires conscious learning and the exercise of choice. The citizens had a particular view of themselves in relation to their organizations. They saw themselves not simply as assets to be managed by the business, but as active investors in the business, choosing when to build and when to leverage their human capital.

From the investors' perspective, great businesses are built from a broad sense of purpose and a deep understanding of current skills and capabilities. The same is true of building and leveraging personal human capital. In each of the stories of the three citizens we saw attempts to create an understanding of what it was that was important to them, their goals and aspirations. For Greg, the goal is to create an exciting, wide-ranging life. He loves working in new places, finds learning a thrilling experience, and wants to operate at the very boundaries of his skills. One of Nina's primary goals is to create a life that balances her work responsibilities with her responsibilities as a mother. For Stewart it is important to understand his own needs for tranquility. Each is unique, each is an individual. The challenge they face is to understand themselves, but also to translate that understanding to attain their unique personal needs.

Life is never linear. There is no clear and easy path to follow. If we asked Greg or Stewart or Nina ten years ago where they expected to be, they would have been unable to predict their current situation. Paths opened which they had not expected, others stopped in dead ends and they had to retrace their steps. But despite these twists and turns, for each of these people there is a thread running through their lives. For them, understanding this thread and making rough plans will be crucial. Without this rough plan, they would be incapable of coping with the unexpected events – the twists in the road – while still moving roughly in the desired direction.

Each of these citizens created a sense of themselves as an investor and an adult by learning from their own experiences. They did this through awareness and reflecting on their experiences by creating concepts, generalizations or 'models' from these reflections. These models and concepts were then tested in new situations and adapted accordingly. In Nina's story we see this cycle of learning very clearly. When she first joined McKinsey her experiences and model of herself were as an ambitious, hard-working analyst. Her first four years passed in a project-orientated way developing a broad range of knowledge, and building close working relationships with colleagues and mentors. During this early experience she took the opportunity to reflect about herself using her mentor as a sounding board and coach. By doing so she began to create a new working model of herself.

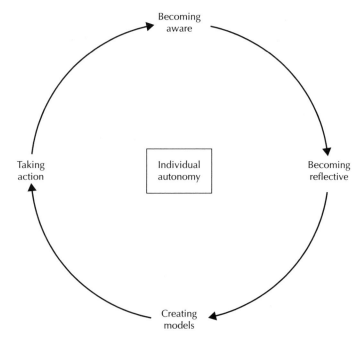

FIGURE 5.5 ◆ **The cycle of individual autonomy**

Nina was engaging in what David Kolb has called 'learning from experience'.[23] Across a period of a decade she engaged in a continual interaction between ideas and experiences that were grounded in the external world, and internal reflections about these experiences and ideas and what they meant to her and her 'model' of herself. For Nina this cycle of awareness, reflection and model creation was vital to her capacity to act in the role of the citizen. Had she not reflected and drawn lessons from her experiences there is a real danger that she would have become caught in an endless cycle of repetition. This could have led to her moving rapidly from one job to another without understanding what it is she was trying to achieve, or accepting the sacrifice of some types of work because she was unaware of their costs and unclear of the other possible options. Unconsciousness erodes human capital and limits the opportunities for personal growth. In building a model of what she could be, Nina engaged in a learning cycle with four key stages. These are: becoming aware; becoming reflective; creating models; and taking action.

Becoming aware: At McKinsey, Nina put a priority on understanding herself and understanding the context in which she worked. In understanding herself she paid particular attention to her feelings, perceptions and her reactions to events. In becoming more aware of her wider context it was important to understand the latitude of discretion within which she operated, and the constraints which would limit the choices she made. While reflecting on her own thoughts and reactions was at the centre of her awareness, the reactions of others to her actions and behaviours was crucial.

Becoming reflective. For Nina, simply being aware of herself, her actions and her context would have little value unless she could assimilate this awareness into her ongoing understanding of herself. By doing so she transformed the information about herself and her world into a more complete picture of herself. This process of reflection through synthesis and assimilation is the basis of the model which creates the thread which connects her past with her future. For Nina, some of her reflection took place when she was alone. In solitude she was able to reflect on her behaviours and actions. At other times conversations with others and her own investment in her 'talking partners' also played a key role. Some of these people were able to bring insight and wisdom to her reflections and by doing so to help her on her way to creating a model of what she could be.

Creating models. Through awareness and reflection Nina was able to assemble information about herself and the context of her life. She then attempted to use this information to construct a notion of herself as a unified whole, as a story-line which described not only what she is now, but also what she could be. For her, this model of 'who I am' acted as a touchstone against which decisions could be made and actions taken.

Taking action. Without action, the cycle of learning remains an internal pursuit. It remains devoid of traction or influence. Throughout her story, we see that Nina was able to use her understanding of herself to take action, and at times, to take courageous actions.

Becoming aware

For Greg, Nina and Stewart realizing their unique potential meant embarking on a cycle of learning which provides the basis for self-awareness and awareness of the environment in which they operate. This requires a much stronger sense of their self-identity than would previously have been either realistic or indeed useful. Their understanding of themselves was continuously constituted, deconstructed and re-constructed through their relationships with others, through their conversations and discourses and through their actions.

Each glimpsed aspects of themselves in casual or unprepared ways. They surprised themselves by their actions and the emotions situations provoke in them. Recall Nina's feeling when she received less than favourable feedback from her team members. Faced with this information Nina asked herself: 'Have I heard anything like this about me before? Does this remind me of any other situation I have been in? What are the similarities; what are the differences?' By asking these questions of herself Nina was deepening her awareness. She was acquiring a sense of self.

Engagement in citizenship demands that these questions are asked. If we look again at the stories of our citizens each had some awareness about their current capabilities and assets, of their weaknesses and development priorities, and of what was important to them.

Each had a view of their *current capabilities and assets*, and what they thought they would be capable of achieving. This belief about capabilities has been termed self-efficacy. Self-efficacy is important as it predicts the motivation to perform a task, and by doing so influences personal goal set-ting.[24] Indeed some scholars have argued that self-efficacy beliefs are the most central and pervasive influences on decision making, goal setting, and the amount of effort individuals apply to a particular task and how long they persevere at a task in the face of failure and difficulty. Greg, Stewart and Nina's image of their capabilities and assets is a function of what they believe they can attain; the strength of their conviction; and their belief that they can generalize the skills they have developed from one situation to another. Each one of them has built this image of their own competency from a whole spectrum of experiences and attitudes. Clearly their experi-ences of mastery in the past are crucial. They will feel even more confident if they have successfully overcome obstacles to achieve the task and attain personal mastery.[25] But in understanding their own likely competence they are also influenced by vicarious experiences. These include their observa-tions of others performing a similar task. By observing mentors and coaches, for example, they gain insight into possible task strategies and on the basis of comparisons with their judgement of their own capabilities, decide whether they can accomplish the task. Imitating models are an important source of confidence about personal ability. At some time each of our citizens have learned about themselves and become more confident when others have shown they believe they can perform a difficult task.

For Nina the experience of being able to turn around her performance helped her build self-efficacy. On at least two occasions in her work she has been faced with tough feedback. Once from a team disillusioned with her work style and inability to focus on their development needs, once with a client who became irritated by the way she had approached an assignment. For someone like Nina – professional, highly skilled, ambitious, with incred-ibly high standards – this negative feedback was particularly tough. But as she reflected on the data, she realized she had an opportunity to take stock and reconsider her actions.[26] This resulted in increased self-awareness and more thoughtful analysis of the problems with which she was confronted. As she recalls after receiving a below average evaluation from a client:

'I got really ambivalent evaluation. I began to search for what to do next and spent two weeks talking to people in the office. I went to see one of the partners and said "I have this evaluation. It doesn't do justice to my abil-ity. I need now to demonstrate a real uptake in performance in the next

*couple of months." He made it clear that I could work on the next assign-
ment without the "overhang" of the previous evaluation. I went to work
with the client and it was a real turning point. I blew everyone's socks off
and really built my confidence and began to really understand my
strengths. I was given lots of confidence and the right kind of coaching from
the people I was working with.'*

For Nina capability and assets are a crucial part of achieving her unique
potential.

Our three citizens also developed a realistic view of their *weaknesses and
development priorities*. They understood where they lacked knowledge or relationships and had some ideas about what it is they had to do to build
resources into these areas. As we saw from Nina, understanding weaknesses
can be tough. There were aspects of herself she knew, and aspects of which
she was unaware. For Nina, illuminating 'blind spots' was crucial, discovering what it is that others know about her, that she did not know about herself. It is often within the darkness of blindspots that weaknesses lurk.[27]
Self-reflection can be hazy and subject to all manner of defence mechanisms.
Blaming others for our behaviour, reflect onto others our personal concerns,
and repressing negative feelings. As the psychoanalyst Sigmund Freud
reminds us, these defence mechanisms are important in the defence of our
fragile self-understanding, but they do little to build our deeper awareness.[28]

Faced with information from her blind spot Nina went through a not
uncommon cycle. The normal cycle . . . of anger (How could they say this?
Who do they think they are?) . . . to denial (They got it wrong. They only
saw me in specific circumstances. They are jealous.) . . . to some form of
acceptance (Perhaps I've heard this before, maybe that's why I could not
motivate in the way I had hoped.) to a determination to do something about
it. By accessing her blind spots she was able to become more aware.[29]

Finally, our three citizens have a view of *what is important to them*. This
begins the dialogue we return to later when we consider the creation of a
dynamic model of oneself. The question of what is important is at the heart
of autonomy. What is important to Greg, is not what is important to Stewart. What is important to Stewart is not what is important to Nina. It is here
that the traditional organizational approach to development falls apart. Priorities vary from one person to the next. Nor can we place a value on their
relative merits. Stewart's decision to put working from home at the top of

his list is no better or worse than Greg's decision to move every two years and work in many different countries. But by understanding and acknowledging these individual differences, Greg and Stewart have been able to craft lives which work for them.

Becoming reflective

The foundation of autonomy is self-knowledge. But self-knowledge on its own is static and can rapidly become obsolete. It takes more than the collection of information to build self-awareness. To make knowledge 'real' each of our citizens engaged with it, to develop 'reflexivity', the capacity to be reflective.[30] Reflexivity has both an internal element and an external element. Internal reflection is the capacity to have internal conversations and by doing so to understand aspirations and goals more deeply. Self-reflection is exactly that, reflecting on personal behaviour and actions, seeking to understand the threads and similarities, building up a 'life narrative' from which a self-description can be built. These 'life narratives' piece together disparate actions and establish the thread that stitch these actions into a cohesive picture.

Reflexivity also has an external element. This is contained in reflective relationships and conversations with others which provide an opportunity to reflect on the choices that have been made. Through working with these 'talking partners' (mentors or coaches, for example) the individual is able to build deeper self-understanding. One of the crucial aspects of the autonomous person is their capacity to reflect through building relationships with 'talking partners' and to have the space and time to engage with them. These reflective relationships not only cast light on some of the darker and less visible aspects of behaviour, but also establish partners for the journey.[31] As Nina found her reflective friends and colleagues saw her more often, observed her more accurately and across many different circumstances. More importantly, within the trust and warmth of a friendship they are able to reflect back on her insights in a way that she might find it hard to take from others.

For Nina, talking partners have always played a crucial role in shaping her 'unique proposition' and in helping her think through the decisions and trade-offs she faced. For her, relationships and friendships are very important. As she reflects:

'Make your choices about who you want to work with. That is a critical choice. More than anything else it has effected my working and personal happiness. The assignment is the easy bit. Making the right call on who your colleagues are is really important.'

Some of these are at work:

'When I am thinking about what to do next and share my initial thoughts with colleagues, I tell them, "this is what I want to do; what do you think?". They help me to evaluate and to monitor; I use them as a sounding board and to bounce ideas off. They encourage me to think more broadly.'

For Nina a group of six women friends outside of work are also crucial talking partners. A friend she met at school at the age of eight, a colleague from her Harvard days, a woman she met on her first day at McKinsey, a family friend, room mate from her husband's time at Insead.[32] Some still working; some have young children. Despite Nina's frantic schedule, finding time to maintain these relationships is a priority: 'They are really good at spotting why I feel as I do and then can empathize with me. I can admit how I am really feeling with them.'

Every autonomous person like Nina has a need for reflexivity. A talking partner with whom a reflective relationship can be sustained provides a vital channel for open and honest feedback. Honest and reflective relationships demand rich and intense conversations. Reflexivity demands conversation. Rational conversation in which information and data is shared and where matters are analysed in a systematic manner, beliefs examined logically and with rigour, can uncover truths. But emotional conversations also have a profound role to play – where aspirations and needs are shared; where people are able to put their deepest fears into words.[33] The philosopher Theodore Zeldin has this to say about the nature of conversation:

'Conversation is a meeting of minds with different memories and habits. When minds meet they don't just share facts, they transform them, reshape them, draw different implications from them, engage in new trains of thought. Conversation doesn't just reshuffle the pack: it creates new cards.'

Theodore Zeldin, *Conversation: How Talk Can Change Your Life*, p. 14

Reflection is a powerful precursor to autonomy and the capacity to operate as a citizen within an organization which is moving towards democracy.

Reflection demands good conversation to build awareness, to explore options and to create models. In the Democratic Enterprise, conversation is crucial to all three building blocks: in the support of autonomy, in the creation of action around organizational variety, and in the crafting of a sense of shared destiny.

Creating models

Self-awareness brings an understanding of the accumulation of the past, and an understanding of the present. But what of the future? Many of the choices our citizens made were based on their awareness of the present. This is an awareness built from an understanding of their current preferences, the opportunities to maximize their current asset base or to meet development needs. But other choices were made on the basis of the possibilities of the future. This relies on being prepared to anticipate in the context of time, and by doing so to create a 'theory' of themselves.

For each of the three citizens, the model of themselves is not static. Rather, it evolves over time, and as such has a strong temporal aspect. What we see at any point in time is merely a snapshot of their model of themselves. In part it reflects their aspirations and interests, what could be called a 'personal strategy'. But there will also be an element of predictability, reflecting not simply individual idiosyncrasies, but also unfolding life-stages.

So in her 20s Nina was exploring possibilities, testing initial choices and fashioning a provisional model of herself and her life. By her late 20s she was beginning to revisit her initial model, with particular urgency since she was deciding whether to become a mother. The questions she asked at this stage were questions such as: what parts must I give up or appreciably change? And what is missing? We observe Nina at a stage when her model of herself has formed an equilibrium. She has built a narrative of herself and has crafted mentoring relationships with others who act as both a host and a guide, but more importantly, can support and help her realize her 'dream'. Looking forward, it may be that over the next decade the structures she has created in her earlier life will become intolerable to her and she may enter a period of disequilibria. All this is unknowable at her current life stage. But what it does suggest is that in understanding model building in life, there is a need to place these models firmly within the perspective of unfolding life stages.[34]

While each of our citizens is located in time, simultaneously, each has a personal philosophy about their life and the ways in which it could unfold. To bring some insight into these personal strategies of model building it is useful to draw analogies with the models or visions which are built at the organizational level and to consider what these strategic processes might tell us about model building at an individual level.

For our three citizens the companies they work for were catalysts in the creation of these models. Nina Bhatia's clarity about what she is and the choices she has made come in part from the reflective process at McKinsey where every three years everyone from partner upwards prepares a written document describing their client history over the proceeding years. As Nina reflects, 'It forces you to think about why you have done certain things. It is a record of what you have done. It forces you to think about what you are.' It is these competencies and this knowledge which Nina believes gives her options. As she puts it using metaphors from business strategy: they 'reserve the right for you to play in the game, they create options around knowledge'.

For Greg, the model he describes as zigzag is what from an organizational perspective could be termed 'strategic flexibility'. Unlike Nina he does not have a clear model or scenario for the future. Instead, he has pursued a strategy of developing options for the future. So over the last decade he has built a vast personal competence portfolio. By doing so he is developing and maintaining the capability to pursue alternative paths. Part of his thinking is that he has no idea what the future will hold. Therefore, he wants to increase his chance of success by creating sufficient flexibility to enable him to pursue alternative paths in response to changing strategic and environmental conditions. At the same time he is keeping close to the marketplace in order to sense as quickly as possible potential changes and to maximize his personal speed of response. Understanding that Azerbaijan could be a crucial part of BP's future oil strategy is a case in point. The same was true of his job with ARCO, he saw it primarily as an opportunity to maximize his breadth of knowledge.

Greg is simply doing what the senior team of a company faced with an uncertain, ambiguous environment will do – he is keeping his options open. In such an environment it is foolish to over invest in building assets and capabilities that are highly specific to a particular strategy and competitive context. Making investment decisions based on 'single line' forecasts of the future would risk becoming a prisoner of existing capabilities and market understanding.

The model which Greg is creating is fundamentally zigzag. The success of this model will rely on his capability to balance two elements: his personal capabilities, expressed as competencies and skills; and his knowledge of the external world and the opportunities contained in this world. The relationship between these two is shown in the model of his challenge (see Fig. 5.6). One possibility for Greg is that he moves up the vertical axis and continuously builds and strengthens his personal capability through developing skills and competencies. He can do this by either continuing to build his current skill base to become expert in a relatively narrow range; or alternatively, he can broaden rapidly and develop some expertise in a broad range of competencies. Both have associated risks. Narrowing and deepening his skill base could leave him a prisoner of the past if the oil sector were to rapidly change. Alternatively, broadening his skill base in a haphazard manner is very costly to him and the company since it results in developing competencies which potentially have limited value.

Alternatively, Greg could move along the horizontal axis, and learn a great deal about BP and the oil sector. He could build his knowledge about the current and future market and the likely paths it could take. But unless Greg also built new capabilities, he would be incapable of using this

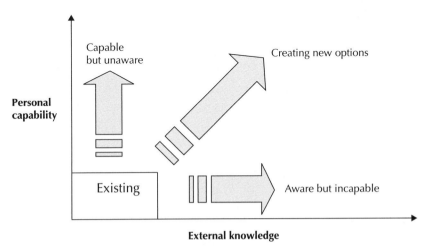

FIGURE 5.6 ◆ **Greg: building options for the future**

market knowledge to create value. Greg needs to both build new personal capabilities and create external knowledge and intelligence. The challenge he faces is how to strike the balance between the cost of creating new capabilities, and the pay-off in his ability to rapidly reposition in a fast moving market.

Greg has achieved this balance by maximizing his opportunities to learn by deliberately taking a number of tasks and projects which did not pay off in the short term, but in the longer term build capability. At the same time he has actively built intelligence around the alternative competencies and capabilities which could be important in the future, and how the market (geography, technology, products) could develop in the future. By doing so he has created a capacity to plan and yet remain opportunistic. Not so opportunistic that he takes roles and projects that would cause him to wander too far from his ideas of his future, but rather 'bounded opportunism'. As the strategist Peter Williamson cautions companies:

> 'To make "bounded opportunism" work in practice, every manager should ask the following question of each tactical opportunity: "Is it a weed or a flower?" An unexpected opportunity that diverts the company pursuing its long-term mission is a "weed". Meanwhile, opportunities that allow it to take advantages of its options to accelerate progress toward long-term goals are "flowers".'

> Peter Williamson, 'Strategy as Options on the Future',
> MIT *Sloan Management Review*, Vol. 40, Iss. 3, p. 117–27

This is good advice to individuals as well as companies. It is at the heart of Greg's own model about himself.

Taking action

Each of our citizens built a model of themselves. This is constructed from what we could term a 'theory of the self'. Within the theory of the self, they are faced with many decisions. For each one of them their personal human capital rapidly erodes, their current knowledge becomes obsolete, their relationships weaken, their courage diminishes. Behaving as an investor required them to take action. None of them took a reactive approach to crafting their lives. Each has made proactive choices. The nature of their action taking depended in part on their model of themselves, and in part on the context of their lives. At some points in time the action they took involved simply continuing along the path of their current realities. Nina experienced this when she became a project leader, and in doing so she continued to work in the same industrial sector, with the same strategic focus. By moving into a related role with a wider span of control she was adding to her current competencies and skills.

At other times, the actions the three citizens took broadened their skills or competencies by extending the boundaries of their current reality. Moving to another part of the business would be a way in which the tasks and competencies remain roughly similar, but the context in which these tasks occur is changed. Similarly staying within the business, but changing the context of the role by moving to another type of job would be a means by which the boundaries of current reality are extended. For Stewart at BT, working from home for a couple of days a week extended the boundaries of his current reality.[35]

But for each of these three citizens, there are also times when the action they took resulted from a significant shift in their assumptions about themselves, or about their work. A key driver for this transformational change can often be fundamental changes in the context of life. For Nina, the imminent birth of her first child led to fundamental changes in her assumptions about herself and about her life. For Nina this changing of assumptions was particularly poignant as her first child died soon after birth. She and her husband found themselves in what Jung has so evocatively termed 'the swamplands of the soul'. Times when security and predictability are lost and when the old assumptions have been destroyed without the knowledge of what the new assumptions could be going forward. Like the trapeze artiste, in this time of profound changing of assumptions, Nina was frozen midflight with no rope to hold.

Karl Weick[36] describes this as a cosmology episode:

'A cosmology episode is when a person suddenly and deeply feel that the universe is no longer a rational, orderly system. What makes such an episode so shattering is that both the sense of what is occurring and the means to rebuild collapse together. Stated more informally, a cosmology episode feels like vujade – the opposite of déjà vu: I've never been here before, I have no idea where I am, and no idea who can help me.'

Karl Weick, *The Collapse of Sensemaking in Organizations*

For Nina, the combination of actively making choices to become a mother, and then losing the baby was a time of deep anxiety and a profound feeling of loss of the past. For her the process of bereavement took the predictable path of denial and isolation, to anger and bargaining, to depression and finally to acceptance. This involved her changing assumptions of a profound kind. But her journey through the swamplands has some bearing on similar journeys that can be taken in the context of work.

For Stewart, coming to terms with what brought him contentment and the impact this would have on his career required a fundamental shift in his assumptions about his work and about himself. In making this transition he had to question some of the assumptions he had developed, often unconsciously, over the period of his life and career. Interesting the word assumption shares linguistic roots with the Latin word *sumptus*, which means to undertake by choice. With collapse of his old assumptions came the lose of meaning, of the building blocks on which his life had been constructed. One such building block was his assumption that as an intelligent, highly educated person he would reach a high level in his company of choice. To find in his mid-30s that to do so would not bring him contentment was a tough call. As a consequence of this changed assumption he had to realign his work and much of his life.

We have considered what it takes from the perspective of the individual to become autonomous. We have looked at some of the questions that are central to the autonomous individual, and we have considered the role of relationships and conversation in supporting life's journey. But individuals operate within the context of organizations. What is it that the companies of which these three people are citizens did to support their autonomy?

How organizations support autonomy

As Nina Bhatia at McKinsey reflected, the primary emphasis for becoming autonomous and building personal capital rests firmly with her. Only she can create her self-awareness; she only can reflect on herself and the choices she makes; and she alone can create a model of what she is now and of what she could become in the future. But at the same time, she acknowledges that her own self-insight and reflection took place within the context of an organization which supported and encouraged her autonomy. Her capacity to become autonomous and to become an action taker was supported by McKinsey in many, often subtle ways. The same was true for Greg. His capacity to be insightful and autonomous rested with him, but there was much about that the context of BP that supported this.

Earlier we saw that the model which supports the creation of autonomy has four elements: the creation of awareness, the support of reflection, the development of models, and the supporting of action. In each of these four elements of autonomy the company context can play a key role.

The companies of which our citizens are members supported the development of their autonomy in many subtle ways. This was achieved primarily by subtle changes in the context of work: in the ways in which performance is assessed and rewarded, in the ways in which feedback is created and communicated and in the ways in which work takes place. None of these companies put bold statements such as 'be autonomous' or 'act as an adult'. Instead there were many subtle cues, which encourages employees to walk the path of autonomy.

Supporting awareness

For Nina, Greg and Stewart, they developed self-awareness by creating an understanding of their past and their present, from accessing their own self-insight, and from seeking and accepting the perspectives of others. This was not easy, as psychoanalytic theory tells us, there are many defences that can be created to keep the view of oneself intact, however unrealistic or inaccurate these views. Yet, in the companies of Nina, Greg and Stewart, there is a real striving to create an environment in which people feel able and confident to engage in accurate and open conversations about themselves and each other.

In each of these companies this process of open feedback has become institutionalized in what has been called '360° feedback' In this process their boss, peers and colleagues, and subordinates (hence 360°) engage in rating their behaviour and performance across a number of key variables.

Parallel to this peer-based feedback, detailed feedback about performance is also elicited and discussed at the completion of each project. For example, at the completion of a project, Nina is given the numerical scores on the factors against which her performance has been rated, the comments made by colleagues and peers, and also a ranking analysis which shows her ranking versus the average for her peer group across the firm, and within the local office. As Nina comments this data can be tough for an individual to accept, but often it serves as a wake-up call for reflection and change.

To achieve this in a fair manner is not easy. The process of 360° feedback itself is fraught with paradoxes: how can a peer be a colleague and a judge? Focusing on one individual potentially puts the entire balance and collegiality of the group at risk. The measurement practice (simple five-point ratings), though easy to rate, is tough to interpret. There are difficulties, too, in gaining honest feedback when the feedback will eventually impact on rewards.[37] Without a sense of trust, peer-based feedback can be seen simply as yet another control mechanism,. Similarly, if peer-based feedback is too tightly linked to the remuneration decision an individual can feel a great deal of peer pressure. This can lead to anxiety about pleasing their peers. Colleague feedback can easily deteriorate into a code of implicit assumptions that 'you say something nice about me: and I will say something nice about you'. In none of these three situations is active learning through self-insight likely to take place. And yet, these are precisely what 360° feedback can deteriorate into under the wrong circumstances.

For Nina, peer and collegiate feedback works because it is elicited by her (rather than 'dumped' on her). Also, because she has personally asked for feedback, she is more likely to take personal responsibility for the outcome. The process of feedback is systematically applied, in the sense that there are clear points at which it is deemed appropriate for feedback to be solicited. And, finally, everyone is part of the process, without exceptions. Whether you are the most senior manager at McKinsey, or a rookie with one-year service, you elicit and receive feedback from your colleagues and peers. So, as Nina found when she was faced with tough feedback, there was a shared understanding of some of the tough calls that have to be made, of how hard it can be to receive negative feedback, and of the courage required to make something of it rather than simply revert to denial.

At the same time, for Nina, there was an enormous emphasis on building real conversations around the ratings and descriptions, rather than simply 'posting' a set of anonymous scores. The ratings of her performance were accompanied by written descriptions of her behaviour and actions. Inevitably it was the written descriptions, rather than the straight numeric ratings, which became the vehicle for deep discussion.

This capacity to talk through feedback is a crucial issue for the development of autonomy and self-insight. Studies, often with young adults as they mature, show conclusively that autonomy is facilitated by what has been termed 'effectance-promoting' feedback and freedom from demeaning evaluations.[38] People are most willing and able to accept feedback about themselves and their performance when it is specific (rather than vague or general), when it is descriptive (rather than value laden and overly general), when it is positive and accurate (rather than demeaning) and when it focuses on a behaviour which the recipient can actually do something about (rather than on characteristics which are not amenable to change).

For Greg at BP, peer-based feedback has certainly been an important part of his path to self-awareness. But for Greg, the foundations of his experiences as a relatively autonomous person were set over a decade ago when the leadership team of BP began an initiative of what was then called 'Career Check'. Over the next decade many thousands of people participated in these workshops. During this two-day workshop Greg embarked on a series of self-assessment tools. Over the course of the first day he completed these inventories and began to build up an understanding of his own profile. The Myers Briggs Type Inventory (MBTI) brought deeper understanding of his preferences, particularly around extroversion/introversion; the way in which he gathered information from his world (sensing/intuitive), the way in which he made sense of this information (thinking/feeling) and his preferences in decision making (judging/perceiving). From these preference profiles he began to gain a deeper understanding of his preferences and the types of roles he would be likely to find engaging.[39] His Career Anchor preferences brought him a clearer view of what was really important to him in his work and types of careers to which he would be naturally drawn.[40] In doing so he began to actively build a 'model' for himself. During the second day of the workshop, he learned more about his predispositions and began to plot his life scripts, the constraints he believed he was operating under, the choices he had made in the past, and his recollections of the assumptions of these choices. At this point he also began to draw a life script for the future, to understand the choices available in the future and how they could benefit from these choices. It was from this insight that Greg really began to understand his need for variety and breadth.

Encouraging reflection

Simply encouraging deep, insightful feedback from processes such as 360° feedback does not on itself result in self-awareness. To have an impact, this information must be brought into the person. It must be assimilated into their view of themselves and turned from data into knowledge. In short, there must be a period of reflection. As we saw earlier, part of this reflection comes from the internal processes of self-dialogue. But potentially more important are the conversations with 'talking partners'; people who have the time and the space to be a reflective partner.

The great conversationalist Socrates conversed as he wandered around the broad avenue of ancient Athens. He was helped by the warm, temperate climate and the scale of Athens that allowed him to traverse across the city in a day.[41] There is something deeply satisfying about walking and talking, the pleasure of momentum, the reassurance as steps synchronize, the simplicity of occasional eye contact. Contrast this with the location in which many work conversations take place. Seated opposite across a table, static, uncomfortable with the need to either establish eye contact or look away. Or worse, many conversations occur over the telephone. Under these circumstances talk becomes dehydrated.[42] My own preference is to walk and talk. Perhaps this comes from my early childhood memories of walking in the hills of the Lake District in the north of England where I spent much of my early life. Many visitors to my office at London Business School are surprised with the speed at which they are taken out of the office and walked around nearby Regent's Park. This is not to suggest that human resource manuals should now contain the words 'ensure that all conversations about people and their career take place during active walks'. But it does suggest that we could become more sensitive to the spaces in which our conversations take place, and be more prepared to ensure that we find ourselves in these spaces as often as possible. This is also of course an argument for being flexible about location.

And the same sensitivity is required about time. As Theodore Zeldin observes: 'The sad fact is that with constant interruptions and phone ringing, there is not enough time in our busy life for real conversations.'[43] The deep reflective conversations of the democratic organization need uninterrupted time, away from the constant interruptions. Conversations need time and space to unfold, they cannot occur in snatched moments.[44]

There is much that companies can do to create the space within which self-reflection can take place. Perhaps most importantly, it can be woven into the very institutional fabric of the organization by being a crucial aspect of the role of the manager. At McKinsey, the role of a senior coach (a Development Group Leader) is to monitor performance, provide professional guidance, coach and feedback. Coaching and mentoring skills are highly prized within McKinsey's apprenticeship model where much of the learning is done on the job. The assumption is that each person will be coached, based on their feedback, for at least two hours, between three or four times a year. It is well understood that without this capability, an Associate Principal will not make partnership.

At McKinsey conversation is woven into both the processes and roles of the companies. At BP, the role of conversation has been institutionalized from the top down. A newspaper reporter once described CEO John Browne and his team as a 'well funded academic faculty'. He was referring essentially to the continual conversations that take place across the company. These are conversations which are marked by both rational content, in the form of information and new knowledge, and emotional content, in the form of passion and interest.[45] While Greg may have not conversed directly with the senior team at BP, he was aware of their working preferences and the importance given to reflection and deep conversation. By behaving in this manner the senior team created role models for Greg, and perhaps more importantly, created the legitimacy of a context in which deep and rich conversation could flourish.

Assisting model building

Creating a life narrative demands self-awareness and reflection. But it is more than this. It also demands a method by which each one of us can make sense of our past and create a vision of our future. This is model building, and implicit in this are the availability of role models and 'templates' against which experience can be calibrated and understood. In the companies of which Greg, Nina and Stewart are members, there has been significant resources focused on the creation and discussion of these 'templates'.

For Nina at McKinsey the availability of role models played a central role in her own creation of what was appropriate and the boundaries she could legitimately create. Much of her model building came from role models. Her first real exposure to making choices and drawing boundaries came with her Korean assignment when she questioned the practice of staying in the office until late in the evening. Her courage to re-define these boundaries came in part from watching how her colleagues behaved:

> *'Boundaries have to be established against absolute standards you want to meet. One of the partners said to me "I will get in the office at 7.00 am but I insist I leave at 6.00 pm because I want to leave time in the evening to spend time with my children". Watching how he policed the boundaries helped me think about my own boundary management.'*

The actions of this manager created for her a model against which she could view her own issues and from which she could make some decisions. In creating a model of herself she was struggling to come to terms with her interest in a tough challenging job and her desire to be a mother. In watching others around McKinsey she was able to see how they handled multiple pressures and she began to create potential models for herself. In the end, she created a model which built on her own predispositions. She choose, as she describes, to be 'unbelievably organized' and to create clear boundaries between the different elements of her life, as she had seen her manager in Korea doing. As Nina reflects,

> *'I learned that you have to make the right bets because you cannot do everything. I had to learn to manage my boundaries and be ruthless about aspects of my life that I consider to be less important.'*

The model played out in various ways. For example, she did not sub-contract all the caring of her children to a third party. This created space to be with her children most evenings. The trade-offs of this model were clear to her and she has faced up to the consequences.[46] She was not able to take clients to dinner with the frequency of other McKinsey partners, or indeed to spend informal time with her team. The creation of this model and an understanding of the consequences was crucial for Nina. Role models within McKinsey remain an important source of model building as she balances family and work. As she remarks:

> *'All women do it differently. When I look at the other women with children working with McKinsey's one thing I am struck by is the multiplicity of models that people have adopted to meet their circumstances. Some work full-time and provide themselves with flexibility at home, others say they*

only want to work 80%, others say they don't want to work on Tuesdays. I found that very encouraging because it means that we as an institution are tolerating different things. But it also means I feel slightly pressured because I have to figure it out for myself. But it is allowable to have conversations. This is a self-governing environment so at the end of the day you have to say what you are going to do and how to make it work. I like that freedom.'

How organizations understand employees

Supporting individual autonomy through self-awareness, reflection, model building and creating space for action allows individuals to express themselves. This in turn enables them to build a deeper 'learning relationship' with their company. This involves the organization learning about the individual through their self-insight. But there are other ways in which the organization can learn about the individual.

Any customer or client orientated organization lives or dies by its ability to understand and predict customer or client aspirations and desires, both now and in the future. Most companies have now created consumer insight methodologies to provide these insights and have detailed profiles of their consumers.[47] Few have invested similar resources in building profiles of employee insights. They know more about their consumers than they do about their employees. As a result, employees are grouped by obvious 'tags'; job level and grade (the foundation for decisions about remuneration), and current job performance (the basis of bonuses and performance related pay). In these companies that are pioneering autonomy and choice there is an ever growing understanding of employees, their needs at any point in time, what it is they desire; but are currently sacrificing, and the choices which will be important to them. They are beginning to understand their employees with as much accuracy as they understand their customers.

They have learned to view employees according to their personal characteristics and traits that predispose them to yearn for, and to make certain choices: so a highly sociable person, for example, may find long spells of home-working extremely difficult and unproductive; while an introverted person could find the same experience rewarding and highly productive. Our propensity and enjoyment of risk taking may profoundly impact on the decision we make. The low-risk taker who craves security and predictability may feel overwhelmed by too many complex choices. They will prefer to be given a smaller range of choices with predictable outcomes. In contrast, the high-risk taker like Greg will want to work on the boundaries of their skills and abilities and will relish choice as an opportunity to create these boundary conditions. They will be more interested in risky stock portfolio and will strive to have a proportion of their benefit package in high risk/high returns.

These personal characteristics and traits are also reflected in the basic values we develop over time. The individual who places great emphasis on their role as a parent or their out-of-work activities will be particularly keen to build their working context around their personal beliefs and values of work-life balance. In doing so, like Stewart, they may well be prepared to sacrifice other aspects of their work life (for example, the opportunity of promotion). We have focused on how companies can support individual self-awareness and reflection in order for each individual to understand themselves better. But what can companies do to understand the individuals who are employed?

Personal characteristics and traits are specific to an individual and reflect a combination of deep-seated predispositions (such as introversion/extroversion; high-risk taking/low-risk taking) and values honed over time (such as attitudes to work/life balance). As Ed Schien's research with career anchors shows, these predispositions and values are relatively stable. They tend to remain over a long period of time, and are unlikely to be radically influenced by the current situation.[48] Overlaying these basic traits and values are predictable events that have the potential to create similar needs across groups of people with very different traits or values. However, the experiences remain similar for the majority of people. The same is true of personal life events. Becoming a parent, for example, is an event which has very specific set of needs associated with it. Caring for aged parents or dealing with personal illness are other life events also have common effects. In each case these are relatively predictable life events which one could expect many employees to experience at one or more times during their working lives.

By looking at traits or life events we are assuming that within any population of employees there will be subpopulations. By identifying people who have just become parents, for example, or women between the ages of 20 and 30 we are focusing on what the marketers call a type – a category of people within the larger population who share some common features. We are able to distinguish types by some aspect of their properties or behaviours that are observable.

So how are companies building this deep learning relationship with their employees? For McKinsey, it is about putting enormous managerial resources and effort into building the relationship on a one-to-one basis. This begins before the individual even signs up, way back when they are still at university and continues through the life of the employee. with, deep, rich involving and challenging conversations, often on a one-to-one basis. At BP, the longstanding intranet proficiency and investment has created a situation in which a 'virtual', e-based relationship enables individual to interact directly with the portfolio of choices as they go along.

But to understand state of the art data on employees we have to move outside the companies of our citizens and look at companies who have leveraged their world-class consumer insight into employee insight. This is precisely what the retail giant Tesco has achieved. Tesco employs over 280,000 people within the UK, continental and eastern Europe and Asia. A large number of these people are semi-skilled and part-time workers with limited access to computers. They have neither the management resource nor power of McKinsey, or the technology infrastructure of BP. But what they do have are world-class competencies in consumer insight. It is leveraging these competencies from customers to employees that has created the beginnings of employee insight.[49]

Building employee insight at Tesco

Tesco is one of the world's most profitable retailers. Recently it was also voted the UK's most admired company. While other retailers fail to meet their profit targets, Tesco has delivered one of the fastest organic growth rates of any major retailer in the world. Its non-food business rose by 18% in 2000–01, and its international business, which began with a launch in Hungary in 1994, now accounts for more than 40% of the group's floor space. At the heart of the Tesco formula is an unstinting and unwavering focus on the customer and their needs and aspirations. David Reid, Deputy Chairman puts it this way:[50]

'We spend a lot of time trying to understand customers. We take that understanding and translate it into detailed plans to add value to customers — be it better service, better prices, home shopping, or a better range of goods. We have a track record of spotting where customers are moving.'

Customer obsession is reflected and reinforced through the values that permeate the thousand stores, it can be seen in the behaviours of managers, and it is the lifeblood of the annual business cycle. Understanding their customer is what makes Tesco tick and each employee relentlessly tries to build employee insight. The focus on the customer is palpable. Of the Tesco employees polled in the 2000 consensus 82% agreed with the statement 'we are first for customers', while 95% expressed a desire to serve the customer by doing their best for the customer.

The Customer Insight Unit (CIU), created in 1995 has over the years used state of the art technologies and data bases to build profiles which support this insight. Each week data from all the stores are collated and trends identified on a weekly basis, while on a day-to-day basis customer shopping habits are tracked and monitored. The success of the Tesco credit card has created an enormous opportunity to build a detailed pattern of the shopping habits of the customer and to triangulate their purchases to build a picture of the key demographic groups with a focus on customer loyalty and lifestyle (values, attitudes and social milieu). As importantly, the knowledge amassed through the CIU helps retail managers extrapolate from current trends to create broad forecasts about the future. For example, the depth of this futuring capacity ensured that Tesco was one of the first retailers to significantly invest in the infrastructure of Internet shopping.

This customer data had fuelled much of the spectacular growth of the company. However, there was growing unease within the management team that the understanding and valuing of customers was running well in advance of the valuing and understanding of employees. While 82% of employees in the 2000 consensus agreed with the statement 'we are first for customers' only 64% felt valued by Tesco. The same discrepancy was increasingly true of management and leadership behaviour. The 360° feedback the company routinely took for its management population showed that employees thought the leadership team performed more strongly at delivering to customers than taking their people with them. The senior team became increasingly clear about the gap between focusing on customers and focusing on employees. And this was not a gap they were prepared to see continue. If Tesco was to continue to be a successful retailer and to meet its stretching expansion targets then a stronger balance between the two had to be created. And the two were indeed related. Earlier store based research at Tesco had shown that there was a strong positive relationship (with a correlation coefficient of 0.42) between customer satisfaction and the employee census item 'we look after our people'. Moreover, like the futures work at BT, the team at Tesco had identified some key employee trends: more people would choose to work freelance, there will be fewer 26- to 44-year-olds, more ethnic diversity, higher levels of education, more women would work in management and there will be more remote working. As David Richardson, a member of the team which led the employee focus initiative, comments:

> 'We increasingly expect to see non-standard employment contracts, with employees "opting-in" because participation rather than promotion drive commitment. Lifelong learning will be a key feature of work and work-life balance will become a hygiene factor.'

To balance employee insight with consumer insight members of CIU worked with members of the HR team to create the People Insight Unit (PIU). Using the CIU's well honed tools of the trade they built a deep understanding of attitudes to Tesco as an employer from both within and outside the company. From outside, they interviewed over 1,000 people to gather perceptions of Tesco as an employer and to understand future work trends. From within, focus groups were held across the country with over 20 groups of employees representative of the total workforce. The primary question in the focus group was what was motivating and de-motivating employees. At the same time the team selected specific targets groups and spent time with them to get to know them better. So deep discussion were held with the young graduates, with young people from different ethnic backgrounds, and with mothers who worked on a part-time basis with the company. Pulling together all these insights the team designed a survey termed 'Your Life . . . Your Future' which was completed by 1,600 employees. The teams were particularly interested in the relationship between what employees valued themselves, what they perceived Tesco as offering, and the trade-off they were currently making between the two. The insights from this survey was augmented by the employee Viewpoint annual consensus of all employees and the bi-annual survey of 3,000 employees which over the

Liberating your business with freedom, flexibility and commitment

preceding seven years had collected information from all the Tesco employees. This data allowed the team to identify employee groups across functions, regions and job levels. They used this data to begin to build case studies of people in the different attitudinal groups and understand their current and likely future needs.

What emerged from the Employee Insight Unit was fascinating. Tesco employees could be grouped into five attitudinal segments with related work commitment and loyalty attitudes. Half of the employees at Tesco fell into two groups, which the team called 'want it all' and 'work–life balancers'. *Work–life balancers* are more likely to be women aged between 45 and 54 who may or may not have children and want to work flexible hours, or part-time. They are not interested in promotion but do want challenging and stimulating work and a fulfilling job with responsibility and the opportunity to learn new skills. The ability of the company to operate flexible time arrangements is crucial to them. *Want it all* work full time and are either aged 25 to 34 with a degree and work in head office, or are older and working in the distribution function of the business. They aspire to a challenging and varied job and are engaged with the company, the success of Tesco is important to them. They are ambitious and want promotion; money is an important part of the deal for them. They are one of the most demanding and mobile groups and leave Tesco if the job fails to challenge them or if they can increase their salary elsewhere.

The third group, are what the team termed *pleasure seekers*. This is the group with the lowest commitment and loyalty to their employee and are often single men with no family commitments. Some are students working part-time in distribution, others are men who have worked with Tesco for about five years and want to maximize their pay by working longer hours. This group is ambitious and keen to travel overseas and to enjoy their leisure time. The nature of the work is less important to them but they do want the opportunity to maximize their income through overtime working and promotion. They do not take enormous pride in their work and do not want work to affect their personal and social lives. They are the most mobile segment, likely to leave Tesco if they can join a higher paying competitor. The future work-studies suggest that this mobile group is set to be a higher proportion of the working population over the coming decade.

Live to work are the most ambitious employee segment and the group with the highest loyalty and commitment. They are either young married men without children or older full-time managers with over ten years' service, typically working in a head office function or in distribution. They are keen to work long hours and want promotion, and challenging, varied jobs with responsibility. Work is not a place for fun or deep friendships and they are prepared to put work before their home life. In contrast, the *work to live* are often women aged over 35 who have worked in the stores for over ten years and may not have children. They are not interested in working long hours or promotion and don't mind working on repetitive tasks; for them the opportunity to work close to home is important. The future work-study suggests that this low-risk, traditional segment will become a lower proportion of the working population over the coming decade.

The employee segmentation gave David and his team a deeper understanding of the aspirations and demographics of the workforce. Next he needed a deeper understanding of what drives value and commitment. The survey and focus groups suggested that there were four major themes that drove commitment at Tesco.[51] The first, and the theme ranked highest across many of the employee segments was the social context in which an individual works. Tesco employees are more committed when they have workmates and a manager whom they are able to work with in a positive and valuing manner. The second theme was termed 'opportunity' and encompassed the benefits and pay package and the opportunities for career advancement. The third theme was termed 'help' and focused on the opportunity the employee had to use training and development to increase their skills, their opportunity to control their workload, and the communications between them and their manager. The final theme focused on the individual's interest in the content of their job and for many employees this was the second most important theme. Workload was quoted as one of the biggest push reasons for people leaving Tesco. At the same time the future research the team had commissioned suggested that companies which are good at making it easy to balance work and life will be the ones who retain people as attitudes to work change over the next ten years.

Building on the methods of the CIU they began to make a number of crucial predictions: that the future proportion of the workforce in each employee segment would significantly change over the coming decade; that the segmentation predicted both current and future retention rates; and most importantly, that commitment profiles varied across the employee segments. The information, presented to the board in late 2001 was startling.

Liberating your business with freedom, flexibility and commitment

Groups such as *'pleasure seekers'*, with some of the lowest rates of retention and commitment where predicted to grow significantly over the next five years. Once it understood the profile of its employees, the next question the board faced was how best to tailor the employment proposition in a cost effective and targeted manner. FedEx, for example, has made spectacular impact on the retention rates of its parcel sorters in its central hub at Memphis by tailoring around the aspirations of 'pleasure seekers', in this case students who work through the night sorting parcels. It was impossible to tailor the remuneration package, but possible to take advantage of the hundreds of FedEx aircraft landing in the Memphis hub every night. With 'jump seats' available in most, those parcel sorters who stay the longest, get to go the furthest. This is choice at its best . . . access to jump seats is of limited value to 'work–life balancers' who value flexibility around time, and it would be an insult to those who 'work to live' who value significant work and advancement, but for the 'pleasure seekers' . . . it is just right!

From this deepening knowledge about employees at Tesco the senior team began to create a portfolio of programmes and initiatives to bring choice to employees where they valued it, and by doing so to differentiate the Tesco deal from the competitors. Earlier initiatives, 'One-Team Rewards', 'Gain and Value Awards', had begun bringing choice to the pay deal. They also began to build on the training and development initiatives, through the Tesco Academy, Talent Spotting, FLM Training. Tesco has understood its employees and is beginning to create a whole portfolio of programmes to bring choice to where it was most appropriate and valued.

Supporting autonomy ensures that agility is maximized as individuals begin to learn to make choices that build their own competence and learning. But autonomy, self-insight and the will to learn can only be exercised when there is variety from within which choice can be made. It is to this notion of organizational variety that we now turn.

CHAPTER SIX

Crafting organizational variety

T he ultimate part of the cycle of building personal autonomy is moving into action, making decisions that build and leverage personal human capital. Action taking is the bridge to the second phase of building the Democratic Enterprise: the creation of an organizational context in which there is sufficient variety for individuals to become the best they can be, and by doing so, to create high performing organizations.

The creation and exercise of variety is at the heart of the Democratic Enterprise. It frames the first tenet, an adult-to-adult relationship, by acknowledging that the citizen is capable of self-determination and through the provision of variety as a resource for self-determination. It reinforces the second tenet, the notion of the individual as an investor, actively building and leveraging the three elements of his or her personal human capital. This active building takes place as the individual configures resources to invest in his or her own development. The configuration of these resources can only take place where there is sufficient variety for choice to be exercised. And, finally, the creation of variety influences both the third and the fourth tenet. Clearly, the expression of diverse qualities requires variety, while the deter-

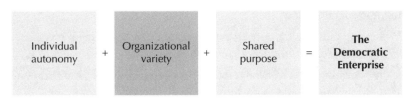

FIGURE 6.1 ◆ **The building blocks of democracy**

mination of the conditions of association requires a relationship in which there is sufficient latitude of discretion for choice to be exercised.

As we saw earlier, responsive, flexible people need both individual autonomy and organizational variety. Without both they are frustrated, confused or inert.

If variety is important to the creation of the tenets of the Democratic Enterprise, then what form should this variety take? The main challenge for the autonomous individual is to build and leverage their human capital. The essence of variety is the creation of practices and processes that support and enable the building and leveraging of human capital. Recall that the building of the three elements of human capital had various processes and practices associated with them:

The key aspects of variety and choice

Building intellectual capital

◆ through accessing training opportunities;

◆ by establishing developmental relationships with mentors and coaches;

◆ through accessing rich developmental opportunities and significant and diverse jobs and projects;

◆ the time and space for reflection.

Building emotional capital

◆ by accessing and seeking personal feedback;

◆ through building developmental relationships with mentors and coaches;

◆ by taking time for personal reflection;

◆ through making choices about the parameters of work, in where and when work takes place.

Building social capital

◆ through networking opportunities created by knowledge of vacancies in project teams, task forces and jobs;

◆ by accessing the knowledge of the key roles in the organization and their developmental opportunities;

◆ through being considered for memberships of project teams, task forces and jobs in functions, businesses and geographies outside the current role;

◆ by meeting others from outside the immediate work area and organization.

There is a great deal of overlap between the 12 practices and processes. For example, developmental relationships positively impact on the creation of emotional capital and social capital. As a consequence, as we saw earlier, there are eight overlapping key practices and processes that can be influenced to support the creation of the Democratic Enterprise.

There are a number of these practices and processes that are important context builders for the three citizens Greg, Nina and Stewart. For Greg at BP, the variety that was brought to the way in which jobs were assigned to people enabled him to zigzag with such elegance across the boundaries of the company. As an autonomous individual, without the variety of job experience and challenge, Greg would have become a frustrated and cynical person. The variety of job experiences at BP ensured that Greg remained flexible, responsive and committed. The same was true for Nina at McKinsey. Her capacity to navigate across the various projects at McKinsey created a context of project variety that enabled her to actively build her personal human capital. For Stewart his capacity to behave in an autonomous manner depended on the variety of location and time choice his employer, BT, was capable of providing. If he was forced to work in a central office at predetermined times, then his capacity to remain engaged and committed would have been severely tested. BT, BP and McKinsey are all pioneering the creation and provision of organizational variety and by doing so are building great organizations on the basis of the democratic tenets.

We have looked at the democratic tenets through the eyes of the three citizens. Their experience is important to this debate, but it is not unique. Many others are crafting autonomous working lives in organizations in which variety has become the norm. As we saw, the creation of personal human capital takes place in a context in which there is a variety of job assignments, project assignments and location choice. But, there are three other elements of variety, which are central to building personal human capital. Variety around how a job is crafted, variety around training, and variety around development relationships. At the same time, there are three elements of variety, which are crucial to the leverage of human capital, reward and benefit variety, and location choice and time choice.

Pioneers of democracy

The making of wise choices is essentially an individual attribute. Greg made choices about the breadth of roles he took because he knew enough about himself to know that variety and breadth were crucial. Stewart made the choice to work at home because he knew that fulfilment would come from being able to concentrate at home and avoid commuting. Nina chose to develop a strong client base in the UK so she could spend less time travelling and more time with her small children. Each made a choice on the basis of awareness of themselves and what really excited them and brought them joy. Each of these choices was not made in a vacuum, but within the context of an organization. There will be other chemical engineering graduates who have not developed Greg's broad skills. There will be other specialists like Stewart who found daily commuting drained their energy but carried on simply because their company did not enable home-working. There will be other women as talented as Nina and in other companies who left work after their first child was born because they could not choose to build a home-based project portfolio.

For each one of these citizens organizational context matters: in the creation of culture; in the crafting of processes and systems; in the education and rewarding of managerial behaviours. To more deeply understand what pioneering companies do to create variety, we focus on eight companies pioneering democracy. Each was chosen because they illustrate the context and processes which support one dimension of variety. Although each company is used to illustrate one dimension, in reality they often have a cluster of dimensions of variety all being pursued. So, while McKinsey is the lead example in project choice, it is also pioneering choice of developmental relationship (with a complex mentoring and coaching scheme) and time choice (with a proportion of associates working flexibly). The same is true of BP. While we will focus on the variety of job assignments, the senior team at BP is also pioneering home-working.

Pioneers of democracy

BP: Job assignments

Multinational oil company, grown through rapid acquisition. Engaged in the extraction, refining and distribution of oil and gas. Has created a transparent internal labour market for jobs for over a decade. Engineered the system on the internal employee web in 2001.

McKinsey & Co: Projects

Strategic consulting partnership, primary growth has been organic. Engaged in strategic advice and support to worldwide clients. Most client work is project based with consultants working for a number of clients at the same time. Has created an internal market for project resourcing now available on the internal web.

Sony: Job content

Electronic goods manufacturer, headquartered in Japan. Operating in a highly competitive electronics marketplace. Development of the VAIO digital system made extensive use of engineers designing their own jobs.

Unisys: Training

Computing company. Re-launched in 1999 to re-focus on services, by 2002, 75% of Unisys University curricula are delivered online through the employee portal.

Goldman Sachs: Developmental relationships

New York based investment bank with significant operations in Asia and Europe. Transformed from a partnership to public ownership in 1999. Has a rich and complex web of developmental relationships with ongoing support to mentoring and coaching.

AstraZeneca: Rewards and benefits

Pharmaceutical company created through merger of a major ICI business and Zeneca. Launched a personalized benefit package in 1999 as part of the merger strategy.

BT: Location

Telecom built from the UK's public telephone operator, now operating in Europe and Asia. Commissioned research in the 1980s on the future of work and has since pioneered location and time choice.

Hewlett-Packard: Time

Computer company grown organically until the recent Compaq merger. Strong ethos of individual development and autonomy. Has a wide portfolio of choice initiatives of which time is one dimension.

Variety of job assignments: BP

For each of the citizens, the opportunity to actively engage with making choices about the jobs that they took was crucial. Actively engaging in job choice supports the first tenet, the creation of an adult-to-adult relationship, and the second tenet, that individuals are seen as investors, actively building and deploying their human capital.

Personal human capital is built and leveraged primarily through work challenges both in the form of project teams and task forces and the relationships associated with this work. Stretching, challenging work experiences are the foundation for the development of social capital by potentially creating the loose and tight network structures in which ideas are exchanged and built upon. At the same time, stretching work experiences build intellectual capital by introducing a new set of competencies and knowledge. The best way to promote and encourage adaptability, as we saw with Greg and Nina, is to provide stretching and challenging job assignments.[1] People who are left in jobs rapidly stagnate as they become skilled at the aspects of the work and unchallenged by its extent. As Greg found, the simplest way to be continuously stimulated and challenged is to move through different assignments that demand different skills and build social capital through accessing and developing a range of networks of relationships. Some of these jobs build on current reality, others extend the boundaries of current reality, or even create an opportunity to change assumptions about oneself and one's work. This sounds simple, but in practice it is very difficult to deliver.

The company profiles in 'democracy at work' show that companies differ greatly in their ability to deliver freedom and space around job choice. Both HP and GlaxoSmithKline created a context in which people were able to have formal and informal discussions about their career development, and they felt they had a choice of career paths, with opportunities for development available to all. For the employees in Citibank and Lloyds TSB, the opportunity to exercise choice around job experiences was very limited. In many companies the variety of jobs available to employees is limited by rules governing when and where an employee can move, how long the employee has to stay in a role, or by lack of transparency in information about job vacancies.[2] These reduce an individual's opportunity to make the decisions necessary to build his or her personal human capital, and ultimately they erode the talent base of the corporation. But, as we saw for Greg, this is not the case for BP where employees have unparalleled transparency, information and access to jobs, and a broad latitude of discretion within which to make choices.[3]

Greg Grimshaw was just one of thousands of BP employees who received e-mails from *myAgent* on the morning of 21 June, and one of hundreds of people who made an online application for a job. The launch in early 2001 of the customized career development processes at BP had as its overriding goal the creation of a flexible internal labour market. Employees are e-mailed the results of jobs searches and presented with a list of job vacancies ranked by the degree of match between their skills, knowledge and preferences and the profile of the job. At the same time, managers are able to access the portal to search for and identify potential team members and to access candidate lists for similar jobs so they can alert past candidates. At any time up to 3,000 jobs are posted, and by mid-2001 most employees had created and posted their job history and competency profiles.

Dave Latin had worked as a geologist with BP and ran the employee portal project before Greg Grimshaw. As he admits, 'I knew nothing about Human Resources when I took the job'. But for Dave the energy and excitement of the project was palpable. As he explains:

'It was the end of 1999 and BP had finished the major mergers with Amoco in 1998 and then with Arco in 1999. By the time we had acquired Burmah Castrol in July 2000 we had a market value of more than $200 billion. The company had doubled in size and was incredibly complex. We saw this as an opportunity to simplify. What got the board excited was the aspiration that e-HR could touch each of the 100,000 employees and cause a real shift in behaviour.'

In late 1999 the team showed John Browne and the top team of BP a video of an integrated career and development system, with *myJobmarket* and *myAgent*. There was a great deal of excitement, but limited technological infrastructure. Browne was adamant that everyone in BP, regardless of their company legacy, could plug in and feel they were part of the same global operating system. The board demanded a simple, transparent process with state-of-the-art, integrated technology. Not easy when there were numerous legacy systems. But there was a strong push to develop the technology platform to support an open internal market for jobs. As Dave says:

> 'We asked ourselves, what can we do to make BP a tremendously stimulating and interesting place to work, where employees feel valued. A lot of it has to do with what we are doing on the web. A lot of talk about e-capability has been about reducing costs. For me one of the key levers is making people's lives easier and making information transparent, and relieving frustrations. Create space for people to be more innovative and do things. If everyone has access to the information they need quickly and easily, then they have the opportunity to have informed conversations and do something valuable with their time. We also see it as an opportunity to reinforce the brand values of BP. It is about openness and transparency within the company and with people we relate to outside. By being open and honest we are trying to espouse what BP is trying to be. In the future we want to recognize that everyone is unique.'

When the system was initially launched managers developed career plans for their team members which were placed on the portal. But this rapidly proved to be both cumbersome and overly bureaucratic. Within months the system was re-designed to enable all individual employees to interact and update their own career details. Within the first six months 17,000 people had placed their competency profiles and the portal was attracting 12,000 users per week and over a million hits every month. CEO John Browne's dream to create a globally connected enterprise was on the way to becoming a reality.

All but the top 200 jobs can be posted, and the rules governing the system are minimal – any employee can apply for any job, in any location, at any time, without consulting their manager. The electronic database is supported by workshops in which employees learn about the types of jobs and possible career options. These educate individuals on how to best manage their development, provide information about the career tracks across the businesses, and use 360° peer-based feedback to build insight and self-awareness.

Opening up the internal labour market and creating significantly more variety has brought real benefits: cross-functional job moves have significantly increased, time taken to fill jobs has reduced, team leaders are positive about their capacity to locate skills. For BP, crafting variety has played a crucial part in integrating the heritage businesses, and creating a flexible and adaptive organization.

Variety of job assignments: the insights

Opening up the internal labour market can be complex and is potentially fraught with difficulties. What can we learn from the experience of BP?

Create a common platform of skills and competencies

The internal job market at BP is complex, large and global. Thousands of job vacancies, and thousands of people. Getting a match between the two is crucial to the agility of the company, and to the capacity of individuals to develop their human capital. At the heart of this matching process is a common platform of competencies, which are used to profile both people and jobs.[4] Competency profiling at BP goes back more than a decade when the senior HR team invested in a research study to establish what made for job success at various levels in the organization and across the business streams. Since then the resulting competency profiles have been updated and recalibrated. They have the advantage of creating a common language to describe what people do at BP. At the same time the element of skill is seen to be more personal and idiosyncratic. So, for example, Greg's competency profile contains both a generic competency descriptor and a specific list of his skills and experiences. The match is made by the classification of these skills in personal profiles and in job descriptions.

The history of the creation and development of competency profiling is long and tortuous. While the creation of a competency profile can require much managerial effort, they can be the basis for variety in job assignments. From the perspective of BP, the key to success was to attempt to go for broad agreement on the competencies rather than try to specify them in minute detail.

Invest in portal technology

Delivering a variety of job assignments is only possible (outside of the smallest company) with technology. Without the employee portal it would have been impossible for BP to create the size and complexity of shared data which enabled Greg and his colleagues to surf the internal job market. The investment in this supporting technology is substantial. In the case of BP, a far-sighted and technologically literate CEO drove much of the resources and energy necessary to deliver this. However, where this is not the case a convincing business case has to be made for the investment. The potential benefits include greater employee alignment (and therefore productivity), faster creation of human capital across the firm, and enhanced retention rates of the most talented people.

Resist the temptation to control

There is an enormous temptation to control the internal market for jobs with complex rules about how long people have to stay in the role, who has to be informed of their job applications, what type of jobs they should move to next and so on. This temptation should be resisted. Order will emerge from this potentially chaotic system as long as there is sufficient information for people to make informed choices. This information mirrors the two axes shown earlier in Greg's Options for the Future. The vertical axis is 'personal capability'. Navigation of the internal job market can only occur if people understand their competencies, skills, aspirations and needs and are prepared to actively build their personal capability. Without this the system can become bogged down with people who have unrealistic expectations of what it is they can achieve and are unwilling to learn.

The horizontal axis of knowledge is the axis of external knowledge. This is knowledge about the world external to the person: the clusters of jobs in the company and their demands and constraints; the capacity of certain jobs to develop specific skills and competencies; the likely changes in roles as the sector evolves; the jobs which are likely to become 'hot' in the future and those which could well lead to the development of dead-end competencies. Without this knowledge, people spend too much time creating needless and costly variety. Armed with this external knowledge they are more likely to be able to target competency areas that excite them and take the risks that would lead to the development of these competencies.

The emphasis here is on a light hand rather than the iron fist of bureaucratic rules and procedures. These will simply tie up the potential agility and flexibility of the internal market for jobs.

Variety of projects and task forces: McKinsey

Increasingly it will be projects rather than permanent jobs that define organizational structure. While job postings, often less elaborate versions of BP's, are rapidly becoming the norm, less emphasis has been placed on creating processes which support variety and choice in project creation and membership. Yet it is often these projects, rather than more permanent jobs, which bring the greatest excitement, challenge and potential for development. As Nina found, projects provide discrete opportunities for the accumulation of new learning.[5]

At McKinsey the acceleration and creation of the distinctive knowledge and skills which takes a rookie from analyst to associate to partner is supported by an emphasis on having a choice of a variety of projects and acknowledgement that individuals are best served when they make educated choices about their development.[6] At the heart of this choice is a belief in what MD, Rajat Gupta, calls 'self governance'; unswerving focus on the client, and the creation of knowledge and skills of each member of the firm.[7] Client projects are at the core, it is these projects which fuel the profitability of the firm and the ability to grow. At the same time, as Nina found, it is the experience of working on client projects that act as the catalyst to the individual development of every McKinsey employee.

This commitment to the development of its member was one of the cornerstones of the strategic review instigated by MD, Rajat Gupta, in 1996. At that time the strategic issues the firm faced were the retention of clients (who were increasingly developing their own internal capability) and the retention of the most talented employees. As Gupta remarks, 'We have always recruited the brightest, but at the time when McKinsey consultant's class peers were earning millions, it was essential to find the means to develop, compensate and retain the internal talent.' To do this McKinsey re-emphasized the role of development as a key driver for recruitment and retention. The focus of the development process was what was called the 'T-shaped consultant' – a broad generalist perspective combined with in-depth knowledge in one industry sector or functional expertise. This is how Gupta describes it: 'McKinsey means the freedom to follow your passions, the opportunity to have multiple careers within a career, all within the unique framework of the global partnership.'

The concept of the T-shaped competence set is based on the assumption that consultants are most able to serve their clients and the firm when they have developed an individually distinctive and valuable portfolio of skills and knowledge. To achieve this combination of generalist perspective and in-depth specialization, every associate is expected to articulate and then design a possible sequence of client and firm experiences which will be capable of supporting the T-shaped proposition. They have to create a coherent story about why they are distinctive and what they can do to support this. There is no structured development process that takes employees from one assignment to another in a clearly defined trajectory. Instead, individuals are asked to create the story-line and then given a wide latitude of choice in their membership of client assignments. At the same time they are provided with sufficient information to chose teams and team leaders who they believe have the aptitudes, knowledge and skills best suited to becoming mentors and coaches. In order to build a longer-term view of themselves and the firm, individuals are able to access a number of sources of knowledge about the future of the firm and the likely client base and consulting focus in order to substantiate their choice of assignments. Nina reflects, 'This is the essence of entrepreneurialism at the firm. You decide what you want to do, you excite people about it so you get the support and leverage that you need, you make it happen.'

People are supported to take big jumps across very different projects rather than incremental shuffles between similar projects. The jumps, like Nina's jump to Korea, can be across countries, across specializations, across industries. Big jumps have the greatest potential for transformation. MD, Rajat Gupta, is clear about this: 'People will tell you, "learn how to say no". In McKinsey I believe it is more important to learn how to say "yes", particularly if this expands your opportunities and your choice.' For Nina Bhatia, this breadth and depth of latitude enabled her to move from chocolate to the oil sector to media and steel, while at the same time focusing on a whole range of strategic and organizational behaviour issues. She also had the opportunity to work on a number of pro-bono assignments, with an educational establishment and a charity. At the heart of these assignments was the opportunity to solve difficult and often complex problems.

The backbone of project choice at McKinsey is VOX the firm's intranet-based talent exchange on which all client assignments, pro-bono projects and other initiatives worldwide are communicated. Consultants are able to interrogate the system by project location, industry, project content, timing and functional expertise. From the day they start, all consultants have a global view of prospective engagements, including pro-bono projects, knowledge building and other initiatives, and can voice their interests and preferences. As their skills and performance grow, so does their degree of influence. At the same time, the experience, knowledge and skills of the team members and project leaders are shared within KNOW, the corporate knowledge portal. This directory stores information on educational and professional experience, on the types of projects an individual has worked on, and language proficiency. To deepen their knowledge of project leaders' potential, project members are encouraged to access KNOW and to talk with people who have previously worked with the project leader to get a feeling of their strengths, working styles and specialist skills. The building of this type of knowledge is actively encouraged. As a result, there rapidly builds around consultants and project leaders 'explicit' knowledge of their career histories and interests, and 'tacit' knowledge of their capacity to coach and mentor and create exciting and stretching working environments.

Consultants are also encouraged to build their personal human capital by pursuing entrepreneurial activities, for example, by helping to establish a new office, or by taking a leading edge issue to found or build a specialized practice. For example, a colleague of Nina's, Stephen Kunz and his associates in the Swiss office started to build client relationships in Greece. In January 2000, the 'new office' in Athens began its operations in a hotel room – just a few months later they moved to new offices and two years later had 20 consultants working with clients from a wide range of industries. Another colleague of Nina's, Matthias Oberholzer, had a passion for sport and in a mountain chalet in the winter of 1999 he and nine other people decided to launch a Sports Practice. Very soon after, the first proposals were written, first potential clients were met and, within a year, McKinsey Switzerland carried out more than ten projects in the sports industry.

At McKinsey the freedom to choose and encouragement to behave autonomously is supported by the remuneration structures. In many professional firms analysts and partners are given individual financial targets which specify the number of client days to be worked, and the fee income generated on each of these client days. This has the disadvantage of encouraging people to focus on simply repeating what they have previously achieved. At McKinsey this focus is discouraged. Employees are compensated in two ways: on the basis of their individual contribution to clients and the partnership, and the performance of the firm. There is no country or regional-based P&L remuneration. This is important since in many professional firms the potential choice of assignments can be severely restricted by the budgeting process in individual countries or regions. At McKinsey employees are free to move unencumbered across borders and, as Stephen Kunz and Matthius Oberholzer did, to collaborate with whoever they believe to be important.

Variety of projects and task forces: the insights

As a professional firm, based on the management of large and complex projects, McKinsey is particularly focused on using projects to extend and stretch the human capital of the firm. Even so, there are lessons for companies for whom projects are currently not a major way of configuring work.

Realize that projects matter

Much of the work of companies has become, and will become, project focused. These are projects which span functions and businesses, geographies and company boundaries. These projects, with their specific timelines and clear objectives, are wonderful learning opportunities. And, to become the best they can be, people need an opportunity to be able to be considered for these projects. Yet, in many companies projects are seen as evening work or work that happens in parallel with someone's main job. As a consequence, even in companies with relatively sophisticated internal markets for jobs, the market for projects is based on proximity (choosing someone in the same team) or convenience (choosing someone who has the time).

In other words, the selection to a project takes place in a haphazard, thoughtless manner. So the first lesson from McKinsey is to treat the selection to projects with the same thought and sophistication as the selection to full-time jobs.

Be prepared to count, describe and monitor

To do so requires companies to learn and put into action the second insight from McKinsey. If projects are to be elevated to the same level as jobs, then they have to be treated in a more thoughtful manner. They have to be counted, described and monitored. The centre of the VOX system at McKinsey is the counting of projects, the description of projects (where they are located, who is the manager, what is it they are mandated to achieve, what is the likely time-frame, what is likely to be gained from them) and the monitoring of projects. This monitoring involved the specific starting of a project, the description of the aims of the project, the timescales of the project, and the ending of the project.

It is only with this counting, describing and monitoring that projects will assume a similar weight as full-time jobs. Without this rigour they will remain on the periphery, an incredible source of rich experiences, but one treated in an ad-hoc and non-specific manner so that the developmental potential of project membership is potentially squandered.

Put round pegs in square holes

One of the enduring pictures from the citizens' stories is the picture of Greg, a petroleum engineer, heading e-HR at BP, and Nina taking the role in Korea advising a chocolate manufacturer. As she reflected, 'The only thing I knew about chocolate was I liked the taste of it.' In both cases BP and McKinsey took a risk. A great deal of the selection processes in many organizations is directed at finding round pegs who can fit into round holes, to discover people who are so exquisitely close to the needs of the job that they fit into it like a hand into a well fitting glove. This severely restricts the capacity of the individual to grow and to be stretched. Instead they are simply working through well-used routines and ways of working, and by doing so rapidly becoming atrophied and bored.

People have to be given the opportunity to work in projects which are outside of their function, which are in businesses different from their own, which are in sectors different from their own, or which are in geographies different from their own.

The only way this can occur is by a combination of a valuing of projects, a systematic project management process, and a capacity to move people across boundaries to take project positions. This take places through a combination of 'pull' and 'push'. In 'pull' the project manager actively looks outside the normal resource pool for potential project members with a combination of skills and competencies that are outside some aspects of the project specification. Clearly the success of the 'pull' strategy depends on the social networks of the project manager and their ability to identify these people. The 'push' scenario is closer to that used by McKinsey. Here, information about current and future projects is made available to all associates and partners and they are invited to apply to be considered for membership of the projects. This has the advantage of creating a wide and varied pool of potential membership.

Choice of job content: Sony

In the machine-like bureaucracies of the 1950s and 1960s managers exercised control by telling people how to do their jobs and monitoring them with constant surveillance to guard against surprises. This level of control is still effective when standardization is critical for efficiency, or when quality and safety are essential to product performance. However, for the agile, democratic company asking managers to spend all their time monitoring others, or specifying the ways in which employees should perform tasks, is neither desirable nor productive. Entrepreneurial employees, capable of moving with agility, do so because, as in McKinsey, they are free to choose the tasks they perform or, as in Sony, they have discretion over the way in which these tasks are performed.

The characteristics of a job can be shown graphically, as in Fig. 6.2. The way in which an individual performs a job has at its centre a set of *obligations and demands* which every holder of the job is required to meet; it is bounded by *constraints*, the factors which limit how the job is performed. These constraints include resource constraints, or technological constraints, or the constraints from lack of skills and attitudes on the part of the job holder. Between the core of demands and the outer rim of constraints is choice, the *latitude of discretion*. Within the latitude of discretion the job holder can choose to emphasize certain aspects of the job, to interact with

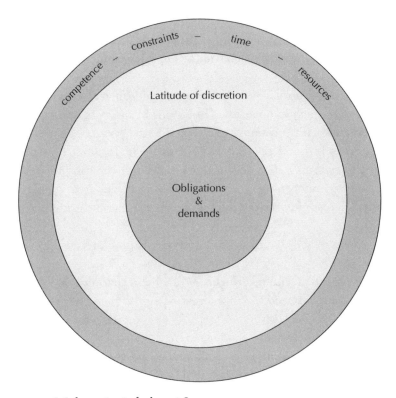

FIGURE 6.2 ◆ **Job content choice at Sony**

a certain group of people, to develop expertise in certain areas of work, or to take part in activities outside the immediate domain of the work. Companies and individuals increase the latitude of discretion by reducing the demands of the job, or by reducing the constraints.[8]

A 'wide latitude of discretion' signals a role in which the individual has much discretion over how the role is performed: what tasks they do and with whom they work. Under these conditions, they specify their actions and they make the choices about what is appropriate. When the latitude of discretion is narrow, the opportunities for an individual to make choices is strictly limited, and they have a correspondingly limited opportunity to exercise their discretion. This latitude of discretion forms part of the wider adult-to-adult contract between the individual and the organization and sends out very strong messages about individual freedom and choice. Moreover, with regard to development of autonomy, we know that individual autonomy is developed only under conditions when the actions an individual takes are made in a context in which they have been self-determining. People must experience their behaviour as self-determined for autonomy to develop.[9]

The democratic profile of the seven companies showed that most people have some determination over the conditions of their association. Specifically, they work with their boss to determine the targets of their job (i.e. those aspects which are the demands of the job). In Kraft Foods people feel they are encouraged to develop new skills and work in jobs that have variety and are interesting. The employees in Parcelforce appear to be least able to create interesting jobs in which they have a wide latitude of discretion.

The notion of self-determination and the shaping of how a job can be performed has a long history. From the 1960s, there has been interest in what has been called 'empowerment'. While the terminology and concepts of empowerment received much interest, in reality many of the studies of empowerment showed that the rhetoric was far in advance of reality. Empowerment experiments tended to have relatively short shelf-lives, fading away when the economic conditions of the firm changed, or when a new management team took the helm.[10]

Part of the problem with empowerment programmes is that they have been exactly that – programmes, not seen as part of the natural, day-to-day way in which people go about their business. Crafting a latitude of discretion is not about programmatic change, it is about slowly, but consciously and wilfully, extending the boundaries of variety and personal discretion. For some companies this has become part of the normal way of working.

This has certainly been the case at the consumer electronics giant Sony.[11] Like McKinsey, the values of Sony were created by the founding team led by Masaru Ibuka and Akio Morita. Their vision was to 'create a stable work environment where engineers who had a deep and profound appreciation for technology could realize their societal mission and work to their heart's content'.

Unlike other Japanese companies, Sony always tried to create a relaxed culture and working environment which avoided rigid corporate rules. Instead, Sony espoused 'ibuka-ism' a belief in a clear and unique self-direction. It also sharply departed from the Japanese corporate norm of focusing graduate recruitment on a strict hierarchy of academic institutions with

Todai (Tokyo University) at the top. Instead it established an open-entry system where applicants were not asked to name their university. The emphasis was not on hiring the best, but rather, as a senior HR manager describes 'hiring those who have something really different from others and own a driving force to achieve their unique dreams'.

The spirit of Sony emphasized the creation and fulfilment of this 'unique dream'. Like BP (and unlike almost all other Japanese corporations) an internal recruitment system was introduced in the 1960s which allowed every employee to apply to any position in which he or she was interested, with or without the permission of their immediate boss. This not only increased mobility, but also ensured that managers created stimulating tasks that could challenge their staff and allow them to do what they particularly wanted to do. And as we shall see in Unisys, there was great freedom in learning, much of which takes place on-the-job. Finally, like many other Japanese corporations, Sony had not implemented highly leveraged incentive systems, but rather used ability-based, or even seniority-based rewards, which gave it flexibility in job assignment without detailed job descriptions. Good performance is acknowledged, not so much by sharply differentiated financial rewards, but the opportunity to work on more interesting assignments, often aligned to personal dreams. As a consequence, there has developed within the company a long history of people working on a task which excited them, even if it failed to get management support. The Sony Walkman was initially developed by an engineer who manufactured an experimental model for his hobby in his own time rather than for his job.

The freedom to choose and to build job tasks was tested severely with the launch of the Sony PC VAIO. In 1995, on the 50th anniversary of the corporation, CEO, Nobuyuki Idei, launched the vision for the next 50 years and announced that, not withstanding past failures, the company intended to re-enter the PC business with VAIO. This was backed by a vision where all content music, movies or whatever would be distributed through a broadband digital network with the PC as the gateway to the Internet, the prototype of the network-centric infrastructure. This was met with horror by Sony engineers, in part because of the memory of the debacle in Sony's previous foray into the PC market; and in part because of the engineers' instinctive aversion to operating the Microsoft Windows platform. As a result, the new project attracted very few applicants. However, rather than assigning engineers to the project, the senior team at Sony began an enormous focus on communication and sharing of knowledge, so engineers could develop a clearer and more engaging picture of the project and its potential outcomes.

A key decision for the project was that it was decided that it would be operating members of the team who drove the process and designed and shaped their own talent and roles. The engineers working on the VAIO product gained mastery over the way in which they chose to work. They were free to make decisions about the priorities they believe to be crucial and had choice in both the access to, and in the allocation of resources. This transfer of power and resources encouraged the engineers to become more self-disciplined. At the same time, much was done to support this latitude of discretion. Clearly, if an engineer is to make confident and effective independent bottom-line decisions, he or she has to have a sense of competence to make that decision. For these engineers their latitude of discretion was supported by a clear understanding of the goals of the project and the mission of Sony, and by deep awareness of their own performance and the performance of the team.[12]

These engineers became confident, independent decision-makers in part because they understood the goals of the project and the environment in which Sony was operating. The strategic intent, or dream, was clear: the PC would be a core catalyst in convergence, and Sony would be a major player in this convergence. The goal was stretching and energizing, every engineer had a sense of ownership about Sony, and understood how their work roles and behaviours affected its success. So while their tasks were not defined, and the decisions not specified, they had a clear view of the end-state.[13] Much was done to create this dream, for example, a virtual organization entitled the 'VAIO Center', was created as the embodiment of the vision. Each group sent a young graduate to this virtual organization to work with the team there and report back to the rest of the team on the mission and current status of the goals. At the same time this dream was not seen as mere rhetoric. On the contrary, they could see senior managers participating in the VAIO Center and understood that the stated intentions and beliefs represented deeply rooted values and intentions.[14] As we shall see in the final building block of the Democratic Enterprise, the capacity to create a shared sense of destiny rests in part on the creation of an exciting and stimulating vision.

Yet while information about the goals of the project and the mission of Sony was important, it was not sufficient. Engineers also had access to information about their own performance, and the overall performance of the project.[15] For example, the team developed an intensive training and feedback programme which matched young graduates to experienced engineer 'tutors' who supervised an assignment to solve a real technical problem. This intense and rapid feedback and coaching created a strong sense of mastery on the part of the young members of the team. At the same time they had a clear view of the performance of their team and, through the Virtual VAIO Center, of the overall performance of the project. They knew where the large project was headed, and felt more personally capable of taking initiatives. They understood how well their team was performing, so were in a better position to make or influence decisions to maintain or improve performance. Importantly, the feedback about performance took place in a supportive environment with a sense of security. Given the clarity of goals and the constant feedback, each member of the engineering team was able to create their own approach to the task and to rapidly adjust it as the team progressed – they had become an agile group. In 1997 the first VAIO notebook model was launched. This established Sony as a presence in the PC market for the first time in its history and was a landmark in Sony's transformation from the analogue-based company of the past to the digital-based firm of the future.

Variety in job content: the insights

Extend the latitude of discretion

In broadening the latitude of discretion there are a number of potential choices for expansion, first, about *how* the work is done and second about *what* work is done. By making a choice about *what* work is done the individual can choose to emphasize certain aspects of the job, they can select some and choose to ignore or delegate others, or they can change the area of work.

There are four major characteristics which influence the expectations of a role and the latitude of discretion individuals are able to exercise. The first is the extent to which the job tasks are clearly and unambiguously defined. The second is the characteristics of the person in the role, in particular their self-belief and achievement motivation, their capacity to take risks and the belief they have in their ability to control and influence their role (what has been termed internal locus of control). The third influencing characteristic is the relationship between the individual and those around them, particularly in terms of their relative power and influence, the strength of their relationship and the independence of the task. Finally, there is the characteristics of the people who have a stake in the job (peers, the boss, colleagues and customers) particularly with regard to their authority, the resources they have available to them and the diversity of their expectations.[16]

The capacity of an organization to extend the latitude of discretion is determined by broadening around one or all of these four influencing characteristics. Variety in roles is created by moving away from fixed job definitions, and allowing jobs to evolve and become an idiosyncratic reflection of the strengths of the individual with sufficient discretion for them to stretch their skills. Next, with regard to people in the roles, they ensure they can perform beyond the expectations of the role by relentlessly increasing their individual competency and motivation. At the same time, they widen the latitude of discretion by making available valued resources (information, visibility, and key task assignments) which motive people to perform beyond current expectations. Finally, they decrease the power and authority distance between the various stakeholders in the job and by doing so encourage them to feel more able to make decisions.

Make the vision clear

The second lesson from Sony about creating variety in work is the focus they put on the centre of the circle that describes work, the obligations and demands. They brought variety to these roles by making clear what might be called the end-state, the vision of what they collectively were attempting to achieve and the role each played in delivering to this vision. Yet while the vision was clear, there was latitude around the path of the journey. So where variety was introduced it was in the means by which the end-state could be achieved. Here the paths were individualistic. Each member of the team was free to choose a personal path that maximized their skill development and made full use of his or her current talents. The co-ordination between the members of the team took place through the shared vision.

Recall also that the vision at Sony was not financial. It was not 'we shall increase productivity by 10%' or even 'we shall achieve a 12% ROCE'. These are business goals, not visions and provide no information at all about the end-state. By creating a vision as a direction mechanism, Sony was able to specify, in the mind of every team member, what it was they were aiming for. This sense of shared purpose, of a common destiny, meant that engineers were continuously able to adjust their performance to the needs of their colleagues and to the overall tasks.

Be aware of the impact of performance metrics

The related learning point from Sony is the profound influence performance metrics can have on the way people perform their task and achieve their goals. The emphasis here is on lightness of touch. Performance metrics which over-specify both the ends (the goal) and the means (the tasks) severely limit the freedom available to people and their personal latitude of discretion. In too many companies the combination of highly specified job descriptions with highly specified goal setting and performance metrics create a limited frame of action.

The lightness of touch at Sony was the combination of a vision of the future that was engaging and energizing, with a very broad description of *how* people were to achieve this vision. Moreover, the *how* description was primarily about the values and culture rather than detailed analysis of the job content. They encouraged people to work in teams, to value sharing knowledge with each other, to build their own personal skills and competencies. They did not detail the specific tasks that should be performed.

Choice of training: Unisys

As we have seen, significant work experience gained through stretching jobs, project work and roles with a wide latitude of discretion are a critical element of enabling people to become the best they can be. This ongoing job-based experience is key. Yet there are times when, focused knowledge and skills can be immensely useful. This is particularly the case if the knowledge in this training is provided at the exact time an individual needs it, and if it is focused on an important challenge. Over the last decade there have been real advances in creating a wide variety of learning activities, paired with a deepening of employee self-insight to make wise choices around their training needs. Many of these advances have taken place as technology links the organization to the individual and the individual to colleagues. This is essential for the second tenet, the individual as investor. Yet, as we saw earlier, companies differ in their capacity to make available to their employees significant training opportunities that develop both their current skills, and also prepare them for the future.

At the computer services company Unisys employees are free to choose from a huge portfolio of learning options.[17] Much of the momentum to learning choice was created from 1992 when CEO, Larry Weinberg, sought to reposition the strategy and change the company from a mainframe computing to a service model. This is a strategic transition which has been attempted by many computer companies and is fraught with difficulties. It requires the transformation of skills and knowledge from understanding software, to understanding the customer. This requires a fundamental realignment between the talent of the company and the business goals. In the space of five years the senior team of Unisys sought to reverse the previous mainframe computing focus by setting a goal of building 75% of revenues through service. The repositioning was begun with the re-organization of the company. The complexity of the new customer-focused structure was immense; a matrix with three major functional groups (outsourcing, network services and systems) and five major industry groups, ranging from telecoms to transport. With the potential fragmentation of the matrix, each of the business units rapidly developed their own training capability with their own language and methodology. As Ettie McCormack, Director of Unisys University, observes:

> 'This was encouraging territorialism – "my business unit made this investment, so I am not sharing it". Eventually the company started to look like a collection of businesses, and it was difficult to trace the skills. In order to maintain the Gold Partner standard[18] you have to have a certain number of people certified. With these different training programmes in each of the business units it was impossible to keep track on the level of capability within the firm.'

The vehicle for much of this re-focus and integration was Unisys University, launched in 1999 with a structure mirroring a business school – the

Chairman of Unisys served as Dean, and nine senior managers headed the functional schools (HR, Legal, Business, Finance, Leadership, Marketing, Sales, E-Services, Technology). By the end of 2002, 75% of the Unisys University curricula were delivered online through the company's employee portal, there were over 2,100 programmes available worldwide, and every year the 37,000 employees participated in over 95,000 learning events.

The capacity of individual employees at Unisys to freely access the knowledge base of a company and to make development choices was supported through a significant attempt by the management team to reduce the complexity of jobs and skills description and to bring greater transparency to the skills and abilities profiling. This transparency enables easy navigation through the training and development options. To achieve this transparency managers from across Unisys worked together to reduce the number of job titles in the company from 5,000 to 400, while at the same time rationalizing the job levels across the world. Every employee at Unisys now starts as a generalist consultant, before moving to a more distinct functional role.

With variety comes choice and it is possible for employees to become overwhelmed by training and development options. At Unisys this potential complexity is simplified by each business unit team continuously benchmarking the skills and knowledge they believe to be most crucial, and creating metrics against which individuals can rate themselves. This transparency and relative simplicity enables employees to understand themselves and make wise decisions. To achieve this, the team created 13 integrated programmes and capabilities which create the framework against which development can be discussed and training needs identified. As a consequence, each employee is able to create a personal career portfolio. This portfolio profiles their role, describes their certification record, their prior work history, formal education and project history. The portfolio approach also enables employees to profile their skills against the business unit benchmarked skills. The profiling of the benchmarked skills results from both self-rating, and team leader rating.

This meant that whenever an employee assumes a new role they are mandated to participate in the learning activities associated with that role. For example, all employees joining Unisys are mandated to attend ethics training in which they explore the behavioural expectations of Unisys. Beyond this core, employees are free to choose the learning opportunities which excite them, and which they judge to be of use to them. Awareness and profiling of personal strengths and development needs is emphasized by participating in a 360° assessment which occurs at the completion of each project, and on a bi-annual basis.

The co-ordination of the learning elements occurs through a single development portal, .com. With the use of powerful search engines, employees are able to interrogate the available learning activities by function, skill, group, or even, by a single word. By the end of 2002 employees were also able to input their learning style preferences to ensure a tight fit between the learning event and their individual learning style profile. The rules of engagement are minimal. As Peter Armstong, VP Commercial Industries, explains:

> 'Employees have a free rein across Unisys. The sign-off to a learning activity is automatic, unless the manager is able to make a case for the employee not to participate . . . very few do. Anything is available within reason if time is available. There are no business-related criteria for vito. We assume employees will make the best decisions for themselves and Unisys.'

Individuals are free to become the recipient of training. But, perhaps as importantly, they are also free to devote a proportion of their time to training and coaching others. This is crucial, as we know that the actual process of training others is one of the key ways in which skills and knowledge are rapidly developed.

Like all companies operating in the computer services sector, Unisys has experienced significant competition and price erosion. Unisys University has cut costs, as have most training establishments in the sector. Between 1999 and 2002 the budget of Unisys University was reduced by 25% and the numbers of faculty and support by 32%. Yet during that same period the number of students grew from 68,000 in 1999 to 95,000 in 2002, an increase of 38%. Much of this has taken place because increasingly employees are choosing online training which enables them to access learning when and where it is convenient for them. The e-learning format has increased by 28% while the class format has dropped by 32% (from 46,000 participants in 1999 to 31,000 in 2002). So from the perspective of the corporation, Unisys has been able to deliver tailored training much of which is online, in an economic climate in which cost cutting is key. During that period the cost per student of training has been reduced by 53%.

Bringing choice and variety in training to individuals has had a real payback for the company. Perhaps most importantly, this learning relationship between employee and employer has brought an unprecedented degree of space and agility. For example, in the crucial pharmaceutical industry sector, many research scientists join pharmaceutical companies from academic communities and have worked on Linux platforms. Historically, relatively few Unisys consultants have this capability and this mismatch in skills severely reduced the capacity of the company to support this crucial sector. Using the shared database Personal Records Online (PRO) the pharmateam leaders were, within a matter of weeks, able to identify all those consultants working across the world in the pharma sector and encourage them to rapidly upgrade their Linux skills. The other payback experienced by Unisys is the low attrition rates at 5 to 6% per annum among the lowest in the industry.

Variety in training: the insights

Begin to classify learning opportunities

Learning and training are broad terms which can encompass activities as formalized as off-the-job training programmes, to those as informal as working with a coach. To create variety in training there needs first to be an understanding of the experiences and opportunities for training that exist within the organization.

As with job experiences, the creation of a shared competency profile against which all training opportunities are classified creates a common platform for choice. These competence frameworks can profile competencies (e.g. the capacity to be decisive), or they can be skill based (e.g. the skills of giving feedback). At Unisys, this classification enabled a portfolio to be created against which individuals could profile themselves and the jobs to which they aspired. The common language of competency profiling created a shorthand against which decisions could be made.

Think memes

We tend to consider training and learning in large event-based 'chunks' – a one-day programme, a three-day workshop, a two-hour event. These chunks are temporal, but they do not refer to the content. The content of knowledge can be refered to as a 'meme'; this is the smallest divisible form of a piece of knowledge. A meme could be a short piece on how to conduct a performance management review; it could be a one-hour video on the acquisition of a specific skill; or a tutored led activity on self-insight. The challenge in creating variety in training is to chunk knowledge acquisition into these memes that can then be re-configured at will to meet the specific needs of an individual. By breaking down knowledge into its smallest pieces the potential for variety increases, not in the memes themselves, but rather in the potential to reconfigure the memes into sequences of knowledge which most closely fit the needs of the individual.

Create flotillas

In the jargon of mass customization, a 'flotilla' is the combination of the standardized modules (memes) which have been rapidly reconfigured to enable customers to have products and services shaped to their needs at a price and speed similar to a standardized product. The keys to mass customization are two interlinked capabilities: to create flotillas of standardized modules and to dynamically link these modules together on demand. It was this combination capacity which enabled the mass customer Dell to deliver computers direct to the customer at a highly competitive price. We can learn much from the technology of mass customization in the creation of variety in learning.[19]

The challenge for creating variety in learning and training is in part the challenge to create content, the memes, but also to build individual flotillas of this content. This requires a deep understanding of what an individual needs at certain times in their working lives. So, in the first six weeks of assuming a new role, the flotilla will look very different from that which is created one year later. The emphasis is delivering exactly what the individual needs, exactly when they need it. We know that this close link between needs and delivery makes for a much more significant learning experience and significantly increases the likelihood of the knowledge becoming embedded into day-to-day activity.

As with variety in jobs and projects, technology has a key role to play through the creation of the memes, and in the stringing together of these memes in an individual flotilla.

Choice of developmental relationships: Goldman Sachs

Each of the three citizens made choices out of deep self-awareness, an understanding of their goals and with the energy and volition of decision making. At the same time they were able to bring important skills and abilities to the organization. At BP the building of competencies occurs with the opportunities to work on stretching tasks; at McKinsey, from the choice of projects far from current capacities; at Unisys from access to learning when it's needed. Each one of these aspects of developmental variety are crucial. But also crucial was the access they had, and their capacity to build a developmental relationship with a number of people who could act as a coach or mentor.

Mentoring and coaching are both important in promoting growth and do so by playing different roles. Essentially coaching can take place at any stage of one's life and is the opportunity to have someone working closely with you focusing on one or more aspect of job performance and competence.[20] Mentoring is also a one-to-one relationship but the dynamics and timing are specific. Mentoring typically takes places at an early stage of life and the mentor (for there is rarely more than one or two across a career) plays a crucial role in being a teacher, an advisor and a sponsor. Mentoring is defined not in terms of formal roles but in terms of the character of the relationship and the function it serves. As a teacher the mentor enhances skills and intellectual development. As a sponsor the mentor facilitates understanding and advancement. As a host and guide the mentor communicates the values, customs, resources and characters of the company.[21] Through their own behaviour and virtues the mentor can be an exemplar. Mentoring can play an important part of the search for personal autonomy and the building of self-awareness. For some companies the establishment of choice around mentoring and coaching has been a key developmental driver.

This is certainly the case at Goldman Sachs, one of the world's great financial institutions.[22] Since the 1980s Goldman Sachs has undertaken extensive globalization efforts, experienced explosive rates of financial and employment growth, and taken the momentous step (in 1999) of converting itself from a private partnership to a public company. Much of the success of the institution comes from a relentless drive to attract, mentor and coach talent. In the words of John Thain, President and Co-Chief Co-Ordinating Officer:

'We have a dream. The dream is that someday – preferably someday soon – that Goldman Sachs is recognized around the world as the institution of any kind – most able to attract and motivate the most talented people anywhere in the world – all cultures, all races, both genders, a plethora of personal talents, viewpoints and lifestyles. The magnet for talent.'

Once recruited to Goldman Sachs young people are given wide latitude of discretion and personal choice to develop their talents and create business opportunities. Co-Chief Co-ordinating Officer, John Thornton continues:

'We basically have a lot of opportunities for individuals to be very entrepreneurial, to help build businesses, to operate on their own. We continue to have great opportunities to expand our business both product-wise and geography-wise – the opportunity for relatively young people to have a lot of responsibility to run or build businesses quickly is one of the huge, big appeals here.'

The founders of Goldman Sachs developed an ethos of 'stewardship'. In the words of Managing Director, Kevin Kennedy, 'You have an obligation when you come here to leave this place better than it was when you arrived.' Mentoring and coaching have always played a key role in this stewardship. Initially this was informal and ad hoc, built from a clear sense of obligations and passed down from partner to partner. By 2001 with 74% of people in Goldman Sachs with less than five years' service and 42% with less than two years' many of the old informal notions of stewardship had began to be systematized. John Thain reflects:

'It is pretty clear to us that in our new, bigger size, we cannot rely on the old method of managing and mentoring people, which tended to be one-off, different people mentored you one by one, and it wasn't formalized at all.'

So, many of the unique processes which had evolved over the years are now being systematized. The grounding for mentoring relationships begins prior to the point of joining. During the selection process potential joiners have discussions with 20 to 30 senior vice-presidents and managing directors. So, even at this stage new recruits build information about the members of the firm, whom they may want to work with in the initial roles, who might be their mentors and coaches and what they may want to do in the longer term. Following recruitment, each new recruit is assigned an official mentor who works closely with them for the first two years of their career – often this is someone whom they have met during the extensive initial selection process. While mentoring remains crucial, after two years of employment the choice of mentor is handed back with the expectation that the individual will actively create strong mentoring and coaching relationships. As Christian Benoit Valentin, Executive Director in the Private Equity Department, remarks: 'I said to my co-heads "guys, I want a mentor, that's the one thing that's missing in my life".' The executives suggested someone whom Christian checked out but did not feel would be suitable 'to get me to the next level of personal development'. The networks of relationships in Goldman Sachs are so extensive that he was able to search on a wide scale before coming to a final decision. 'It's a push, not a pull strategy, about 25% (of mentoring relationships) result in a close personal bond', says Christian.

While the choice of mentor is broad, the obligations of the senior members of the firm to stewardship are described and reinforced in many aspects of the culture and processes. For example, managing directors are expected to balance time spent generating revenue with time nurturing and mentoring of talent. Their performance on nurturing talent is informally discussed, but also formally appraised through 360° peer-based feedback that includes feedback from mentees. This culture of open access to senior people, and the co-head arrangements (where all the senior posts are performed by two people) ensures that there are many opportunities for leveraging mentoring relationships.

To support the mentoring process, mentors receive documentation and can attend a short training programme which provide a broad context on the responsibilities of mentoring, but most learn how to mentor through the mentoring they themselves received and through the actions of the senior members of the firm. The three senior members of Goldman Sachs spend over 40% of their time speaking to and presenting to people from across the company. During their own careers each was actively mentored and they see this as a key part of their own current role. For most of the current managing directors there are strong memories of being mentored. This is how Managing Director, Tim Dattels, remembers it:

'My mentor, who came over to California from New York, was the guy who taught me about Goldman Sachs. He, in many ways was a spiritual, emotional and business leader. We just synched up beautifully; he was one of the greatest mentors that I ever had.'

With such a heritage of mentoring and coaching, the supportive culture is strong. Yet, at the same time mentoring and coaching is seen as an important part of performance appraisal and crucial criteria for the selection to managing director.

While there is much diversity on the process of performance appraisal across each of the businesses, each requires one annual formal performance review and the use of 360° feedback. Those who aspire to be managing directors are assessed over a two-year period during which they are nominated by the current managing directors and then enter into discussions with members from their own business, and more importantly, what is termed 'cross-ruffers' a senior member of another business stream or geography. Promotion to managing director is based on commercial success, but as importantly, the ability of the individual to work as a member of a team and to coach and develop people around them.

For Goldman Sachs, the establishment of mentoring and coaching relationships is at the very heart of the development of individual potential and organizational capability. Creating a context in which choice can be exercised is central to the philosophy of development.

Variety in relationships: the insights

Create clear relationship obligations

Relationships are crucial in the Democratic Enterprise. It is relationships that enable information to be rapidly shared across the company and relationships that enable and encourage each individual to become the best they can be. The qualities of these relationships are crucial. The parent–child relationship cannot be the basis on which the Democratic Enterprise is created or sustained. In creating variety in relationships Goldman Sachs made explicit to people the nature of relationships and their importance to the development of individuals and to the firm. Part of this obligation was specified and embedded into the practices and processes of the organization. So the recruitment process, the performance management processes and the mechanism by which individuals achieved partnership are all occasions when the formation of relationships play a key role.

But it is more than this. Not only are relationships embedded into the key practices and processes of the organization, they were also part of the daily life of every employee. Senior partners create strong relationships with their peers and team members. Those people not able to create relationships rarely progress within the company. The emphasis is continuously on 'us', not 'I'. The learning point from Goldman Sachs is that if relationships are important then their valuing has to be built into the processes and practices of the company, and also be the operating standard for all the senior team as role models.

Encourage tacit and explicit knowledge

What is striking about the relationship structures at both Goldman Sachs and McKinsey is the combination of people's tacit and explicit knowledge.[23] McKinsey's VOX system creates an explicit description of the project team leaders, their backgrounds and competencies. While the process may not be computerized, much the same level of explicit knowledge is available at Goldman Sachs. The depth of this knowledge creates a shared data set about people which enables others to make relatively thoughtful judgements about their style before approaching them to be a project leader, a mentor or coach.

But the interesting aspect is the depth and complexity of the tacit knowledge that surrounds relationships. There is much about a person which is not contained in their CV or detailed description of their projects. How do they behave under pressure? What is their attitude to working long hours? How flexible are they about the way in which tasks are achieved? Yet while this information will not be contained in the CV, it may well be crucial to the capacity of someone to form a mentoring or coaching relationship with them. This is tactic knowledge, and in the creation of variety it could well be as important as explicit knowledge.

At Goldman Sachs, this tacit information is shared as a matter of course. People are open and able to engage in describing people which goes way beyond the structure of the CV, yet at the same time does not simply degenerate into negative asides. The openness of sharing this information at Goldman Sachs is a strong part of the adult-to-adult relationship.

Allow churn

There are occasions when mentor or coaching relationships don't work or when a project leader is unable to bring out the best in a team member. Under these circumstances at Goldman Sachs it is appropriate for the individual to move on without carrying the burden of a 'failed mentor'. Clearly, if this became an ongoing problem then the signs would be that the individual couldn't work in teams. But, for the majority of people, relationship churn is acceptable.

Choice of rewards and benefits: AstraZeneca

Becoming an investor implies creating opportunities for people to exercise choice about the way in which they work, and the jobs and projects they focus on. The focus is on building personal human capital. But, there is a second element to being an investor – the opportunity to leverage from the value created. By leverage I mean the freedom to use the value created within work to build a life outside of work which has meaning and enables balance to be created. The primary means of leverage in organizations are rewards and benefits. By making choices about the composition of rewards we are more able to exercise our will and craft satisfying lives.

Rewards play a key and often subtle role within an organization. While the outcome of rewards are important, of potentially greater importance are our experiences of the process of being rewarded and our perceptions of the fairness of the rewards we receive compared to others.[24] We become disengaged from the company if we believe we have been treated unfairly. At the same time, we want to use rewards and benefits in a manner which meets our needs. Tesco discovered that, for example, the rewards which were motivating and engaging for a parent of young children who is primarily working to live, are very different from someone who is highly ambitious and work orientated. The young parent values discounted childcare vouchers, while the highly ambitious person will value share options.

Companies have generally shied away from individualizing rewards, save for those who lead the organization. Bringing choice to rewards has been seen as overly complex and potentially unjust as it opens up the possibility for divergence. Not so at the pharmaceutical company AstraZeneca, which has pioneered reward and benefit choice.[25] The company was created in

1999 from Zeneca (which had demerged from ICI) and the Swedish-based Astra. For CEO, Tom McKillop, the capacity to integrate the two companies and in particular the talent rich research and development groups was critical to success. He was well aware that this would be no easy task. Integrating R&D and marketing teams across two companies is fraught with difficulties. Many years after integration a competing pharmaceutical company still had two heads of R&D, operating from two locations.

At AstraZeneca the issue of talent integration was taken very seriously. HR Director, Malcolm Hurrel worked as a member of the integration team to ensure that pace and performance was sustained during the integration. The issue of integrating rewards and benefits was seen as an important lever to the success of the whole process. Faced with potential remuneration integrating costs of 10 to 15%, the team decided instead to go for a zero-based option. All employees, whatever their heritage, had equal and transparent access to a range of remuneration and benefit options.

The remuneration programme launched in April 1999, created a platform which enabled all 54,000 employees to build personalized reward and benefit packages. This was initially pioneered with the 10,000 employees in the UK who were able to make trade-offs between lifestyle options which included increased holidays (22 days plus 10 days that can be bought out), childcare vouchers (which include a built-in subsidy), retail vouchers, (negotiated at a 5% to 10% discount), company car (there are currently 5,000 models available), and company bicycles (33 models available). The health options include health and dental insurance, while the financial options include cash, share options and pension. The initial take-up of these options was monitored in the first year and a broader portfolio created to reflect changing employee needs and to maximize the benefits of current fiscal conditions. Since the scheme was launched, over 85% of employees have created their own unique package.

At the centre of the personalized reward and benefit package is web-based technology that calculates and communicates to every employee the cash equivalent (termed the Advantage Fund) of their current deal. Each employee is then given three weeks to model various scenarios around this baseline and come to a final decision about their total package. Expert, on-demand resources support the individual modelling. A set of built-in warning triggers alert employees to the risks they are taking. The final enrolment remains for a year unless the employee experiences a life event such as the birth of a child or changes in marital status. There are no rules, apart from statutory requirement. Individuals are free to create a personalized portfolio.

Employees are not simply provided with the capacity to operate as an investor, they are also supported in their ability to make wise decisions. This support takes a number of forms. Complex intelligent systems in the employee portal enable each participant to make an initial choice of options and then create scenarios around how these options could play out. During the same period employees can participate in Insight Workshops which help them develop a deeper self-awareness of what is important to them; their risk profile, their likely financial needs, and their lifestyle aspirations.

This level of individualization has brought the company real competitive advantage in the market for talented pharmaceutical scientists, on occasions making the difference between joining AstraZeneca and joining a competitor.

Variety in rewards and benefits: the insights

Be prepared to experiment

While the initial project planning for the launch of the remuneration package at AstraZeneca was meticulous, the team operating the system became more confident and at ease and more able to experiment with ideas. In the second year, for example, they experimented with people taking bicycles as part of their remuneration and with various retail outlets.

By experimentation and tinkering the project team increasingly cast the relationship between the organization and the individual as a learning relationship.[26] As people were faced with variety, they were more able to exercise their choice, and by exercising their choice, more able to communicate to the company precisely what was important to them. This double loop of self-awareness and learning sent out clear messages of an adult-to-adult relationship and of the employee as an investor able to exercise their rights.[27]

Monitor and learn

By continuously experimenting and by monitoring the choices people made, the teams at AstraZeneca were able to create a more detailed and insightful picture of the various demographic employee groups and their likely needs, desires and aspirations. At the same time, they held many workshops and in-depth interviews with people to establish whether there were areas of sacrifice that would be important for them to eliminate. This enabled them to build deeper precision in the adult-to-adult relationship.

Educate, educate and educate

Perhaps one of the most surprising lessons from the AstraZeneca team was that within a relatively short period, employees became extremely sophisticated decision-makers in their financial affairs.[28] The transformation to the investor mindset was faster than anyone could have hoped for. In the first iteration of the scheme people made relatively conservative choices, mirroring to a large extent their previous packages. Within a year, they were making more varied and individual choices that enabled them to reduce and eliminate areas of sacrifice in a way they had not been able to do.

Another surprise was employee sophistication in areas such as pension provision that had previously been seen as the financial area in which people either needed professional assistance, or alternatively where the company made the decision for them. At the centre of this adult-to-adult relationship about rewards was a continuous focus on employee education. The employee portal, workshops, telephone information lines, posters and advisors were all brought in to create a wealth of information which educated employees in the options that were available to them, and in their personal needs, aspirations and risk profile. By treating people as adults, AstraZeneca rapidly increased employees' mastery of their financial affairs and their general feeling of autonomy.

Choice of location: BT

In the third tenet individuals are able to develop their nature and express their diverse qualities, and in the fourth tenet, they are able to determined the conditions of their association. In the development and expression of 'individuation' choice about location and time will be crucial. In the earlier profiling of the six tenets, only HP gave significant choice. Few people we surveyed had a choice of location when they where initially offered their job, although this increased significantly at the time when their annual objectives were set.

For Nina and Stewart making time and location choices enabled them to create greater meaning in their life. For Stewart the opportunity to work from home meant that he avoided the stressful commute into central London, and allowed him to structure his daily work in a more meaningful manner. For Nina, the opportunity to work in London enabled her to make the commitments to her children that she valued. For both BT and McKinsey the opportunities they have given to allow people to work flexibility has ensured that they have retained the talents and engagement of both Stewart and Nina.[29]

Location choice can be central to well-being and job performance. Yet many employees sacrifice valuable time and resources commuting to work, and then working in an environment which may not be conducive to high performance.[30] In the 1980s BT commissioned a report, *The Future of Work*, to help the senior team understand the ways in which they should prepare for their clients' future and their own future. There were three messages from the study: the growing diversity of society; the potential technology developments; and the rise of the 24/7 customer environment. BT began a journey to create flexibility and choice that was to take over 20 years.

Stewart is one of many tens of thousands of people at BT who choose to work from home for some part of their working day.[31] BT has pioneered home-working since the 1980s when the nascent technologies began to make this possible. If BT was to become one of the world's leading technology companies then it needed to demonstrate to clients that mobile technology could indeed work for them. The future study showed the working world would be one in which location and time choice would be increasingly seen as a key factor in becoming an employer of choice. As a result, BT was an early adopter of location choice.[32]

For BT, the journey began in 1984 with the launch of the first home-working trials. These were a mixed success: the supporting technology was unreliable, employees were not used to using their home for working, and there was a strong 'attendance' managerial mind set. Ten years later with the advent of e-mail, the technology of location choice became feasible. During the intervening period, the attendance issue had been tackled by placing enormous emphasis on measuring the *output* of performance, rather than *input*. As a consequence, 'hours worked' was no longer an important metric, and with a focus on output, home-workers where able to have their work assessed from the same basis as those working in an office environment.

By 2001, 5,200 employees were working permanently from home, and 60,000 people had the technological capacity (remote access, EIN passwords and electronic signatures) to work periodically from home. The rules for home-working are simple and transparent. Employees develop a business case on the implications to customers and performance, and bring this business case to their managers and team members for discussion. The final decision is made on the basis of operational viability and customer focus. A recurring issue for home-workers is the difficulty of building communities of practice. To tackle this, BT is currently supporting a network of smart buildings in towns and cities that enable employees to go to an office near their home with hot desks and remote access.

Variety in location: the insights

Start small and get the technology right

One of the key learning points for the BT team was that they started pilots on the periphery of the organization before they rolled out location choice to a wider audience. They initially chose work groups for whom they knew location choice was an issue and worked closely with them to understand their concerns. By establishing an early learning relationship with employees they were able to identify potential points of friction and confront and solve them prior to the scheme going live to a wider employee group.

Many of these pilots failed because the technology was not sufficiently robust to work with the scale and complexity of data used by many of the home-workers. As Stewart recalls, these early trials were immensely frustrating as systems crashed and data was lost. However, they provided a window in which home-workers could become more sophisticated users of mobile technology, and the BT team could learn what was required.

For a telecommunications company, creating mobile working is crucial to a long-term strategy of supporting mobile working in client organizations. Much of BT's early investment in mobile technology was built on a strategy of learning with its own employees before involving the employees of other companies. So, it is likely that the sophistication of technology at BT exceeds the platforms in all but the most advanced company. Nevertheless, the mobile technology which BT pioneered is now widely available. The second lesson for location variety is that investment in technology is key.

Encourage an adult-to-adult relationship

As we saw in the tenets of the Democratic Enterprise, establishing a relationship that has an adult-to-adult basis is about being up-front and open in negotiating and enabling individuals to have the opportunity to determine the conditions of their association. Beneath this are the accountabilities and obligations the individual has to themselves, and also to colleagues and to the company. The emphasis here is in the establishment of conditions in which the liberty of one individual is not at the expense of another. This issue is particularly pertinent to location choice. When one member of a team chooses to work from home, there may be circumstances when that member's liberty negatively impacts on other team members. One way to monitor this balance is for the management team to agree a set of rules which determine what constitutes benefits to the company, and what constitutes benefit to the individual. The disadvantage of this is that it puts the individual clearly into the parent–child relationship and potentially encumbers the company and the decision-making processes in complex rules and procedures.

BT has simply and effectively short-circuited this potential problem. Rather than the company, it is the individual and their colleagues who make the call. It is they who consider whether there is a balance of outcomes, and whether the solution to which they are working is acceptable to those around them. Location choice is made on the basis of a business case developed by the individual to show their working at home will benefit themselves, their colleagues and the firm. These business cases are relatively complex documents and support is available in their preparation through information, web-sites and hot-line telephone advice. It is expected that people will work with their colleagues to ensure that the business case is accurate and viable, and then prepare a document which describes the way in which they will work flexibly. Through engaging colleagues in the process, there is an opportunity for others who feel that they will be negatively effected to have their voice heard and acknowledged. At the same time, the process of preparing and presenting the case puts the relationship firmly onto an adult-to-adult basis.

Sustaining the autonomy of the individual, enabling them to become an investor rather than an asset, can only take place when there are also benefits to the wider community and ultimately to the organization. Without this balance of benefits the liberty of the most powerful is at the expense of the weakest, or at the expense of the whole community, the organization.

Monitor the intended and unintended consequences of choice

Earlier we saw how AstraZeneca actively learned about employees as a consequence of monitoring their choices and engage in conversations with them about their choices. Creating a learning relationship was also evident at BT as it piloted and then rolled out its location initiative. Throughout this time the aspirations, needs and concerns of people working at home or in different locations was monitored through online surveys, focus groups and in-depth interviews. As a consequence of this learning relationship, the project team began to identify some of the downsides of location variety. People felt isolated, it was more difficult to convey some of the tacit knowledge which co-workers typically convey within the first couple of weeks, and it was more difficult to get the message across about the business goals of the company.

Consequently, the BT team rapidly constructed alternative relationship structures. So, for example, home-workers remained in an office environment in the first couple of weeks of a new job so co-workers could convey the tacit knowledge of the roles. Home-workers were assigned office locations near their homes so that it was possible for them to meet other people. Video-links were established between key home-workers so they could see their colleagues and speak with them on a frequent and informal basis. In the future, BT plans to create a network of informal office spaces equipped with advanced technology to be used as centres for people to drop in so that relationships are formed as much on location (people who live near the office spaces) as they will be on peers (people who work on the same project).

The lesson was that the BT team was prepared to monitor the aspirations and expectations of people who had decided to exercise choice, and was able to create a platform of innovative services to ensure that their choices resulted in maximum performance, and maximum commitment.

Choice of time: HP

Like any company operating within the computer and service sector, HP faces a highly competitive marketplace, characterized by intense competition, very fast product cycles and convergence.[33] In this context adaptability and flexibility are key. As European CEO, John Golding, described it:

> *'Managing HP is like driving a highly powered car through the winding road of a forest, in the middle of the night, with the rain coming down. We can only see a short way ahead and we have no idea what is behind the next corner. All we can do is keep our hands on the steering wheel and our foot on the accelerator and steer as well as we can.'*

Much of the power that drives HP has been attributed to the strong culture enacted through The HP Way.[34] Founders Dave Packard and Bill Hewlett had a clear guiding philosophy which became the company's credo:

> *'We made an early and important decision. We did not want to be a "hire and fire" company, that would seek large numbers of short-term contracts, employ a great many people for the duration of the contract, and then let these people go . . . we wanted to be in business for the long haul, to have a company built around a stable and dedicated workforce.'*
> David Packard, *The HP Way: How Bill Hewlett and I Built Our Company*, p. 129

This initial commitment to jobs-for-life began to fade in the downturn of the computer business in the late 1980s when the company was forced to cut costs and make redundancies. Yet much of the HP culture remains – a firm commitment to the development of individual potential within a wide latitude of discretion.

As a senior manager observed, 'This is an environment where we try to get organized chaos. What we want is for people to understand the overall goal and then feel free to achieve them.' The freedom to achieve is palpable. Flexible working patterns are increasingly the norm. In 1993 then CEO, Lew Platt, set three key goals to reinforce the HP culture. By 1995 one of these goals had become a global goal within the Hoshin performance management process – to improve the balance between life and work. But as Platt said at the time in a communication to all employees:

'We will never move into slow growth, low pressure industries, I promise you, we are always going to be in high growth, high pressure industries – I cannot promise you a job with no stress in it.'

Achieving this is difficult. In the fourth tenet we asked the sample of employees from the seven companies whether they agreed that, 'This organization does what it can to help its employees maintain a healthy work/life balance'. As the data show, HP had the highest percentage of employees who believed this was so.

For Hewlett-Packard, as for many companies, this is the conundrum. Employee stress and burnout has been and continues to be one of the major issues at HP. As one manager remarked, 'The treadmill works quicker and quicker each year. People are stressed and get almost numb by having to repeat the exercise over and over again.' At HP, like any other high-growth, successful organization (and few other companies have sustained organic growth rates, over such an extended period as HP), people work long hours, the work is intense, the customers demanding, and most people have what is called 'a day-job' and an 'evening job', the latter being the project teams and task forces which run in parallel to their main role.

Location choice is in the very blood of HP. As Janice Chaffin, a senior manager in the Enterprise Systems group, remarks:

'Historically the HP environment has been very open, very progressive. People are use to working with others all over the world, with different cultures, different languages, and different locations. So you have to learn to work in many different ways. Historically we have been open to telecommuting, to video conferencing and teleconferencing and working part-time.'

In part this flexibility has reflected the international nature of the company and its tradition of respecting individual preferences about working style and location. Unlike other multinational companies, HP prefers not to uproot people, but rather to find ways to flex around the needs of its high performers. This includes working flexible hours, job sharing and working from home. Job sharing, for example, is a well-tried method at HP to enable individual flexibility while supporting the needs of customers and partners for ongoing support and continuity of relationships. As Janice, a veteran jobsharer, remarks:

'The most important factor of success is the personality of the individuals. If you are sharing your job, you literally have to be prepared to put your ego aside. It is based on complete trust and willingness to say "I am willing to take credit equally with my partner and for me alone".'

Building flexibility is tough. But flexibility has increased. Part of the momentum for change was research about stress levels in the organization and the impact of stress on performance. The result was a programme of stress reduction based on the location of workstations in the office, physical fitness and healthy eating. Another result was the acknowledgement that for people to operate at their peak of performance they needed to control the times at which they worked.

Variety in time: the insights

Reduce constraints

Constraints act as the outer boundary of the way a job can be performed. The obligations are in the inner core which describes the aspects which are non-negotiable. Much of the lack of variety of time in organizations exists because the outer boundary of constraints determines the hours people should work. Some of these are obligations. For example, customers must be served at specific time. But many of these constraints are simply the assumptions of colleagues and team leaders about when the job should be done. As the early time trials at BT showed, the major constraint to flexible working was the managerial preconception that if someone is not present in the office, then they cannot be working.

The cultural aspect of time flexibility is shown clearly in the earlier analysis of the six tenets. As we saw in the fourth tenet, companies differ in their capacity to bring flexibility to location or time. The actual work between these companies is not radically different. For example, the work of an employee in Citibank is not radically different from the work in HP. We can only surmise that the difference we see has more to do with the difference in the culture of the companies, rather than reflecting a fundamental difference in the jobs.

So the first lesson for HP and BT was that for flexible working to become a reality, the constraints of the job had to be considered, and the latitude of discretion extended. Some of these constraints were technological, some were the sheer complexity of getting the job delivered, but much of the constraints were cultural and attitudinal, particularly the 'presenteeism'. To tackle this, both companies had to learn a lesson about performance.

Re-shape performance metrics

When performance metrics are weak, 'presenteeism' is the only legitimate means by which managers can account for the performance of their team members. The assumption is that if people are present, then they are working. The reduction and ultimate elimination of 'presenteeism' as a monitoring device requires two changes to performance metrics. First, the performance metrics should be adept at accurately measuring what it is people do – the quality of output. Only when output is measured does input (i.e. the time and location of work) become less important.

The second change in performance metrics has to occur to the description of how work is performed. Earlier we saw how over specification of work reduces the opportunity individuals have to achieve the goals in an idiosyncratic manner. The same is true for time choice. If the tasks are over specified then there is limited opportunity for people to exercise choice about how and when they perform tasks. In the Democratic Enterprise, there is an acknowledgement that working teams can create a way of working which enables each one of them to have some freedom and flexibility. Both BT and HP have learned that the combination of the business case (which describes the obligation of the individual to benefit themselves and the organization) and a wide latitude of discretion about roles, creates an environment in which personal potential can flourish.

The lessons of building variety

Each one of these companies has attempted to build variety in one or more dimension. As we saw earlier from the human capital model, there are eight potential dimensions of variety. So the issues are where to start and how to start.

In thinking about this we can consider the approach of customer service companies which map what they label 'the terrain of sacrifice'. These are the characteristics of a product or service which would be important to a customer but which industry practice and norms do not enable them to obtain. Hence, the sacrifice. For example, forcing babies into one size diapers was a sacrifice which they and their parents made before multi-sized diapers. Treating all bicycle riders as if they have the same length of leg forces them to sacrifice comfort and speed.[35]

Each company is different, each workforce is different. By mapping the terrain of sacrifice companies establish where sacrifices are being made. By doing so they gain a clearer view of what stops people from being the best they could be. Once this has been achieved the organization can then expand variety by deepening it in a single practice, or by broadening variety across practices. Be prepared in doing so for variety to educate. Once the pendulum begins to swing from the parent–child to the adult-to-adult relationship, the momentum quickly gains velocity. Once people have experienced choice in one aspect of their life, their expectations of choice expand.

The overriding and generalizable lessons of the creation of variety are drawn from the world of 'self-organizing systems', the emerging science of nuclear physics, biology and astronomy. The parallels are interesting because, like the emergence of order from the possible chaos of BP's self-organizing job market, many of the systems in nuclear physics or biology are potentially chaotic. Three lessons come directly from self-organizing systems.[36]

The first is that in these systems variety is created in the boundaries on a continual basis, this is what some have called 'tinkering'.[37] This is the continual, small-scale experimentation we saw at BT or at AstraZeneca. The second lesson is that these systems are capable of directing themselves precisely because they are rich in information and relationships. This enables the continuous mutual adjustments we saw, for example in the business case Stewart and his colleagues prepared to support flexible working. They were able to engage in deep conversations with their colleagues in order to come to an agreement that met the needs of the individual and of the group. The final lesson is the extent of the rules that govern action within the system. The emphasis here is on the development of few, simple rules. We saw this clearly at BP where the navigation of Greg around the job market is marked by surprisingly few directives.

1 Map the terrain of sacrifice

How does an organization know where to start to build variety? There is no common starting point. One way to know where to start is to map the terrain of sacrifice. This allows a company to clearly understand what it is that employees need to develop and leverage their human capital which is not currently available to them. Mapping the terrain is not straightforward, much of the sacrifice an employee bears is invisible to them because it is such an established industry practice they do not anticipate anything different. Mapping the terrain of sacrifice involves surveys and in-depth conversations with individuals and groups and really exploring what is crucial to them. The employee survey data presented earlier give some idea of the terrain of sacrifice, both in terms of the actual opportunity employees have to make a choice, and in their attitude to the choice they are given. For example, the survey item 'this company helps me to balance my work and life' gives a good indication of the attitudes. Although I have not presented the demographic data for these survey items, much more detailed analysis can come from analysing the responses of specific groups (by age, gender, job level and education level) to identify those where the greatest sacrifice is being felt. The in-depth analysis that Tesco undertook helped it to map the terrain. The early results of the BT, project began to map the terrain of sacrifice and to understand the huge impact industry norms has on expectations and aspirations. Once established industry practices began to crumble at BT, so the extent of sacrifice became clear to employees.

2 Continuously expand variety

Variety is created through continual trial and error. These establish the dynamic systems in which variety is expanded both within specific process and across processes. By continuously creating variety organizations are institutionalizing experimentation, enabling people to prototype new behaviours and creating new ways of working. By doing so they are maximizing diversity and creating the opportunity for people to rapidly reconfigure both the creation and leverage of their human capital.

At AstraZeneca, for example, every year the HR team expands variety within the rewards process by adding choices to the remuneration and benefit package. At the same time, they take away benefits that create limited value for employees. Clearly continuously expanding variety has a cost associated with it. So, on an annual basis the team takes a close look at both the costs and the value of each of the variety of benefits and adapt the total package accordingly. This is expansion of variety within a process or practice.

There is also an attempt to expand variety across processes. So, for example, BT began initially to pilot variety around the location of work. As it became more adept at understanding the mechanism of variety and as employees became more adept at making wise choices, so BT was able to expand the variety to other processes such as time and remuneration choice.

3 Prepare for variety to educate

These companies have learned that creating variety helps them to understand their employees better and also expands the horizons and human capital of employees. As companies learned more about their employees, they began to create small, incremental changes and variety to meet the specific needs of groups of employees. At AstraZeneca, for example, the take-up of the different remuneration packages enabled the company to create a deep understanding of the various groups in the community. The company began to understand that there were certain groups (women with small children, for example) who needed a completely different configuration to enable them to balance the aspirations of their work and home life.

At the same time, these companies learned that in exercising choice, employees became more confident about themselves, more aware of their needs and aspirations. This should be no surprise, recall John Stuart Mill's words written in the nineteenth century.

> 'When people are engaged in the resolution of problems affecting themselves and the whole collectively, energies are unleashed which enhance the likelihood of the creation of imaginative solutions and successful strategies. In short, participation in the social and public life undercuts passivity and enhances general prosperity.'
>
> John Stuart Mill, *Considerations*, pp. 207–8

As the early Athenians discovered, involving people in the conditions of their association encourages and enables them to take responsibility for themselves and to practise the art of citizenship. As they exercised choice in one domain of their life they became more aware of the sacrifices they were making in other parts of their working life. Creating variety fundamentally shifts the relationship with the employee to an adult model. As these organizations made this shift, so too they educated their employees to become more self-determining and insightful. They saw the iterative nature of the learning model which is at the heart of the autonomous employee.

4 Be prepared to tinker

One of the striking aspects of the creation of variety in each of these companies is their capacity to invent variety quickly, often in relatively isolated parts of the business, and to then accelerate the roll-out of success and then to monitor the consequences. This is clear in both BT and AstraZeneca where projects were created around the ideas of variety and then allowed to run. After a period of time the value of these initiatives was considered and those which failed to create value were discarded. Clearly there is a balance to be stuck between continuous churn and experimentation, and stasis, between exploration and exploitation. Experimenting with variety is difficult. Rather than the pristine creation of tried and tested predictability, these companies were prepared to live with redundancy, fuzziness and trial and error. They were prepared to play with ideas, experiment, focusing on what was viable. The practices and processes that framed the individual were continuously moving.

How did these companies maximize the value of tinkering? First, they had a clear view of the practices and processes that they would work on at any time. Next, they set up the experiments as projects with clear timelines, accountabilities and metrics. Finally, they were prepared to stop the experiment once they were convinced it was incapable of adding value. The capacity to know when to stop and reduce variety was as important as the capacity to know when to start.[38]

5 Create rich information

The capacity of the members of a self-organizing system to rapidly adjust to each other depends on the nature of the relationships between them, and on the amount of rich and meaningful information. Without information their decision making is blind. With rich information they are able to make the continual modifications and adjustments which ensure that they are on track with the other members. The same is true in the creation of organizational variety. As we saw in the tenets of the Democratic Enterprise, there is a potential conflict between the fourth tenet 'individuals are able to determine the conditions of their association' and the fifth tenet 'the liberty of some individuals is not at the expense of others'. This conflict is solved in part through the obligations and accountabilities of individuals, but it is also solved by pumping sufficient meaningful information into the system so that people are able to exercise choice and remain autonomous and yet not impinge on the liberty of others. Again, this plays to the concept of continual mutual adjustment. In the Democratic Enterprise citizens have a deep understanding of the current reality of the organization, of the future and of the goals, that they are able to exercise choice in a realistic and appropriate manner.

These companies supported people to use variety to make wise choices through the creation and maintenance of rich and deep seams of information. It was this information that enabled Nina, Greg and Stewart, and many thousands of others to navigate variety. Without this information it would have been impossible for them to do so, to make active choices individually or collectively. Without information they had no capacity to adapt, even if the variety was available to them. This information had two distinct elements: the explicit knowledge about the actual choices available to them, and the more implicit or tacit knowledge of the likely consequences of these choices.

With regard to the explicit knowledge, each of these companies had created transparency around the open exchange of information from all parts of the organization, not simply top down. So for Nina, the information on which she decided to take the next job had an explicit content, the companies intranet gave her the information. But more importantly it had an implicit or tacit part – information about the likely configuration of the job, about what it was likely to lead to, about the consequences of taking the job. This information came from her peers and colleagues across McKinsey. For Nina, it was the quality and quantity of this explicit and implicit or tacit information which enabled her to make wise and informed decisions.

Each one of these companies had used recent developments in technology to mediate the flow of information from one individual to another.

These employee portals were a key source of explicit knowledge. But as important was the information which Nina, Stewart and Greg received through internal connections and relationships. Each one of these companies was sufficiently open to allow them to be connected to people dissimilar from themselves, and by doing so to create a rich tapestry of information about the choices which arise from organizational variety.

6 Keep the rules simple

In the world of self-organizing systems the agility and flexibility of the system is maintained by experimentation around the boundary and by rich tacit and explicit seams of information. But it is remains agile and mutually adjusting by the nature of the rules that bind it. The emphasis is on the minimal conditions by which the system can operate. Too many rules and it becomes slow and moribund.

An illustration of this concept of simple rules can be found in the natural world. Whether it be a shoal of fish, a flock of birds or sub-atomic particles, these systems are governed by the application of a number (usually a very few) guiding principles. For a flock of birds, for example, there are three simple principles: stay close to all the birds around you; travel at equal speed; and let the leadership of the flock rotate. Early computer programs used agents, termed 'boids', which were able to generate flocking patterns of birds with these three simple rules. What is striking is that none of these rules are about forming a flock. They are entirely local, referring to what an individual bird should do in their vicinity and in relationship to others.

Faced with a variety of practices and processes the temptation is to create rules and procedures to meet every possible configuration. The internal labour market is one process that has in many companies been put into a state of near atrophy through the tangled web of rules and procedures which bind it. Rules about the amount of time an employee has to stay in a job. Rules about whom they have to inform if they are applying for another job. Rules about the type of job they should be considered for. Rules about the applicable distance between the current job and any future job. The temptation to create rules can be overwhelming.

But these companies have resisted the temptation to entangle choice and variety through complex rules and procedures. Instead they have taken the very least number of rules which could be used to define the boundaries of the space in which individuals can exercise choice. At AstraZeneca, employees are free to choose across the variety of remuneration and benefits they have created. The only boundary conditions are created by legal and statutory requirements. The same is true at BT where there is a judgement that people will make wise decisions and the boundaries are that they have to make a business case about the potential benefits to the organization.

CHAPTER SEVEN

Shaping shared purpose

T he Democratic Enterprise is founded on employees who are autonomous and capable of making wise choices. It is they who drive innovation, create new ideas, and can anticipate and re-form to meet changing business goals. Individual autonomy is the first building block. But by simply supporting individual autonomy, organizations risk creating frustration. Autonomous individuals also need the freedom and scope to exercise choice. This is organizational variety, the second building block. Together, individual autonomy and organizational variety are the basis for adaptability and choice. But this is not enough. A fundamental challenge facing contemporary organizations is what binds these autonomous, skilled and self-determining people together? What is the glue that holds it together?

The question has profound significance for the organizations of the future. Once the genie of democracy is out of the organizational bottle, it is no longer possible to rely on traditional hierarchical control or paternalistic arguments to lock people in. Something else is required. I believe that this is best understood in terms of citizenship.

What holds the Democratic Enterprise together is explored in the fifth tenet. It states 'that the liberty of some individuals is not at the expense of others'. There is potential for the organization to make choices which exploit the individual, and potential for the individual to make choices which exploit their colleagues, and ultimately the organization. How can this balance between the two be sustained? What is it that keeps these autonomous individuals together and glues together the Democratic

Enterprise? This question plays directly to the sixth tenet, that individuals have accountabilities and obligations to themselves and to the organization.

This is the third and final step to democracy and one that every management team needs to understand. The solution to this dual challenge lies with the notion of shared purpose. These autonomous, self-determining employees do not exploit their colleagues or the organization because the purpose and destiny of the company is also their purpose and destiny. And, they choose to stay and provide their resources because the company, or their business unit, has a purpose that engages and interests them.

With a shared sense of purpose people understand what the organization is trying to achieve and its short- and long-term goals. Perhaps more importantly, they also understand what it is they personally have to do to contribute to the success of the company. These are the survey items we saw earlier in the sixth tenet. In particular, 'my work goals are clearly defined' and 'there is a common sense of purpose among employees'. In the purposeful company goals are clear and unambiguous, employees have something to aim for. This, more than any other factor, reduces the dangers of drift. Second, as in any democratic order, choice and the exercise of choice brings with it accountability and obligations. In these companies with a strong sense of purpose these are often made explicit and adhered to. Third, there are strong ties between any one individual and other members of the company. Looking around their working teams, individuals feel they are with people with whom they have strong relationship ties and whom they trust and respect. And at an organizational level, they feel trusted and respected. In effect, they believe themselves to be party to an adult-to-adult relationship, which contains the elements of respect and dignity.

Goals

A Democratic Enterprise has both individual autonomy and a sense of shared purpose. The importance of these two elements was clearly demonstrated by the empowerment movement of the 1980s. At that time, a number of companies attempted to free workers from constraints and to significantly increase the space and choice in which they operated. The aim of these endeavours was to move to a democratic order.

The empowerment movement derailed for a number of reasons. A key issue in some companies was that the freedom to choose became a freedom from goals. Or where there were goals, they were ambiguous and overly flexible. People were left with a broad canvas, but very little idea or compass on which they were required to act. They did not understand what it was they were free to choose from. Highly flexible and ambiguous goals simply created uncertainty and anxiety. This anxiety arose from goal conflict across various stakeholders, as individuals tried to fulfil the expectations of numerous stakeholders. Faced with ambiguous or conflicting goals and with conflict across stakeholders, the empowerment movement ground to a halt.[1]

We now know that in a Democratic Enterprise with autonomy and variety there must be some idea of the purpose of the enterprise. There must be a goal. In some situations the driving goals will be *intrinsic*. Stewart, in deciding to exercise choice around location, did so because his intrinsic goals were to work from home. The same was true for Nina when she decided to restructure her working life. Certainly there was negotiation with the company, and as we shall see in the following section, there were clear obligations and accountabilities. Nevertheless, the reasons behind the choices they made came from inside of themselves. They encompassed 'the dream', or what we described earlier as the model, the vague yet palpable idea of what it was they could become. The choices they made where in part determined by an internal articulation of this dream.[2]

For the Sony engineers on the VAIO project some of the goals on which decisions were made and choice exercised were also intrinsic, based on their 'dream'. For example, an engineer may have decided to take on a particular task because it added substantially and in a positive manner to their skill and competence portfolio. But, at the same time, much of the focus of the goals was *extrinsic* in the sense that they defined the external outcome, in this case a product.[3] For the engineer at Sony the goal was clear. These engineers became confident, independent citizens of Sony in part because they understood the goals of the project and the environment in which Sony was operating. The strategic intent or dream was clear: the PC would be a core catalyst in convergence, and Sony would be a major player in this convergence. The goal was stretching and energizing. Every engineer had a sense of ownership about Sony, and understood how their work roles and behaviours affected its success. So while their specific tasks were not defined, and the decisions not specified, nevertheless, they had a clear view of the end state. Much was done to create this dream. For example, a virtual organization entitled the 'VAIO Center', was created to be the embodiment of the vision. Each group sent a young graduate to this virtual organization to work with the team there and report back to the rest of the team on the mission and current status of the goals. As a consequence this 'dream' was not seen as simple rhetoric lacking substance. On the contrary, each engineer could see senior managers also participating in the VAIO Center and understood that the stated intentions and beliefs represented deeply rooted values and intentions. This inspired the engineers to create new opportunities and to search for new ways to create value. In doing so the leaders were able to tap into the engineers' deepseated need to contribute, to devote their time and energy to this worthwhile endeavour.[4]

The study of democracy presented in Chapter Three shows clearly the sense of purpose which pervades HP. The clarity of goals is embedded in the performance management processes of the company which date back to its inception. As founder, David Packard, remarked: 'No operating policy has contributed more to Hewlett-Packard's success than the policy of management by objective.'[5] From the inception of HP there has been a performance process in which employees are discussed and agree clear targets and then have the freedom to reach these targets in ways they determine for themselves.[6]

The details of the performance management system have been in place for many years and the continuity and consistency of the process has brought great employee awareness of its principles and linkages. The long range plan has ten steps: statement of purpose, five-year objective around customers, competition, products and services; a developmental plan, financial analysis, potential problems, recommendations and first-year plan. The annual plan is made up of two components: the Hoshin plan and the Business Fundamentals. The Hoshin identifies those areas that need immediate and substantial attention; the business fundamentals focus on day-to-day management of the business. The Framework initiative introduced in 1991 maps out performance targets, key result areas, job analysis, skills analysis, ranking criteria and training needs analysis. At the same time, there is a formal requirement for employees to be evaluated annually (an HP fundamental) at which time self-appraisal takes place accompanied by evaluation from peers, clients, team members and managers. As a consequence of this and broader performance data, the performance of all managers is ranked against each other. The performance management creates a broad set of objects in which performance can take place, but there is also a strong value set of what is appropriate. A team leader put it this way:[7]

> 'There is no great rulebook that tells you what to do when you come in the morning. You know what has to be achieved, and you know when you have to achieve it by, and most of the time nobody is too bothered how you do it, as long as it is ethical. The company's stance on ethics is incredibly strong. You find in HP after six or nine months that if people cannot cope with the business ethics, then the antibodies reject them – they just cannot work in the environment.'

If we are to learn anything from some of the failures of the empowerment movement it is that giving choice without clear parameters of goals simply creates ambiguity and anxiety. Some of these goals will be created intrinsically, within individuals as part of their dream or model of what they are and what they can become. Other goals, as we saw at HP and Sony, are created extrinsically by the organization. Both intrinsic and extrinsic goals serve the purpose of focusing individuals and teams on the direction they could and should be taking. But, while goals specify the end state, they say nothing of the means by which this end state is achieved and the parameters within which the journey takes place. This is the sphere of accountabilities and obligations, which specify for every individual the space within which the goals are achieved.

Accountabilities and obligations

The freedom to choose in the Democratic Enterprise is a journey with many forks in the road. At each of these forks a choice has to be made. In this final building block we have explored the basis on which a choice is made. A shared sense of purpose creates a long-term vision of the aims and goals of the organization; it points to the general direction the journey could be taking. But it is more than this.

Vision and goals specify the end-state, but say nothing of the journey itself. The specification of ends and the non-specification of the means are a crucial aspect of the creation of autonomy and the exercise of choice. In Autocracies, both the ends and the means are specified and in doing so choice and freedom of action is severely constrained. So the question is this: should there be any specification of means, or should each individual be able and capable of reaching the goal in any way he or she sees fit? In each of these companies that are moving towards a democratic order we see clarity of end-states and some specification of means. The word 'some' is used with care, for the crucial issue is the balance between under and over specification of means. What we see is this balance being struck through the notion of obligations and accountabilities. That is the means by which the goals are achieved. These obligations are few, but in them are held the essence of the organization, what gives it a unique culture and differentiates it from competitors. These obligations and accountabilities, in particular, specify the relationship between key stakeholders. To illustrate this let us

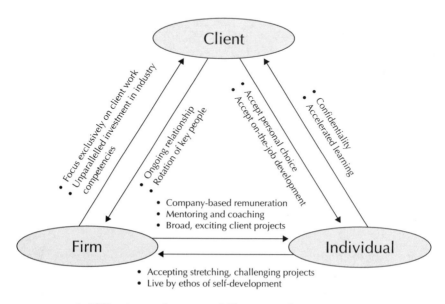

FIGURE 7.1 ◆ **Obligation and accountability at McKinsey**

look at the web of obligations and accountabilities that hold together McKinsey and which are a day-to-day reality for Nina.[8]

At McKinsey, this notion of accountabilities and obligations is at the heart of the Democratic Enterprise. The explicit knowledge of projects created through the VOX system, and the implicit knowledge developed through conversations ensures that every member of the company is faced with a latitude of discretion on a regular basis. Faced with this broad latitude of discretion, on what basis, how do people act? They make decisions for action in part by reference to the explicit balance between the needs of the client, the needs of the firm and the needs of every individual within the firm to become the best they can be. As a consequence, the destinies of each member of the firm is closely linked and aligned through mutually reinforcing obligations and accountabilities. A schema of these overlapping obligations is shown below which specify the obligations of the clients, the obligations of the firm, and the obligations of the members of the firm.

The obligations of clients

Clients commission the partners and directors of McKinsey in the knowledge and understanding that their capacity to understand and advise on complex strategic situations is unparalleled. They know that the team who will be advising them will have experience of their own and other industry sectors, and in all likelihood will have encountered a similar set of strategic issues at some stage in their development. But there are explicit obligations to the firm and its members in being a client of McKinsey. First, as a client there is limited choice of specific resources. It is partners and associates who are free to choose whether they want to work with a particular client. Second, as clients they cannot demand that the same team of associates and partners remain with them for the duration of the project. Members of McKinsey (at least up to associate level) are able to leave a client assignment at any time if they believe they are not learning from the assignment or contributing to it. At the same time, no associate stays on a project for more than nine months. Finally, as clients they are obligated to accept that while there will be collective knowledge of their context, individual associates may not have explicit knowledge of the specific area, or indeed of their sector. As a consequence on the basis of these obligations, there are clients who choose not to engage McKinsey and projects that the partners of the firm decide not to accept.

The obligations of the firm

The second set of obligations are those the firm as a whole has to its clients and its individual members. To clients the obligations are to focus exclusively on serving clients. As MD, Rajat Gupta, explains:[9]

> *'We are a client-serving firm and will be nothing else. We are not a VC, or an incubator, or a technology company. McKinsey does not want to be in competition with its clients. Thus, we do not invest in new ventures. Our primary investment is in industry competence to service our clients better.'*

The obligations of the firm to individual members are expressed continuously, but there are three obligations that are made at some potential short-term cost to the firm. The first obligation is true commitment to people. On the face of it 'true commitment to people' is an overused phrase, appearing as it does on every CEO's annual business report. The obligation of 'true commitment' is tested, not when times are good, but when times are hard. Such a test came for the partners of McKinsey in the 2001 downturn when it had recruited new joiners on the expectations of continuing substantial growth. By mid-2001 it was clear that this substantial growth would not take place and the company had made promises to new recruits which it was unable to deliver. At this point in the recruitment cycle many of the other consulting companies reneged on previous promises. Not so at McKinsey. The firm honoured every offer it had made to new joiners despite a reduction in attrition rates and an increase in acceptance rates. It met its obligation of 'true commitment to people' despite the short-term costs.

Next, the obligation of the firm to individual members is to continuously develop every member of the firm. Members are given the opportunity and freedom to broaden their experience and to develop deep knowledge in an industry sector or area of expertise. This begins at the point of recruitment. Recall Nina's career:

> *'The first two years as a 21-year-old was very exciting, the learning curve huge, I did eight or nine assignments in four or five industries. The expectation that you would be working with clever people and would be stretched was more than met.'*

As a consequence, partners become expert in managing the trade-offs between the immediate obligations to the client and the longer-term obligations to develop the human capital of the firm. The means by which consultants are chosen for projects is a complex balance between the obligations to the clients and the obligations to the developmental needs of the consultant. The emphasis always is on helping consultants choose roles in which they are currently unskilled or lack knowledge in one or more aspects to provide fast-paced development opportunities. The choice can be complex and this balancing capacity is seen as a key attribute of managerial effectiveness. So much so that one of the core management training programmes for all second-year associates uses a simulated decision-making tree in which associates choose people who they believe are most appropriate for selection to a project. After making the choice they spend time with coaches discussing their rationale for choice.

Finally, the partners are keenly aware of the impact financial demands and remuneration strategies can have on the latitude of discretion and the capacity of individual members to making wise choices. This consideration has led them to create a remuneration strategy which goes against much of the common folklore of reward practice in professional and service firms. Perhaps most significantly the obligations of the firm to individuals have profoundly influenced the ownership structure of the firm. Over the last decade many professional and service firms have chosen to go public, primarily to increase the financial asset base of the firm. The partners at McKinsey have retained a partnership structure. In making this choice they have limited the personal wealth which a public flotation would have brought. However, by doing so they believe that the partnership structure provides the greatest opportunity for the development of members unencumbered by individual financial targets.

The partners have also been very specific about their choice of remuneration strategies. Most companies of this size would target and remunerate senior managers on the basis of their personal performance (measured primarily through client-hours worked) and the performance of their immediate team or region. These performance targets create what has been termed 'line of sight' between the working hours of the individuals, the goals of the business, and individual pay. This targeted remuneration has been adopted as something of an industry standard. At McKinsey, associates and partners are not set individual time-based performance targets which target client working hours. Instead compensation depends on a combination of individual performance and the overall performance of the firm; there are no regional P&L accounts. In the words of Rajat Gupta, 'You have to do what is right for the client. If the country is going through a difficult time period, you do not push for more work.' The same is true for individuals. What is remunerated is their overall performance with the client, not their hours of work.

The obligations of the members

The primary obligation of individuals is to themselves and to their personal development . . . all other obligations flow from this. Individuals are obligated to become the best they can be. As Nina Bhatia comments:

'We have clear standards and boundaries of working together, but we basically trust each other to do the right thing. With our clients, with respect to each other and with respect to the people we develop. But we also take responsibility for our careers and what happens to us . . . We have to take choices and sometimes we have to take a chance and a risk. We have a lot of support around us to make these choices.'

The first step of this is to develop a high level of self-awareness through attending programmes and courses (for example, the associate course Nina took early in her career), but more importantly, through conversing with sponsors, mentors and colleagues. Next, since stretching project work is the primary developmental tool, as we saw earlier, individuals are obliged to make wise and informed choices about which projects to take. Certainly the firm as a whole supports this latitude of discretion by creating enormous transparency: through constant personal feedback with the VOX system; through the openness of partners to discussing their projects and the projects of others. Thus, there is a frame within which an individual can tap into both explicit and implicit knowledge. But, ultimately the obligation for development rests firmly with the individual, and the emphasis is on rounded rather than narrow development. Creating rounded development can sometimes mean walking knowingly into 'the swamplands'. As London associate principal, Jessica Spungin, recalls of her own development:[10]

'One of the first projects I did had a very strong analytical and numeric component. I worked incredibly hard on it, but frankly did a really bad job . . . the spreadsheet was all over the place! At the same time, the project feedback showed the client really appreciated my client management skills. I remember having long conversations with my mentor. I told him I had really had it with this complexity of financial analysis and wanted to ensure that I avoided projects with this component. He told me I needed to get over this hurdle or it would limit what I could do next. So the next project was even more analytically complex, but I was ready for the challenge and got through it.'

Finally, members are obligated to understand and live by the ethos and values of the firm. And the primary value is that members make choices for themselves, but ultimately for the greater good of the firm. The antithesis of this is 'employeeism', a derogatory term used to describe behaviours that focus on the individual rather than the firm. As Nina remarks: 'very early on you learn that this is a place where "I did this" or "I should be paid more" or "I am doing more than others" just doesn't work.'

At McKinsey the freedom to choose, has within it responsibilities and obligations, for clients, for the firm and for individuals. These obligations can be expressed explicitly, or understood implicitly. Here we see both, in terms of the values and remuneration practices and implicitly in the use of descriptors such as 'employeeism'. Much of the contracting of obligations takes place primarily in conversations with mentor, coaches and talking partners. It is at these points that individuals learn what it is they have to do to stay and flourish. As the psychologist Denise Rousseau describes:[11]

'Contracts . . . are rich in assumptions as well as facts, uncertainly as well as predictability. Balancing these makes it possible for organizations and people to operate more effectively. Contracts are a way of both groups to know and create the future.'

Rousseau *Psychological Contracts in Organizations*, p. 223

The contracting at McKinsey starts at the point of selection where a great deal of emphasis is placed on people who will flourish in this autonomous environment, yet have the self-motivation and ambition to continue to strive and remain engaged. Even when Nina Bhatia was at Harvard she kept in contact with the partners about her options.

'I did not feel under any pressure to come back. I felt that McKinsey had an option on me. We definitely want you back, but we want you to make the right decision. While I was away I had a lot of conversations with partners here about the other options I was considering. I think that says something about the self-confidence of an organization. The desire to have people because they want to be there, not because they have no other option. That made me feel confident about my decision to come back.'

It then proceeds in a tacit and explicit manner. Explicitly there are courses and workshops which describe in some detail the emphasis placed on personal development and the manner in which a set of projects is strung together to create depth and breadth of experience. At the same time, and perhaps more importantly, mentors and coaches devote a considerable amount of time reflecting back to individuals their choices, and the consequences of these choices. The feedback people receive following each project ensures they are crystal clear about their current strengths and development needs and the basis of resources against which choice can be exercised.

For many organizations, particularly those operating as Autocracies or Bureaucracies, the rights and duties of individuals have evolved along a set of basic values, the primary one being the implicit value of paternalism. Senior managers operate in a quasi parental role, making the most appropriate choices for individuals. In McKinsey while the partners play an important role in contracting, the role they play is one of illumination rather than direction.

Trust and power

Paternalism and the parent–child relationship imply that collectively senior members of the organization are in a better position to make choices for the individual than the individuals are capable of making for themselves. The re-appropriation of choice from senior members of the organization to individuals themselves implies trust on both parts, but particularly on the part of the senior members. It is they who have to cede power to individual employees and to trust them to behave in an autonomous manner and make decisions and take action that serve their personal good and the good of the organization.

Democracy implies the giving of authority to individuals to make choices within the context of obligations and accountabilities. Authority, obligations and accountability are deeply bound up with trust. Trust without accountability and obligation is likely to become one-sided, that is, to slide into dependence. Accountability without trust is impossible because it would mean the continual scrutiny of the motives and actions of individuals. We can only encourage autonomy and build choice if we trust each other. That requires us to credit others to be trustworthy without the need to continuously audit their behaviour and the choices they make.[12]

The democracy study showed the extent of differences between companies in their ability to create an environment in which people trust each other, their manager and their colleagues. In the data on the fifth tenet, HP and Kraft Foods are the highest trust companies, and Lloyds TSB and Parcelforce the lowest trust. For those companies with high trust there are subtle ways in which the management processes of the organization reinforce the adult-to-adult relationship and treat people with dignity and in a manner which they believe to be fair and equitable. In high-trust companies, such as HP and Kraft Foods, trust is also nurtured in the means by which feedback and information is made available to employees, and the means by which power is shared within the organization.

The management processes such as performance management and career management are primary ways by which trust or mistrust is most clearly expressed. In the process of setting targets, appraising performance, giving feedback and reward, and discussing job moves and careers, senior management are sending out strong messages about control and trust. In high-control/low-trust environments, the performance management and career processes are largely concerned with articulating operating procedures which are initiated top-down through a centralized framework. Employee performance is closely monitored, with appraisal used chiefly as an auditing device to correct deviations from the norm. There is no mechanism to credit others to be trustworthy without the need to continuously audit their behaviour. Career development is controlled and centralized with an emphasis on the careers of high potentials rather than the average employee.

While each of these pioneering companies is fundamentally different, they have each made important decisions about the way in which they audit the performance of their employees and manage career development.[13] In particular, they have made decisions about audit through the measurement of time, and the measurement of output. In doing so they are striving to create a low control/high trust environment. In fostering trust and crafting more democratic organizations, both BT and McKinsey have moved away from the common practice in their respective industry sectors of measuring time and have created more equitable and fairer ways to measure individual performance. In both cases this is an extremely resource and time-consuming decision. Measuring elapsed time is relatively simple and easy to administer, employees themselves simply complete a timesheet. More elaborate performance management systems are extremely difficult to support, often being overcome by managerial apathy and cynicism.[14] At BT, for example, measuring the output of 3,000 engineers working alone or in small teams across the UK posed a real problem. The company solved it by building information systems that measured the performance output of each job the engineer completed. The system emphasized the quality of workmanship, and team working and support. The same is true at McKinsey where the quality of the output of individuals is measured with a range of sophisticated performance management tools. Moving from time to output has been at the creation of trust and an adult-to-adult relationship. At BT, time and location flexibility would not be possible unless employees felt they would not be penalized under the old rules. At McKinsey, measuring output has broadened the space within which individuals are free to develop their personal human capital.

Management practices, such as performance appraisal, have a real impact on the development of trust. One aspect of these management practices is feedback and communication. The trust an organization has in individuals is expressed through the emphasis on meaningful and realistic feedback. Giving meaningful information is crucial to procedural justice and to the feelings of respect and trust between the individual and the organization.[15] It is in the conversations with managers that individual gauge the trust of the organization in their competence, and ultimately, in their latitude of discretion. Distorting or suppressing information prevents individuals building self-awareness and reflexivity. It is meaningful feedback which enables individuals to learn about the consequences of their actions, and by doing so, to learn to be trusted citizens of a Democratic Enterprise.

Trust in the individual to the organization is built through processes and practices such as the measurement of performance, the allocation of rewards, and the discussions of careers. Here both the nature of the conversations, the processes themselves, and the outcomes can build or indeed destroy trust. This nature of the implementation of management practice and processes is crucial to the creation and sustaining of trust. When employees perceive the performance and career management to be fair and just and when they are treated with personal dignity, then their trust in their colleagues and the organization is built. When they believe these practices are unfair, or when they are treated in an undignified manner, then trust is destroyed.[16]

Trust is also built or indeed destroyed through the mechanisms by which power is exercised within the company.[17] The move towards an adult-to-adult relationship, the notion of the individual as an investor, are based in the distribution of power from the organization and the manager to the individual. The re-assignment of power is crucial to supporting autonomy and building democracy. This is not simply the rhetoric of power sharing and information distribution. If the rhetoric is that power has been ceded but the reality is that it has not been, then employee's consider the organization has breached the contract. Trust and commitment then decline as employees withdraw from their obligations.[18] One of the guiding principles of democracy in these pioneering companies is that individual autonomy is the realization of equality in influencing the outcomes of decision making. This is the basis of the final tenets of the Democratic Enterprise.

Forging variety and autonomy subtly shifts the locus of power within the organization. In the parent–child relationship power rests with the parent; in the adult–adult relationship power is negotiated. These shifts of power may be subtle, but they are played out at all levels in the organization. By shifting power, these pioneering organizations are stimulating a positive sense of self-discipline by enabling employees to secure their sense of identity, meaning and reality. Through the process of gaining the power of choice, employees gain mastery over their affairs.[19]

Take BP as a case, where opening up the internal job market and advertising the majority of job and project vacancies has fundamentally shifted the power structures of the organization between the individual and their boss. In the past the internal labour market had been a source of control and power available to managers at BP, as in many other large companies. Through their power of veto a manager could block a subordinate's application to a job outside their group on the grounds that they had been in their current role for less than two years. The rationale was that team leaders could retain their highest performing members for at least two years and thereby build some degree of team and performance stability. At BP, as in many other large complex organizations, managers also gained power from their ability to access a network of colleagues across the corporation. They were able to place their most favoured team members into positions of power and influence. This bestowed on them the power of the king maker.

With the opening of the internal labour market both sources of managerial power have been severely depreciated. Greg Grimshaw's manager has no control over whether Greg stays for two months or two years. There are certainly organizational norms and stories that discourage people from moving too rapidly. But that is a judgement call that Greg, as a mature adult, will take for himself. In the past Greg's managers have played key roles in placing him in preferential jobs. This is particularly the case as Greg is one of the 150 young high potential people at BP. When Greg chose to apply for a job in the HR team he certainly asked the advice of his manager, but it was not his manager who made the vacancy known to him, and this depreciated his king-making power.

Despite having the technology to create an open internal labour market, many other large companies have chosen not to invest in this degree of personal autonomy.[20] The reasons given for this vary – 'it would not be good for the individual', 'people could make the wrong choices', 'everyone would change jobs every couple of months and that would have an impact on productivity'. Of course, the answer to all of these rational arguments is 'yes'. In the case of BP, Greg Grimshaw could indeed make the wrong choice and move into a dead-end career limiting position, or work with a manager who destroys rather than builds his personal human capital. He may decide to change jobs every two months and leave a trail of debris in his wake. But as the theory of self-organizing systems suggests, giving sufficient meaningful information enables individuals to make wise choices.

Certainly the nature of this information is important. It allows individual to make informed choices. But in a sense this is a first-order effect. The second-order effect is that by making deep and meaningful information available, the organization is signalling the type of relationship it expects to develop with individual members and the way in which power will be distributed. It speaks firmly of the adult-to-adult orientation, rather than of the parent-to-child. In sharing this information the organization is attempting to treat the individual on an equal footing with itself. It is the recognition that individuals have the right to certain types of information previously withheld, and can be trusted to arrive at a judgement based on their self-knowledge and information. It develops what Barbara Townley has termed authenticity:[21]

> 'The individual is neither an object of knowledge for the organization, to be examined to see if there is the likelihood of a good "fit"; nor is the individual a "subject" to be manipulated in order to fit into the organization, but there is an authentic subject who can exercise independent judgement . . . It is the creation of dialogue . . . it is a recognition of the degree of honesty with which the relationship is conducted.'
>
> Townley *Reframing Human Resource Management: Power, Ethics and the Subject at Work*, p. 156

In the creation of a Democratic Enterprise, in which individual potential flourishes and people are free to choose, there is a subtle move from parent-to-child relationship to an adult-to-adult relationship. Nowhere is this more apparent than in this notion of 'shared purpose'. In the parent–child relationship a shared purpose was seen as inconsequential. In this new relationship type, what was once assumed has now to be discussed and negotiated. At the heart of this negotiation is clarity about what it is the individual is trying to achieve, and what it is organization has constructed as goals. It is unambiguous goals that create a focus for choice and attention. Goals speak less about the means of creation; this is the domain of obligations and accountabilities. These are obligations individuals have to themselves, to their colleagues, to the organization and to their customers. As we saw in the case of McKinsey, these obligations may hold within themselves paradoxes: about the rights of the individual and the rights of the organization, about trade-offs between the two, about what can be gained and what has to be sacrificed. Accountabilities and obligations, as we saw, are not simply blue-sky, soft-centred wishes and desires. They are adult, mature decisions about what the individual and the organization can be, and more importantly perhaps, what it is they cannot be. The forging and understanding of these accountabilities and obligations can only occur in an organization which is self reflexive and which is party to a level of conversation and dialogue which enables these paradoxes to be understood. People are only free to converse and be reflexive in a space where they feel trust and respect for one another and in which power has been distributed. As the fifth tenet puts it, this is a place were people are involved in 'determining the conditions of their association'.

CHAPTER EIGHT

Leaders and citizens at work

Democracy and the Democratic Enterprise is fundamentally about the relationships between employees and between employees and the organization. In the first building block the organizational challenge is to support the creation of personal autonomy. In the second, it is to craft organizational variety. And in the third it is to shape shared purpose. Each of these building blocks involves roles and responsibilities for all levels of the organization. The CEO and leadership team has a role to create the broad philosophical context of democracy and to become the architect of shared purpose. For the manager, the roles across the three steps of democracy are to mentor and coach and to be prepared and capable of entering into a relationship that is firmly adult-to-adult and creates space and freedom to the team. Finally, much of the process context of democracy – the supporting of individual autonomy and the crafting of organizational processes – requires a highly competent and sophisticated HR function.

The role of the leader

The leader as philosopher

Leaders are faced with day-to-day decisions that subtly shape the context and processes of the organization. At the same time, they are called upon to create and articulate a sense of the longer-term purpose and goals. In making these day-to-day decisions and in articulating their view of the future they are inevitably making constant reference to their own assumptions and beliefs. This will include their personal theory of the firm, their beliefs about the nature of people, and their views of the competitive environment. These assumptions or what we might call philosophies develop from the leader's past experiences, their biases and their personal views. The philosophy of leaders if often assumed rather than articulated. But whether they choose or are able to articulate these personal theories, they exist as a set of beliefs.

So a major role of the leader in a Democratic Enterprise is to create and communicate a philosophy which embraces the adult-to-adult relationship and individual autonomy of the first tenets. They do this primarily by engaging those around them in a conversation and debate about the company which has both intellectual rigour and insight.

In BP for example, the adult-to-adult relationship was championed, developed and sustained by the CEO and the top team in many subtle ways. In the ways in which the leaders of the firm interacted, mentored and coached their own team and the members of the organization. In the role model they themselves created as thoughtful, discursive and autonomous people. In the manner in which conversation and dialogue flourished within the organization. Every day the leaders send out subtle clues that reflect their attitudes and beliefs about the role of the employee and the nature of the relationship between employee and corporation. In supporting the creation of individual autonomy, those leaders who believe in democracy make substantial investments in supporting substantive conversation and reflection about individuals and the organization.

At BP the relationship which CEO John Browne seeks to create between the individual and the organization is reflected and made apparent in a myriad of subtle ways. At the centre is the role of intellectual curiosity, the importance of conversation and the means of engagement. Browne and his colleagues were aptly described by a *Financial Times* journalist as 'an unusually active and well-financed university faculty – earnest, morally engaged and careful of other's sensibilities'.[1] As Browne comments:

> '*This company is founded on a deep belief in intellectual rigour . . . Rigour implies that you understand the assumptions you have made – assumptions about the state of the world, of what you can do, and how your competitors will interact with it, and how the policy of the world will or will not allow you to do something.*'[2]

His appetite for knowledge is insatiable, and he himself is a crucial creator of knowledge. Through conversation and reflection he has built a model of the role of the CEO and of the structure and aspirations of BP. By engaging in conversation and knowledge creation on his own behalf, he sends a clear signal about the appropriateness of these activities to others. At the same time, the striving towards individual autonomy is something he reinforces in the way the senior team works together. This is how he describes his relationship with deputy CEO, Rodney Chase:

'Rodney and I have worked together since 1984, and we have worked close up the ranks and it is a very close relationship. You would think that we would be so familiar with each other that we would know the way each other thinks, but it is actually the reverse. We challenge each other very hard, in a very appropriate way, but it is the purpose of the relationship to get a better result, and we do that. And that, in turn, encourages others to do that.'

The intellectual curiosity he role models legitimizes intellectual curiosity in others – curiosity both about themselves and about the corporate community. What Lord Browne and his team have achieved at BP is to elevate the importance of intellectual discovery and the creation of self-awareness. By doing so he has championed the role of the citizen and the power of individual autonomy.

The leader as visionary

Perhaps more than any other aspect of the creation of the Democratic Enterprise, it is in the creation of a shared purpose that the role of the leadership team is most vital. Without this 'containment' of a sense of purpose independent people simply go their own way and the organization rapidly becomes an adhocracy. In the Democratic Enterprise the leader plays a key role as the integrator, the force operating against random drift.

What stops random drift is a sense of purpose which pervades the company. Here is how John Thornton, President and Co-Chief Co-Ordinating Officer of Goldman Sachs articulates this sense of purpose:

'I believe that anyone with any depth and any talent has to ask the question "what am I doing with my life?" The purpose of my life is to use my

talent for some larger and better purpose. I believe that some form of that sentiment is what motivates most highly talented people.'

These are not a sense of purpose built on ROCE or growth rates. They are a sense of purpose which engages the emotions and beliefs of employees. For Sony CEO, Nobuyuki Idei, it was his absolute clarity of the purpose of the business which created the space in which experimentation could take place. His was a vision of the digital universe:

'We have to shift our thinking toward developing, along with the PC and software industries, what in effect are audio/visual-orientated computers and components and the software to play on them. If we can do this, I believe Sony can become the master of the digital universe.'

This broad vision of the future and sense of shared purpose in the journey acted as a continuous beacon to the engineering team working on the VAIO project.

The role of the team leader

In the Democratic Enterprise the leaders' personal philosophy pervades the company, and their sense of purpose articulates a common vision for the realization of freedom and choice. Theirs is the broad, encompassing articulation of the meaning of the company. However, while this is important, it is the leaders of the teams across the organization who make this vision a reality on a day-to-day basis. They do this primarily by expanding the space in which choice and freedom can be exercised. Yet at the same time as expanding the space, they also delineate it with the obligations and accountabilities contained with the business goals. Finally, while the leader has a role in setting the philosophy of autonomy and personal development, it is the team leader who brings this to realization in the manner in which they mentor and coach. The team leader can become an active block to individual autonomy and organizational variety. Alternatively, they can become a role model for how citizens can behave.

The team leader as creator of space

Recall that at BT it was managers' inability to support people making personal choices that grounded the early attempts at location and time choice.

Having grown up in a bureaucracy, many were uncomfortable at supporting the variety and choice that are central to the third and fourth tenets of
the Democratic Enterprise.

The day-to-day behaviour of team leaders sends out pervasive messages
about what is valued. Perhaps most importantly they send out clear messages that people are free to choose, creating freedom within jobs, but also
by encouraging people to take roles and responsibilities which are far from
their current capability. Rajat Gupta speaks for many when he says:

> *'Each associate at McKinsey must have the freedom to follow their own
> passions, to have the opportunity to have multiple careers within a career.
> In McKinsey . . . everyone needs to learn how to say yes to opportunities
> which expand their competencies and knowledge.'*

This was supported by team leaders across McKinsey. Recall how Nina
Bhatia's experience took her from chocolates to steel, from media to oil. At
many of the points of her assignment she entered roles which were outside her
knowledge and experience base. By being prepared to accept her, the team
leader was signalling that she would have freedom to develop within the role.

The same is true of Sony. There were many points in the VAIO project
when people moved into very different roles. Enabling people to take roles
far from their current skill set became something of a norm. As team leader,
Kazumasa Sato, recalls, having entrusted the task of prototyping the channel strategy to someone in her mid-20s, 'I chose her because she knew nothing about supply chain management. Because of her very lack of knowledge,
I expected her to come up with a completely new idea.' She was able to
create the freedom which allowed her to become the best she could be.

The team leader as goal setter

The wide latitude of discretion which choice creates can be a real invigora-
tor. But it can also create confusion. The sense of purpose created and communicated by the leader sets the broad context, but it is the goals agreed
with the team leader, which shape choice making.

At HP, for example, the CEO drives down the cascade of the corporate
goals. At BP, John Browne and his team periodically review the performance
of each of the business unit managers and agree on the next targets. Here is
how Deputy CEO, Rodney Chase, describes the process:

'The actual performance contract is relatively simple, a few financial goals – profit before tax, cash flow, investment, return on invested capital – I have never seen more than four. Then there are two or three high-level non-financial targets. Once the contract is decided, people are free to achieve them in whatever way they find appropriate.'

Team leaders work within the broad corporate goals to create a 'line of sight' in which every employee understands exactly what is expected of them. Moreover, these performance expectations are articulated primarily as outcomes, so while the *what* is clearly articulated, there is space around the *how*. These broad business goals set the parameters and create the frame within which choices can be made. These performance contracts clearly and unambiguously articulate the accountabilities and obligations of every employee as a member of the corporation.

The team leader as role model

As we saw at BT, managers who ignore the diverse needs of members of their team or who reinforce presenteeism are a significant barrier to the creation of the Democratic Enterprise. Managers support choice and variety in many subtle ways; by what they say; and by their actions. Many have very actively demonstrated conscious choice in the ways in which they have configured their roles or in the breadth of projects and jobs with which they have been involved. A few have become role models for location or time choice. As one of the senior team at BP reflects:

'About 12 months ago I came to the realization that something had to give. The only possibility was to leave the organization. Following the BP brand launch, I said to myself, there is another possibility – I can work less hours and it will be OK for me to do so. And that is what I am doing. Twelve months ago if you had asked if that was possible, I would have said absolutely not.'

The same is true of a growing number of team leaders at BT and HP where location choice and job-sharing have been pioneered by members of the senior team. These tend to be highly idiosyncratic choices rather than main stream. But, by doing so, the members of the team are signalling that variety is tolerated, and in some cases, actually celebrated.

The team leader as mentor and coach

Developing personal potential is a crucial focus in the Democratic Enterprise. The cues and signals team leaders send are subtle but profound. For the team leaders at McKinsey this relentless building of human capital is tied closely to the individual's attitude to their own self-development. As Rajat Gupta says:

> *'If you are an industry leader, you are there for three to five years: this is not a life-long position. I do not have a discussion with the head of the London office about this. It is an obligation for industry leaders to give leadership opportunity to other people.'*

The same is true at Goldman Sachs, where choices and support for mentoring and developmental relationships are seen to be crucial to the culture of the firm and are assigned importance for all team leaders. The history of Goldman Sachs, from the days of Marcus Goldman and Sam Sachs, has demonstrated a clear and unflinching belief in the need for team leaders to actively engage in supporting each one of their talented employees to become the best they could be. Stephen Friedman, co-leader in the period 1990–94, says, 'Our success is directly related to six things – people and culture, culture and people, people and culture.' Across the history of Goldman Sachs, the actions of team leaders continuously reinforce the relentless building of human capital. This is demonstrated most clearly by the way in which the team leaders choose to spend the time, perhaps the most valuable commodity in this investment community. Each team leader of Goldman Sachs chooses to spend an enormous proportion of his or her time in supporting, evaluating and coaching other members of the firm. Their dedication to this is far beyond that associated with other managers in the financial sector. Every year, for example, a vice-president will participate on average in a series of in-depth performance and coaching conversations and from these conversations prepare performance review documents for between 50 and 60 people. They will participate in between 15 and 30 conversations with prospective new hires. They will be members of the cross-ruffing teams (responsible for the selection of partner managing directors) for up to eight people. At each step of the creation of human capital the time involvement is substantial. Current partners who are members of the cross-ruffing teams speak with the colleagues of those nominated, prepare a detailed report on the nominee and then participate in the various meetings at which selection decisions are made. Partners can demonstrate their values by no clearer means than through their allocation of their most precious resource; their time.[3]

The same is true at Sony where team leaders actively and publicly engage in building human capital. Founder, Masaru Ibuka, initiated 'Sony *juku*' in which 20 middle managers, typically in their mid-30s worked closely with him. In small taskforces they identified an organizational challenge and worked with him to develop a set of organizational actions. From this beginning successive leaders have personally given their time and energy to supporting the development of others.[4]

At BP, coaching and mentoring starts at the top. Each member of the executive typically coach and mentor up to ten group vice-presidents who then coach and mentor their own teams. Rodney Chase, deputy CEO of BP, describes it this way:

> '*I gossip with them about what is really going on within the inner cabinet, I share confidences, I tell them about my discussions with John Browne. I build trust with them. I agree with them what their weaknesses are, and agree to work with them. You have to take the time to engage them with examples that will make them broader and wiser. To develop their sense of responsibility for the firm; who they are developing. The greatest pleasure I get is the development of talent.*'

Consider how close Rodney Chase's description of how he sees his role is to the picture of the 'talking partner' so crucial to forging individual autonomy. By engaging in a deep conversation about strengths and weaknesses he is supporting the creation of self-awareness and understanding. And by engaging in this way, Chase and the executive team are ensuring that this 'talking partner' becomes a model for relationships and conversations across the corporation.

The HR role

It is the leaderships teams of the organization who are best placed to describe and support the tenets that together create the Democratic Enterprise. However, the journey to employee autonomy and organizational variety is not simply built on aspirations and vision. It is also built upon a sophisticated platform of processes and practices. Much of the development of these processes and practices rests within the remit of the HR teams. Most importantly the creation of the Democratic Enterprise needs a level of employee insight rarely seen in many organizations. Next, it requires a number of relatively sophisticated practices, perhaps the most important of which is the practice of discovering and learning through trials and experiments.

At the heart of the Democratic Enterprise is a subtle and articulated belief about people and assumptions about their behaviour and development. This focus on the human side of the enterprise places a particularly key role in the hands of the human resource function. In each of these pioneering companies the members of the HR function played key roles as business champions and employee advocates. More specifically, they developed the techniques and processes to create insight about employees and they built trials and experiments which enabled them to create variety and test the benefits in a relatively low risk environment.

Creator of employee insight

The capacity of leaders to actively build a Democratic Enterprise requires both a depth and breadth of information on which decisions can be made. The leadership teams need to understand what motivates individuals and build a picture of their capacity to exercise choice and the most appropriate means by which variety can be created. The creation of this information lies within the domain of the HR function.

The major interventions which Tesco and BT undertook to build variety began with the HR team presenting to the executive committee insight about present and future employees. At BT, successive employee surveys showed that people increasingly felt under stress, that their work and life was out of balance and, as a result, many would not take further managerial responsibility. When the HR team presented this information to the executive committee of BT it caused the team to seriously reflect on the current situation. It was an opportunity for the team to have a realistic and sensible discussion about the engagement of employees and the factors, such as stress and work imbalance, denuding this engagement. Moreover, when the HR team went on to commission a study about the future of work it became clear that these issues would increase rather than decrease. This data can be as simple as that collected in the democracy study described in Chapter Three. Reliable, comparative data on important factors is enormously useful as an aid to decision making.

At Tesco, access to reliable and timely information about employees gave the senior team the opportunity to have a realistic conversation about the needs of employees across the organization. What emerged from initial employee surveys was an understanding that the axis of the company had tipped towards the needs and aspirations of customers without a similar appreciation of the needs and aspirations of employees. This was one of the key drivers behind the creation of the Employee Insight Unit. In their presentations to the Tesco board, the HR team used statistical modelling and data-warehousing capabilities to present a complex and comprehensive view of employees. The sophistication and depth of this data enabled the senior team at Tesco to make hard choices about where scarce resources could most usefully be deployed.

In both BT and Tesco employee insight was created using highly sophisticated methods. This included employee survey analysis techniques, focus groups and the use of data warehousing to integrate data on 360° feedback with leaver data and performance measures. Clearly the capacity to create such a depth of employee insight is crucial to steering the course of the Democratic Enterprise and is a key role of the HR function.

Builder of trials and experiments

Many of the early experiments to bring variety and choice began one or even two decades ago as specific projects or trials. The BT location and time flexibility trials, for example, began in the 1980s. At about the same time, the BP open internal labour market began with the 'green box' with access restricted to the high potential group. For Sony, the extension of the latitude of discretion in the roles and responsibilities became as a key part of the VIAO project.

These initial trials served a number of important functions. Perhaps most importantly they allowed experimentation to take place at the periphery of the organization. This created the possibility of variety that is so important to the evolution of adaptability and ultimately of self-organization. Through trials and experiments, the HR and leadership teams in these companies were in a stronger position to make accurate evaluations and to take a bet on what will work best. These trials create opportunities for new ideas to be tested in a relatively low risk environment.

For the HR team at BT, the development of location and time flexibility that was so important to them at the beginning of the new century began ten years earlier as a series of discrete trials. These trials enabled the team to monitor the problems as they emerged and to take 'before' and 'after' measures of key variables, such as performance, commitment and satisfaction with work-life balance. As a result, the team understood that technology could be a major problem and were able to specify the technological development resources necessary for these trials to be rolled out on a company-wide basis. The clear measure of performance outcomes the HR teams collected also enabled the team to write detailed business cases about the potential business savings and the costs of location and time flexibility.

Together leaders, team leaders and members of the HR function create the context in which citizens can become the very best they can be.

The five good reasons to become a democratic enterprise

We began this journey to the Democratic Enterprise with Toc-queville's reflection that 'the field of possibilities is much more extensive then men living in their various societies are ready to imagine'. We can also recall Warren Bennis's challenge to each one of us to get our heads together to develop what he called 'delightful organizations'. In a sense this book is about 'getting our heads together'. It is about the role that we can play in supporting the tenets of democracy. About the means by which the six tenets can re-energize our working lives and re-invigorating the organizations of which we are members.

Creating 'delightful' organizations is surely a good thing to do. As we have seen, those companies who follow some, if not all of the tenets of the Democratic Enterprise create places where people want to be. Think of Nina as she engages with excitement and pleasure in the challenges with which she is faced. Or of Greg as he zigzags from one interesting assignment to another. Or Stewart as he experiences the joy of a balanced life.

But is creating what Warren Bennis called a 'delightful' organization for the common good of employee a sufficient reason? The Democratic Enter-prise certainly has the potential to engage and excite employees. But employees are only one of the constituent stakeholders in organizational life. For the financial stakeholder the question is one of sustainable perfor-mance. Can the support of the six tenets of democracy build financially suc-cessful organizations?

My answer here is an unequivocal yes. Our research suggests that the democratic tenets can play a crucial contributing factor to the longer term

The five good reasons to become a democratic enterprise

sustaining of that organizational health. The most democratic companies in our Democracy Study (HP and Kraft Foods) are also among the highest performing companies.[1] There are good reasons for every organization to embrace the tenets of the Democratic Enterprise. But there are two distinct contexts or events in the life of an organization in which supporting the six tenets of democracy could make a real and significant impact to long-term financial sustainability.

The first context is when the company is experiencing unstable and unpredictable markets and economic events. It is during these periods of turbulence that organizational agility is crucial. Agile companies are able to respond faster, to move quicker, and to accelerate with grace. For any company entering into a period of uncertainty, the ability of each employee to remain agile could well become the overriding determinant of success. Democratic enterprises are more agile.

Second, there are times in the history of many companies when financial success depends on the capacity for rapid integration. This could be the integration of a newly acquired business or joint venture. It could be the internal integration of the various strategic business units of the company. At this moment the speed and viability of integration will be a contributory factor in long-term financial performance. Democratic enterprises are more able to successfully integrate.

There are numerous reasons why companies that attempt to live the six tenets of democracy are more agile and more able to integrate. Many of these reasons have been explored through the eyes of the three citizens or in the description of these companies who are pioneering choice and variety. But beyond these there are three good reasons why every leader, every management team and every HR professional should be actively working to create a more democratic workplace.

The first is that employees who experience democracy are more engaged, committed and willing to give their potential to the organization. Second, the notion of democracy in organizations reduces the potential for conflict and posturing and instead creates a win–win solution. Finally, organizations that attempt to live the six tenets are places where justice and fairness flourish. Not only is this positive on its own count, but is a significantly contributory factor to employee engagement.

Employees who experience democracy are more engaged

At the heart of the Democratic Enterprise are citizens who are committed to the organization and have aligned values and beliefs. This is a prerequisite to the sixth tenet, the accountabilities and obligations which citizens are able and willing to shoulder as a consequence of their sense of shared purpose.

When people are engaged and committed they are more likely to behave in the interests of the company and they have less need to be controlled and measured. In essence, engaged people can be trusted to behave in the interests of the company, in part because they perceive their interests to be the same as, or aligned with, the interests of the company.

The engagement of the citizen in a democracy has always been central. Recall the engagement of the citizens of ancient Athens as they actively played a role in their own fate and the fate of the state. Or consider those such as John Stuart Mill who wrote about liberal democracy and their belief that it is participation that undercuts passivity and enhances general prosperity. The industrialization and mechanization of the twentieth century reduced participation to the role Weber and Schumpeter described for it. Participation became simply the participation in the election of decision-makers in a bureaucratic organization.

In the companies we have studied the act of participation has encompassed many dimensions of working lives. Do we have any evidence that participation has had any significant impact on the performance of individuals or teams?

The evidence of the link has been most clearly articulated at BT. For Stewart the opportunity to actively engage in the conditions of his association and to experience the variety of BT has been a significant decisive factor in his remaining with the company. But has his performance increased? We don't know the answer to this in the case of Stewart. But we do have a glimpse of this through the lens of a series of pilots in location and time choice that the BT team ran from the 1980s. From their initial design of time and location choice the team at BT were scrupulous about measuring the performance of the teams who were involved in the pilots.

Since the initial projects the BT team managing the pilots have systematically collected and analysed the performance data. This has included performance measures such as customer satisfaction, the amount of time a task actually takes and the rates of completion. It has also included metrics around the feelings and attitudes of those people who have participated in the pilot studies. This has been collected through the annual survey of every employee and also through in-depth discussions and focus groups. The results of these performance measures are clear proof that those people who are members of the pilot studies perform at a higher level than parallel groups of people who are doing the same job but not in a context of choice.

For example, the Freedom to Work initiative was launched in 1998 with just 18 people, 9 men and 9 women, in the UK's Cardiff Engineering Centre, a software team with high market value. At the time this was not a team that was performing at the top of their ability. As one manager who worked on the initial projects reflected, 'They had relatively high turnover, their performance and attendance were not the best either. They certainly weren't the worst, but they weren't the best either.' Conversations with the team at that time showed that each individual member had a particular set of requirements and needs – and often it was the pressure on the balance between their working life and their personal lives which was at the heart of much of this dissatisfaction and turnover. Taking what was at the time a great leap of faith, the management of the team described to individual members the standards of performance output that was required and invited the team to develop their own attendance pattern. Members of the team worked individually and then collectively to come up with attendance schedules that suited them. This attendance schedule then became the document against which people worked. At the end of the first year the management team surveyed customer satisfaction, the views of colleagues, of internal customers, and examined all the performance data routinely collected through the BT performance management systems. They also focused on the team's turnover rates and levels of attendance. The manager takes up the story:

> 'The people moved to being top performers, they had debugged the system
> that had been giving us problems with an incredible amount of speed and
> flair. They struck up an amazing relationship with the Indian Software
> Engineering Centre because lots of people were working in the night,

whenever it suited them, so we had no time zone. Productivity went up, turnover went down. We had individuals turning down higher paid jobs just to keep the flexibility they had developed.'

On reviewing this initial BT story cynics may recall the Hawthorne studies in the US in the 1930s which showed that any intervention, whatever its nature, creates initial increases in performance simply because the subjects of the intervention feel valued and trusted. This could be one interpretation of the Cardiff story. But what is interesting is that these initial results have been replicated across the other initiatives rolled out across BT from 1999 onwards, and more importantly, they have been sustained over time.

In late 1998 the Freedom to Choose pilot was rolled out across 3,000 field engineers working in different locations across the UK. At that time the remuneration system for the field engineers paid extra overtime for weekends and evening work. This had encouraged a culture of poor performance where engineers failed to complete jobs properly so their bonuses would be maximized through repeating work at the weekends. Like the initial group this pilot enabled field engineers to work in teams to make decisions about what jobs they were going to do, and which team member would work on each job. Many of these conversations take place on the portable laptop – used since 1999 with dynamic scheduling technology. This scheduling technology enabled different data to be brought together to make a scheduling decision. This included the tasks to be achieved, the capabilities of each engineer, the location of each engineer, the availability of engineers, and their preferred work schedule. From the perspective of the engineer, at the heart of the scheme was a system of points, which could be earned by completing extra jobs and through coaching others (termed 'buddying up'). So engineers get the choice of earning more money, or working fewer hours. The pilot finished in March 2002, and at that point became part of the normal working practice for 20,000 engineers. The performance advantages were clear. On average engineers earned more, they worked two hours less per week, productivity was up by 5%, and quality of service was up by 8%. As one engineer remarked 'I earn my bonuses through improved productivity rather than through overtime.' Another adds, 'My wife works shifts as a paramedic so it has helped us make more time to be together. I also have time to ride out on my motorcycle.'

During the same period BT also piloted home-working. The studies showed that commitment and engagement also increased substantially for people working from home. By 2002 there were about 6,000 people working permanently from home and many thousands working sporadically from home. On average, home-workers at BT are 20% more productive than their office-based colleagues; 7% happier and more satisfied; and provide higher levels of customer satisfaction and quality of service. Retention rates are higher for those who work from home. This focus on choice and flexibility has had a real impact on the way in which BT is perceived both by investors and by potential employees. In 2001 BT was ranked eighth in the FTSE4GOOD ethical trading index; it was ranked the top telecoms company in the Dow Jones Social Responsibility Index; and won the UK Employer of the Year Award.

Democratic enterprises give people choice. In the words of the third tenet, 'individuals are able to develop their nature and express their diverse qualities' and in the fourth tenet, 'individuals are able to participate in determining the conditions of their association'. It was the chance to work flexibly that gave the engineers at BT the context in which they could fulfil their own needs and at the same time fulfil the needs of the organization. It was the context of location choice that enabled BT employees to create a working life in which, like Stewart, they could express what was important to them. Beneath this broad statement of facts are two ancillary factors that together support the increase in engagement and performance observed by the BT pilot team. The first factor is that by giving choice, companies and employees are engaging in what we might call win–win solutions. The second factor is that by entering into an adult-to-adult relationship, the organization is behaving in a more fair and just manner.

Democratic enterprises create win–win solutions

For Greg Grimshaw at BP the opportunity to take many different roles was a win–win solution. He 'wins' because his zigzagging is aligned with his own desires and wishes. BP 'wins' because the company gains a person with broad skills and is able to resource jobs in far away places. The same was true for Stewart Kearney at BT. He 'wins' because he is able to work from home and create the balance in his life that is crucial to his well-being and sense of personal meaning. BT 'wins' because the talents and insight of Stewart remain with the company rather than going to a competitor.

The best possible relationship between the individual and the organization is a win–win solution where both win and neither loses. In a sense the citizens of ancient Athens were engaged in a win–win solution. They gained relative security and stability from the state and an opportunity to express their talents. The state gained a responsive, participate citizenship. In the writings of John Stuart Mill and John Locke we see the same win–win. Through participation, citizens 'energies are unleashed' and 'imaginative solutions and successful strategies' created. And through this the state 'wins' as the talents of citizens are focused on the purpose of the state. For Marx and Engels the world would never be a win–win place. On the contrary, the owners would always win and the workers would always lose. The only way the balance could be re-addressed would be through what they called 'collective action' in which the power of the owners could be balanced by the collective might of the workers.

The tenets of the Democratic Enterprise provide an opportunity for win–win solutions to be created without the need for collective action. This is achieved because the organization engages with individuals on a one-to-one basis rather than collectively. The implication here is that by engaging in this adult-to-adult relationship, the individual is able to fashion what is important to them within the context of the business case of the organization.

The choices which frame the relationship between the individual and the organization can be described around two key axes. The first axis is the value these choices bring to the individual. Some of these choices may be of high value and others of less value. The second axis is the cost that the company has to bear by engaging in the variety necessary to create choice for employees. There will be some aspects of variety which is of high cost to the organization and there will be others which are less costly.

As the model in Fig. 9.1 illustrates, there are two fundamental and costly errors the organization can make. The first is the error of *high company cost/low employee value*. This is the error of wasted resources. These wasted resources occur because individuals are given resources by the company that are of little value to them. Giving costly pension benefits to the people who do not value them would be a case in point. This was precisely the lesson that the reward team at AstraZeneca learned. As the new reward

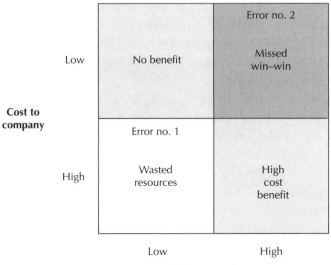

FIGURE 9.1 ◆ **The win–win solution**

scheme was rolled out, the variety it contained allowed employees to make individual choices. As a consequence, the team learned, for example, that for some young, mobile employees the cost the company bore in providing costly pensions to them was perceived as having very limited value. Like AstraZeneca, many other companies are making this type of error. For AstraZeneca the consequence of this is simply that they waste resources on giving people something they do not value. However, the other aspect of this type of error is fundamentally more problematic.

This occurs when companies give a costly resource to an employee which is not simply of any value to that employee, but which actually destroys value. This can be the case with providing office space. Not everyone wants to work from home, and not every job can be fulfilled at home. However, there are some people, like Stewart, who really value working from home and there are some jobs which can be fulfilled from home. By giving office accommodation to people who value home-working, the company not only has no benefit, but is also potentially destroying the engagement and performance of those individuals. Take the case of BT, where the senior team found that when they gave people an opportunity to work from home over 6,000 people took that opportunity. The wasted resources (in this case office accommodation) which they saved amounted to in excess of $300 million per year. But more importantly, as the team discovered, those people who valued home-working and were able to do so were more productive and engaged. The company had moved from a situation of wasted resource to a win–win solution.

The second error is the error of *low company cost/high employee value*. This is the error of missed win–win. There are some choices which are relatively low cost to the organization but which are of significant value to the individual. Many of the seven dimensions of variety fall into exactly that category. Opening up the internal market for jobs is relatively cost free for BP but enormously valuable to Greg Grimshaw. Enabling people to share jobs is a relatively cost free choice to the organization, but as BT found, can significantly increase the quality of the working lives of some people.

Understanding what employees value is crucial to the win–win solution. For the team at AstraZeneca, which modelled the choices made by employees, the real surprise was the extent to which employees differed. For example, the opportunity to buy time off with Holiday Choice differed markedly across employees. With Holiday Choice, over 30% of employees took the base, 30% flexed to the maximum, while the remainder spread across the days. Each employee has a unique reason why they had chosen to do this, and these reasons changed from year to year. Typically, in the first year employees made conservative choices, mirroring their previous packages. As they become more aware of their needs and knowledgeable about the options they realized how to derive value from their choices. For a young mother the package she chooses could be made up of £8,000 of retail vouchers, £6,000 of child care vouchers, £1,000 of pension and health care, a company bicycle, £8,000 of cash, and buy-out of the maximum ten days' holiday. For a young salesman with the same cash equivalent, the package could be £15,000 for the car of his dreams, £3,000 in retail vouchers and £7,000 in cash. By building learning relationship, these companies offered only and exactly what each individual employee needed and by doing so maximized the win–win solution.

Much of the relationship between the individual and the organization is framed either within the 'collective action' of Marx and Engels or the Schumpeterian vision of minimally engaged individuals. In the Democratic Enterprise we have an opportunity to build the engaged, participative adult-to-adult relationship which leads to win–win solutions.

Democratic enterprises are more just and fair

The value of the Democratic Enterprise is viscerally experienced through the engagement and alignment of citizens and the creation of win–win situations. Beneath both of these lies the third value of the Democratic Enterprise. The capacity to create and support justice and fairness.

Justice and fairness lie at the heart of the Democratic Enterprise. It is described in the first tenet: 'the relationship between the organization and the individual is adult-to-adult'; in the fourth tenet: 'individuals are able to participate in the determining the conditions of their association'; and in the fifth tenet: 'the liberty of some individuals is not at the expense of others'. As the democracy study shows, the capacity to deliver on justice and fairness differs markedly between the companies. But however difficult it is to deliver justice and fairness, the value of doing so is clear.

Justice and fairness matter to companies since they are one of the key drivers of employee engagement and agility. Typically we assess justice and fairness across three dimensions. The first termed *procedural justice* is a response to the question: 'Is the procedure fair?' Is the process itself, its mechanisms and rules actually fair and just? The second, termed *distributive justice*, is a response to the question: 'Is the distribution of resources arising from the procedure fair?' This distribution of resources could be the allocation of time, or the allocation of money or indeed other resources. The issue here is not the means by which allocation is made, but rather the results of allocation. What is the outcome for each individual? The final aspect of justice, termed *interactive justice*, again refers to the means rather than the ends. The question is: 'During the process am I treated in a dignified and just manner?' These concepts of justice and fairness have been much researched over the last decade and there is now a clear consensus on the role they play in organizations.[2] Specifically employees who believe they have been treated in an unfair or unjust manner are less committed and engaged, they are less likely to be innovative and are less inclined to work in an agile manner. Similarly, those who believe they have been treated with justice and dignity are more likely to be engaged and committed.

Justice and fairness is operationalized and built in the Democratic Enterprise primarily through the mechanism of choice. When we are given a choice before making a decision we perceive the process itself and the outcome we experience in a more positive way. The process could be the process of reward allocation; it could be the choice of mentors, or the choice of working arrangements.

For example, the choice we have on whether company stock options are included in our total remuneration package impacts on our perceptions of justice and ultimately our commitment to the company.[3] Specifically, if a choice of investment strategy is given, as is the case of AstraZeneca, then employees feel positive about the outcome, even in the event that the stock price falls. However, when there is no choice about the allocation of stock options, then employees feel aggrieved when the stock price falls. In the first case, choice is exercised and as a consequence people are prepared to live with the consequences of that choice, whatever the outcome. In the second case, choice is not exercised and so people feel powerless in the face of the outcome.

These single incidents of procedural unfairness (the individual was not given a choice) can have an impact far from the point of unfairness. Employees who believe they are treated badly in one situation generalize to another. Take the case of two research scientists at AstraZeneca. After the company merged they sat on opposite sides of an office and talked about car policy. It quickly became apparent that one research scientist has a significantly bigger and more luxurious car than the other. The second scientist felt aggrieved. It is clearly unfair. Although they sit in the same office and have the same job title, his colleague clearly gets a better deal. Interestingly, when it comes to feeling aggrieved, the past history of why this occurred (the other company traded cars for salary, for example) is not considered. The primary consideration is that at this point in time one car is bigger than the other. The research scientist with the smaller car is then inclined to generalize this feeling of injustice to other aspects of their working lives. The way performance is ranked may also be seen as unfair; or holiday entitlement is not as it should be. The psychological phenomenon underlying this is simple to understand. He has lost faith in the company, and the process of losing faith means they can no longer 'take for granted' what was previously taken for granted. Incidentally, as AstraZeneca found, the transparent giving of choice solved the car problem at a stroke. One scientist could still have a larger car, but the other would know that it was a matter of personal choice. As a result, he felt OK (perhaps a little smug even) that they made different choices. The point is this – be aware that one slip in creating one practice that is seen to be unfair can have much wider consequences.

Of the three aspects of justice and fairness it is the third aspect interactive justice that has the greatest impact on employee attitudes of commitment and engagement.[4] This refers to the way in which people perceive they are treated during processes, such as applying for a job, or discussing their performance with their manager, or negotiating a salary increase. These perceptions are crucial to an individual's beliefs about justice and fairness, and ultimately, to their engagement and commitment. People want to be treated with dignity and to feel that their voice and concerns have been heard. In essence, they want an adult-to-adult relationship, rather than a parent-to-child conversation. People who perceive they have been treated as children, or in a disrespectful manner, are less likely to pay back to the organization in terms of flexibility or involvement beyond the call of duty.

A major impediment to building choice and crafting democracy is a real concern on the part of management that it would open up a Pandora's box of unfairness – the choices of the strong would be made at the expense of the weak. In fact what we have observed is the opposite – that crafting democracy increases justice and fairness. Historically, companies have abounded with choice of a kind; the result of preferential, one-off side-deals struck between managers and their team members. Typically, these are based on power, politics and favouritism or the assertiveness of the employees.[5] In these side deals the criteria of deal making was opaque, the rules of engagement rarely communicated, and the outcomes unclear. This creates perceptions of injustice and unfairness to those excluded from them.

By building choice, creating transparency and making the rules clear, these companies are eliminating many of the aspects of unfairness and injustice. They increase procedural fairness because the procedures of choice inevitably bring transparency and information. As HR Director, Malcolm Hurrell, remarks:

> 'At AstraZeneca building transparency has in one stroke removed all unfairness. For example, everyone gets the same total amount of holiday. So there are no side deals to be made. People see the processes as fair. Every employee has the same rules, the same 18 options, the same process of selection and the same transparency of information. Anyone can log online and model a set of scenarios that are similar to their colleagues or completely different.'

The freedom to choose has a positive impact on distributive justice because people make active choices about the distribution of resources. For example, in the BT engineering teams an engineer with a lower bonus does not feel aggrieved about the way BT is distributing bonuses since he had the choice to increase his bonus, but decided instead to take time rather than money. And finally, choice impacts on interactive justice because the very process of giving choice moves the relationship from parent/child, to adult/adult. So at McKinsey, for example, the developmental discussions take place in a context of full knowledge about the individual, about mentors and coaches and about possible projects. These types of discussions shift the axis of maturity and responsibility firmly to the shoulder of the employee.

The fundamental value proposition of the Democratic Enterprise is that employees are more committed and aligned with the organization, more capable of entering into win–win solutions and more capable of operating in a just and fair manner. But what is the impact on the bottom-line of the company? As the democratic study showed, the two companies that are most democratic are also financially successful. Both HP and Kraft Foods have outperformed many of their competitors over the last decade. I believe that there are two over-riding reasons why this is the case: the Democratic Enterprise is more agile, and the Democratic Enterprise is more able to grow through integration.

Democratic enterprises are more agile

Autonomous, insightful employees working in a context of variety and with a shared sense of purpose collectively create agile, adaptive organizations. They are responsive to the first signs of changes in the operating environment and are able to adapt and respond to the information. Consider Greg at BP and his interest in working in Azerbaijan. With the information about the future business trends and purpose he received in BP's regional briefings, Greg was able to identify the strategic importance of Azerbaijan for oil exploration. On the basis of this information he began to look for opportunities in the region and applied for jobs as they arose. At the same time other colleagues with access to similar information and a similar sense of purpose were taking similar action. So when the Azerbaijan fields became productive many skilled professionals were able to 'flock' there. As a consequence, BP was able to focus talented people rapidly in this crucial region. Remember there was no corporate edict illuminated the path to Azerbaijan. Neither Rodney Chase or John Browne manipulated the reward structures of the company or commanded people to move to the region. Instead it was more like a flock of independent professionals acting independently using organizational purpose and information as a compass for their choice of direction.

In these examples of companies behaving in a democratic manner we have seen many such instances of agility. How might we understand this agility? Consider the way in which associates at McKinsey search for and find projects; the engineers at BT agree a time schedule which covers over 3,000 people; geologists at BP find their next job; or working mothers at HP develop a rhythm of time and location. In each of these situations these people are operating within what has been termed 'open systems' in which there is much variety and they have wide latitude of discretion.

The mechanisms of agility are numerous. For example, what happens in some of these situations is what could be termed small wins.[6] As we saw, the BT engineering team in Cardiff learned how to negotiate a collective working schedule with their parallel team in Bangalore in India. By doing so they made small incremental adjustments to their day-to-day working which enabled their collective performance to increase. At the same time, managers at BT were experimenting with working from home and working from the office. At first the technology was not in place, but as it developed they too had small wins and were able to rapidly adapt in a manner which suited them as much as their clients. Or consider how Matthius Oberholzer at McKinsey was able to move rapidly when he saw an opportunity in the sports client segment to rapidly developing his own knowledge, while building up the collective knowledge base.

In each of these companies agility was created in part because people made choices, and there was sufficient variety from which they could choose. Variety is crucial since in the complex environment in which these companies operate, major changes are harder to control. They typically entail the simultaneous manipulation of so many variables that one must strain to learn anything from experiences. The environment in many instances is changing faster than major planned change attempts. It would take huge, and probably undeliverable, corporate change programmes to specify the career trajectories for everyone at BP, or indeed to create a controlled process of project allocation at McKinsey.

The alternative, which we can see across these companies, is to enable small, incremental changes to take place by many people, in many locations. By doing so people learn rapidly what works, and what does not work, they allow exploitation, exploration and learning.[7] Although there is a tangible outcome, the meaning and significance of that outcome are not fixed. By becoming free to choose and operating in a situation of variety employees have the opportunity to uncover new opportunities, and breach old assumptions. These small steps were experiments, diverse rather than homogeneous explorations, providing learning and basic momentum. Each person we saw making choices did so individually. Yet within a context of rich information and a sense of shared purpose they began to act as a flock and to adapt more rapidly to changing circumstances. Through the exercise of choice these individuals become agile, both individually and collectively.[8]

Democratic enterprises are more able to integrate

Organizations growth primarily occurs along two major axes. The first is the axis of mergers and acquisitions; the second is the axis of innovation through integration. For both growth strategies the integration capabilities of the Democratic Enterprise is well positioned to deliver.

For many of these pioneer companies building a shared and transparent platform of variety was a crucial part of their merger and integration strategy.[9] When BP's John Browne decided to invest over $100 million in creating a global platform for employees to access job and project opportunities his aspirations were clear, 'Everyone in BP, regardless of their company legacy, could plug-in and be part of the same global operating systems.' This meant integrating over 150 legacy payrolls and 275 intranet sites, heritage from BP, and the four companies with which it had merged over the preceding five years. Only then was BP able to leverage the technology to bring the opportunity of choice to all of its 160,000 employees.

Integration was also a key driver for choice at AstraZeneca. Zeneca demerged from ICI in 1993 and merged with the Swedish-based firm Astra in 1999. Consolidating the two companies created real inequalities – for example, two scientists, sitting in the same office, could have very different car and holiday allowances. As HR Director, Malcolm Hurrell, recalls:

> 'Those who had worked for Astra believed the Zeneca scientists had a better deal – and those who worked for Zeneca believed the Astra scientists had a better deal. The reality was that if you looked at the total package they were roughly the same.'

Post-merger negotiations about car policies and pensions take a disproportionate amount of management time, with limited payback. And even after this management time, there is inevitably suspicion that one group came off better than the others. Hurrell's experience with previous mergers had taught him that merging two remuneration strategies can be costly as inevitably the higher pension or allowances are the new standard. As a consequence, the cost of merging remuneration plans has been calculated to increase payroll costs from 10% to 15%.

Like John Browne at BP, AstraZeneca CEO, Tom McKillop, saw the opportunity to bring choice and transparency as a major integration lever. His strategy was to create an industry-leading package, integrating terms and conditions of employment while protecting the legacy arrangements. To do this, the new remuneration process, launched on the heels of the merger in April 1999, was built on transparency and equal access to choice. The cash equivalent for every employee (called 'The Advantage Fund Statement') was calculated to give an underlying logic that was open and understandable to all. By doing so, a shared baseline for choice was rapidly created. Next, the same 18 options were available to all employees. The mechanisms to build employee understanding of the choices available to them were rapidly rolled out across all the parts of the merged company. A half-day pension workshop, education packages and phone lines, all created a platform of shared experiences regardless of an individual's heritage. Employees rapidly learned that they could make choices that reflected their aspirations and personal circumstances, not their company heritage. By doing so, the company was able to reduce the cost of mergers from the normal 10% to 15% of payroll, to 2% of payroll in the first year, and zero in the second year, as the initial start-up costs were absorbed and the scheme became self-financing. From an employee perspective, the advanced financial planning available to them, combined with their greater knowledge of the options and choices, increased the actual value of their total remuneration package by 5%.

At Unisys University the open choice of training was a key driver in the re-integration of functional and industry groups. While the matrix structure may have made sense from a measurement and accountability perspective, it created an unprecedented level of competition and bad blood between the business units. Recall Ettie McCormack's words, 'The business structure was encouraging territorialism – "my business unit made this investment, so I am not sharing it".' Creating a common platform of choice enabled them to use a common training vocabulary to create a language of competencies and skills capable of directly linking the content and the competencies of roles and activities across all the businesses. The full value of mergers is rarely realized for a variety of reasons including mutual suspicion and lack of rapid sharing of knowledge. By creating transparent platforms of choice these companies moved rapidly into a high productive mode.

The tenets of the Democratic Enterprise and the three building blocks create a structure to grasp the organizational possibilities that are tantalizingly within our reach. The democracy study illustrates that for some companies democracy is indeed tantalizingly within their reach, while for others the journey to democracy will be longer. The challenge is primarily the challenge of creating variety. Of building space for people to act and freedom for them to choose. Yet as BT, BP, Goldman Sachs and others have shown, it is indeed possible to create space and it is indeed possible to build freedom.

We have seen that the term Democratic Enterprise does not have to be an oxymoron – a company can be both democratic *and* economically viable. The Democratic Enterprise is far from being an oxymoron; rather each reinforces the other.

Should this be the primary reason for adopting the six tenets? Invariably from the investor community this has to be a primary reason. But for the employee community the possibilities of democracy are the possibilities of creating lives of meaning and lives of sustainable productivity. Lack of personal autonomy, restricted choice and vague mis-aligned organizational purpose has a corrosive effect on us all. As we enter an era in which we live longer and can expect to work for the majority of our lives we must build organizations which are capable of bringing us joy and meaning. If we cannot do this then we condemn the majority of people, for a majority of their life, to corrosion and distress.

But beyond the realms of the financial community and the employee community I believe there is an overarching reason why those of us employed in large companies should question whether the six tenets could be even more fully realized. Organizations are increasingly becoming as important in our lives as the states of which we are citizens. Many of the companies we have considered such as BP, BT, Kraft Foods, Goldman Sachs have a global footprint and opportunity for influencing the lives of many millions of people. Large companies, particularly multinational companies have a crucial and exemplary role to play in our societies. Much has been made of the role they play in the environment, particularly in sustaining and destroying environment resources. More should now be made of their role in sustaining and destroying human resources. The tenets of the Democratic Enterprise have the potential to create a blueprint against which this role can be evaluated and described.

This is a particularly crucial issue as state democracy evolves. State democracy has indeed become the preferred governance structure of an increasing number of countries around the world. At the same time, the foundations of state democracy are being rocked by powerful lobby groups, by misinformation and in some nations, by an increasingly cynical and disaffected citizenship. As the political theorist, David Held, concludes his own examination of state democracy: 'The explosion of interest in democracy: in recent times has all too often . . . assumed that democracy can only be applied to "government affairs", and presupposed that the nation-state is the most appropriate locus for democracy' (p. 359). He was addressing the idea of widening the aperture of democracy to include the relationships across nation-states. But perhaps we can also narrow the aperture. To see organizations as potentially fertile ground for the seeds of democracy to flourish, at a time when many of the flowers of nation-state democracy appear to be wilting.

Notes

Preface

1 de Tocqueville, A., *Democracy in America*, two volumes. London: Fontana, 1968.

2 For an insight into these three contemporary thinkers see, for example: Bennis, W., *Managing the Dream: Reflections on Leadership and Change*. New York: Perseus Publishing, 2000; Drucker, P., *Post-Capitalist Society*. New York: Harper Business, 1993; Handy, C., *The Hungry Spirit*. New York: Broadway Books, 1998.

3 For an overview of the democratic ideals in ancient Athens see, for example, Held, D., *Models of Democracy*. Cambridge: Polity Press, 1996.

4 Mill, J.S., 'Considerations on Representative Government' in Acton, H.B. (ed.), *Utilitarianism, Liberty, and Representative Government*, London: Dent, 1951.

5 See, for example, Weber, M., *The Protestant Ethic and the Spirit of Capitalism*. London: Allen and Unwin, 1971. Schumpeter, J., *Capitalism, Socialism and Democracy*. London: Allen and Unwin, 1976.

Chapter one

1 For an overview of participative practices and some of the challenges of embedding these principles see, for example, McLagon, P. and Nel, C., *The Age of Participation*. San Francisco: Berrett-Koehler, 1995 and 1997.

2 For descriptions of democracy in relatively small companies see, for example, Leadbeater, C., *The Weightless Society*. New York and London: Texere, 2000 and Law, A., *Creative Company: How St. Lukes Became the 'Ad Agency to End All Ad Agencies'*. John Wiley and Sons, 1999.

3 Perhaps the most widely celebrated charismatic founder of a Democratic Enterprise is Ricardo Semler of Semco. For an insight into this thinking see, Semler, R., *Maverick! The Success Story Behind the World's Most Unusual Workplace*. Random House, 2001.

Chapter two

1 The proposition that the ancient Greek democracy has implications for the modern corporation has been explored by Manville, B. and Ober, J. in *Company of Citizens: What the World's First Democracy Teaches Leaders about Creating Great Organizations*. Boston: Harvard Business School Press, 2002.

2 Held, D., *Models of Democracy*, Cambridge: Polity Press, 1996, p. xi.

3 See Lively, J., *Democracy*. Oxford: Blackwell, 1975.

4 This Pericles quote is cited in Held's 1996 book, p. 17.

5 See Pericles' Funeral Oration, in Thucydides, *The Peloponnesian War*, trans. Rex Warner, New York: Viking Penguin, 1972.

6 See Manville, B. and Ober, J., *Company of Citizens: What the World's First Democracy Teaches Leaders about Creating Great Organizations*, Boston: Harvard Business School Press, 2002, p. 95.

7 Mill, J.S., 'Considerations on Representative Government' in Acton, H.B. (ed.), *Utilitarianism, Liberty, and Representative Government,* London: Dent, 1951.

8 See Marx, K. and Engels, F., *The Communist Manifesto* in *Selected Works*, vol. 1. Moscow: Progress Publishers, 1969.

9 See Polan, A.J., *Lenin and the End of Politics*. London: Methuen, 1984.

10 For an insightful overview of the thinking of Joseph Schumpeter, see Heilbroner, R., *The Worldly Philosophers*. New York: Simon and Schuster, 1953 or Schumpeter, J., *Capitalism, Socialism and Democracy*. London: Allen and Unwin, 1976.

11 Douglas McGregor's immensely popular book *The Human Side of Enterprise* (London: Penguin, 1987) posed the mechanistic concept of authority (Theory X) against the humanistic, relationship view of business (Theory Y). See also William Whyte's seminal work, *Organizational Man*. New York: Simon and Schuster, 1956.

12 The rise of the notion of people as 'interchangeable parts' was the basis of the construction of jobs in the first automated assembly lines. See, for example, Crozier, M., *The Bureaucratic Phenomena*. London: Tavistock, 1964, for a deeper description of the genesis and impact of this stance.

13 This book represents one step in a long line of scholars who have attempted to play out some of the tenets of state democracy within the context of contemporary knowledge-based organizations. See, for example, Ackoff, R., *The Democratic Corporation*. New York: Oxford University Press, 1994; Bennis, W. and Slater, P., 'Democracy is Inevitable' in *The Temporary Society: What Is Happening to Business and Family Life in America Under the Impact of*

Accelerating Change. San Francisco: Jossey Bass, 1998. Warren Bennis returns to ponder his initial thoughts on democracy in *Managing the Dream: Reflections on Leadership and Change.* New York: Perseus Publishing, 2000; while Robert Putnam, takes an essential social capital view in *Making Democracy Work*, Princeton: Princeton University Press, 1993. For a view of how the democracy of ancient Greece can have modern implications see Manville, B. and Ober, J., *Company of Citizens: What the World's First Democracy Teaches Leaders about Creating Great Organizations*, Boston: Harvard Business School Press, 2002.

14 This criterion presupposes an understanding of the 'current state' from which a notion of viability can be described. In the third chapter an analysis of the 'current state' in a representative number of companies is described.

15 Much of the writing on the participate element of democracy does not meet the criteria of practicality. While I believe participate decision making is a legitimate aspiration, our research suggests that it is very far from practicality in most company. For a view of the possible mechanisms of participative democracy in contemporary organizations see, for example, McLagan, P. and Nel, C., *The Age of Participation.* San Francisco: Berrett-Koehler Publishers, 1995 and 1997; Purser, R.E. and Cabana, S., *The Self-Managing Organization.* New York: Free Press, 1998; Greenberg, E.S., *Workplace Democracy: The Political Effects of Participation.* Ithaca, NY: Cornell University Press, 1986.

16 The possible workings of participative democracy founded on ancient Athens is compellingly described in Manville, B. and Ober, J., *Company of Citizens: What The World's First Democracy Teaches Leaders about Creating Great Organizations.* Boston: Harvard Business School Press, 2002.

17 This form of democracy is described at length in ch. 9 of Held, D., *Models of Democracy.* Cambridge: Polity Press, 1996.

18 John Stuart Mill believed that it was the combination of liberty and democracy that created the greatest possibility for what he termed 'human excellence' see, for example, Mill, J.S., 'Considerations on Representative Government' in Acton, H.B. (ed.), *Utilitarianism, Liberty, and Representative Government,* London: Dent, 1951.

19 The categorization of parent/child and adult/adult is drawn directly from psycho-dynamics. See, for example, Harris, T.A., *I'm OK, You're OK.* London: Arrow, 1995.

20 This was the view described by Marx in Marx, K. and Engels, F., *The Communist Manifesto* in *Selected Works*, vol. 1. Moscow: Progress Publishers, 1969.

21 The significant differences associated with the knowledge-based economy and the organizations operating within it have been described by many. See, for example, Nonaka, I. and Takeuchi, H., *The Knowledge Creating Company*. New York: Oxford University Press, 1995 and more recently Eisenhardt, K.M. and Santos, F.M., 'Knowledge-Based View: A New Theory of Strategy?' in Pettigrew, A., Thomas, H. and Whittington, R. (eds), *Handbook of Strategy and Management*, pp. 139–64. London: Sage Publications, 2002 and Cairncross, F., *The Company of the Future: How the Communications Revolution Is Changing Management*. Boston: Harvard Business School Press, 2002.

22 This notion of the asset and investor has been developed and described in Gratton, L. and Ghoshal, S., 'Managing Personal Human Capital: New Ethos for the "Volunteer" Employee', *European Management Journal*, 21 (2003): 1–10.

23 The changing nature of the relationship between the individual and the organization has been described by a number of commentators, see, Cappelli, P., *The New Deal at Work: Managing the Market-Driven Workforce*. Boston: Harvard Business School Press, 1999.

24 Much of my thinking about individual autonomy comes from Jung's beliefs on the subject of the individual and the journey they take. Jung's concept of individuation is described by Edward Edinger in *The Creation of the Consciousness: Jung's Myth of Modern Man*. Toronto: Inner City Books, 1984. For the original see Jung's psychological factors in 'Human Behavior, The Structure and Dynamics of the Psyche', *The Collected Works*, Vol. 8, Princeton: Princeton University Press, 1953–79. My own thinking has been enormously enriched by the work of the Jungian analyst James Hollis. All of his books bring insight to Jung's work, but perhaps most thought provoking is *Swamplands of the Soul: New Life in Dismal Places*. Toronto: Inner City Books, 1996. I used the metaphor of the 'swamplands' to describe aspects of Nina's story. James Hillman has also acutely observed the world through the Jungian lens, see e.g., *The Soul's Code*. New York: Random House, 1996. The political philosopher, Anthony Giddens, has made a connection between Jung, and autonomy and democracy, from the perspective of modern relationships, in *The Transformation of Intimacy: Sexuality, Love and Eroticism in modern societies*. Stanford: Stanford University Press, 1992.

25 See Schumpeter, J., *Capitalism, Socialism and Democracy*. London: Allen and Unwin, 1976.

26 See Mill, J.S., 'Considerations on Representative Government' in Acton, H.B. (ed.), *Utilitarianism, Liberty, and Representative Government*. London: Dent, 1951.

27 The concept of 'rights' and 'duties' has been a central aspect of the debate on the nature of democracy. See, for example, the debate in Burnheim, J., *Is Democracy Possible?* Cambridge: Polity Press, 1985.

28 There is a growing literature on accountabilities and obligations. For an overview of the foundational issues, see e.g. Etzioni, A., 'The Responsive Community: A Communitarian Perspective', *American Sociological Review*, 61 (1996): 1–11.

29 We return at length to this issue of accountabilities and obligations later in the book. Much of my thinking on the topic evolved from interacting with the companies of the three citizens and from scholarly work on the nature of the relationship between individuals in organizations, see e.g. Burt, R.S., *Structural Holes: The Social Structure of Competition.* Cambridge, MA: Harvard University Press, 1992; Coleman, J.S., *Foundations of Social Theory Cambridge*, MA: Harvard University Press, 1990; and Granovetter, M.S., 'Economic Action and Social Structure: The Problem of Embeddedness', *American Journal of Sociology*, 1985, 91 (1985): 481–510.

Chapter three

1 This democracy data was collected as a sub-set of a larger research endeavour called The Leading Edge Research Consortium. The findings from the 1994 and 1997 study are described in Gratton, L., Hope Hailey, V., Stiles, P. and Truss, C., *Strategic Human Resource Management: Corporate Rhetoric and Human Reality*, Oxford: Oxford University Press, 1999.

2 See Marx, K. and Engels, F., *The Communist Manifesto* in *Selected Works*, vol. 1. Moscow: Progress Publishers, 1969.

3 Mill, J.S., 'Considerations on Representative Government' in Acton, H.B. (ed.), *Utilitarianism, Liberty, and Representative Government*, London: Dent, 1951.

4 Schumpeter, J.A., *The Theory of Economic Development: An Inquiry into Profits, Capital, Credit, Interest and the Business Cycle.* Cambridge, MA: Harvard University Press, 1934, 1962.

5 Held, D., *Models of Democracy*, Cambridge: Polity Press, 1996.

6 Personal autonomy is a crucial prerequisite to self-esteem and to learning. See, for example, Ryan, R.M. and Deci, E.L., 'Self Determination Theory and Facilitation of Intrinsic Motivation, Social Development, and Well Being', *American Psychologist* (1) 2000, 69–78.

7 These various organizational forms have been described by a number of

commentators. For an overview of the machine bureacracy see Mintzberg, H., *The Structuring of Organizations: A Synthesis of Research.* Englewood Cliffs, NJ: Prentice Hall, 1979. For a broader view of organizational studies see Katz, D. and Kahn, R.L., *The Social Psychology of Organizations.* 2nd edn, New York: McGraw Hill, 1970.

Chapter four

1 The pressures for democracy have been described by a number of commentators. The primary pressure is seen to be the rise of the knowledge economy. Warren Bennis and Philip Slater describe what they call the 'reinforcing factors' in their enormously insightful piece, published initially in the *Harvard Business Review* in 1964 and reprinted in 'Democracy is Inevitable' in *The Temporary Society: What Is Happening to Business and Family Life in America Under the Impact of Accelerating Change.* San Francisco: Jossey Bass, 1998.

2 Average hours of work for pay in the US have risen significantly from 1979 until 1999 by a factor of almost three and a half weeks. *Report on the American Workforce,* Washington, DC: US Department of Labor, 1999.

3 For a review of the experience of successful women, see Carr, N., Cliffe, S., Champion, D. and Collingwood, H., 'The Choices That Confine Us', *Harvard Business Review,* 80 (2002): 10.

4 There is a growing body of evidence to suggest that the experiences of BT are mirrored in many other organizations. The *Catalyst Studies* reports that 80% of participants had increases in morale when working part-time or telecommuting; 46% reported productivity gains; 48% reported increased commitment, *A New Approach to Flexibility: Managing the Work/Time Equation,* New York: Catalyst, 2000.

5 Reich, R., *The Future of Success: Working and Living in the New Economy.* New York: Random House, 2000.

6 In the US, for example, 30% of Generation Y are minorities, 25% grew up in single-family households, 75% had a working mother, in Wolburg, J. and Pokrywczynski, J., 'A Psychological Analysis of Generation Y', *Journal of Advertising Research,* 41 (2001): 33–45.

7 See, for example, Loughlin, C. and Barling, J., 'Young Workers' Work Values, Attitudes and Behaviours', *British Journal of Occupational and Organizational Psychology,* 74 (2001): 543–58.

8 Cates, K. and Rahimi, K., *Financial Times,* 19 November 2001.

9 These profound changes in the work structures have been a central theme in the writing of Charles Handy, see in particular *The Hungry Spirit*, London: Hutchinson, 1997.

10 Much of this insight on the potential impact of the technology of 'bundling' on the creation of choice and variety is taken from the earlier impact of technology on mass customization. For an overview of this, see for example, Gilmore, J. and Pine, B.J., *Markets of One: Creating Customer-Unique Value through Mass Customization*. Boston, MA: Harvard Business School Press, 1988.

11 Christensen, C., *The Innovators Dilemma*. Boston: Harvard Business School Press, 1997.

12 The impact of technology on the way we work has been described by a number of contemporary commentators. The case for the impact of technology and the creation of the freelance, autonomous worker has been made by Pink, D. in *Free Agent Nation: How America's New Independent Workers are Transforming the Way We Live*. New York: Warner Books, 2001; while the wider impact of technology has been described by Chandler, A., Jr. and Cortada, J., *A Nation transformed by Information: How Information Has Shaped the United States from Colonial Times to the Present*. Oxford: Oxford University Press, 2000; and by Grantham, C., *The Future of Work: The Promise of the New Digital Work Society*. New York: McGraw-Hill, 2000.

13 *Into the Future*. February 2000 vision paper prepared by the American Society for Training and Development (ASTD).

14 Morris, S. and Johnson McManus, D., 'Information Infrastructure Centrality in the Agile Organization', *Information Systems Management*, 19 (2002): 8–11.

15 See, for example, Walker, A.J. (ed.), *Web-Based Human Resources*. New York: McGraw-Hill, 2001.

Chapter five

1 This model was first described in Gratton, L. and Ghoshal, S., 'Managing Personal Human Capital: New Ethos for the "Volunteer" Employee', *European Management Journal*, 21 (2003): 1–10.

2 Of the vast amount of literature on this topic, I have found the books by Quinn (Quinn, J.B., *Intelligent Enterprise*. New York: Free Press, 1992) and Nonaka and Takeuchi (Nonaka, I. and Takeuchi, H., *The Knowledge Creating Company*. New York: Oxford University Press, 1995) to be the most insight-

ful from a practical point of view, and the article by Spender (Spender, J.C., 'Making Knowledge the Basis of a Dynamic Theory of the Firm', *Strategic Management Journal*, 17 (1996): 45–62) as a useful contribution and idea review.

3 Polanyi, M., *The Tacit Dimension*. Garden City, NY: Doubleday, 1967.

4 Argyris, C. and Schon, D.A., *Theory in Practice: Increasing Professional Effectiveness*. San Francisco: Jossey Bass, 1992.

5 The issue of the additive nature of intellectual capital has been debated at length. Simon, for example, argues that knowledge is the learning of individual members, or the ingesting of new members who have knowledge that the organizaion doesn't previously have. However, with the rise of the theories of social capital it is now apparent that the social network is itself a creator of knowledge, and that learning is inextricably located in the complex collaborative social practices. Simon, H.A., 'Bounded Rationality and Organizational Learning', *Organizational Science*, 2 (1991): 125–34.

6 See, for example, the research on communities of practice, Brown, J.S. and Duguid, P., *The Social Life of Information*. Boston: Harvard Business School Press, 2000 and Weick, K.E. and Roberts, K.H., 'Collective Mind in Organizations: Heedful Interrelating in Flight Decks', *Administrative Science Quarterly*, 38 (1993): 357–81.

7 We return to the context of facilitating learning, but for a detailed analysis of the relationship between intellectual and social capital see Nahapiet, J.E., *Towards a Theory of Dynamic Firm: Knowledge, Learning and Social Relationships*. Unpublished doctoral thesis, University of London, 2003. For a focused overview of her thinking see Nahapiet, J.E. and Ghoshal, S., 'Social Capital, Intellectual Capital and the Organizational Advantage', *Academy of Management Review*, 23 (1998): 242–66.

8 What I have termed here 'emotional capital' borrows from disparate literature streams. At the individual level the notion of emotional intelligence has been described by Goleman (Goleman, D., *Emotional Intelligence*. New York: Bantam, 1995) and earlier by Salovey and Mayer (Salovey, P. and Mayer, J.D., 'Emotional Intelligence Imagination', *Cognition and Personality*, 9 (1980): 185–211) and loosely defined as the ability to monitor one's own and others' feelings and emotions. It is described as essentially individual and partly innate. By emotional capital I have broadened the concept to include integrity, to understand the emotions of others and to acknowledge and be sincere about one's own emotions (Hochschild, L.E., *The Managed Heart: Commercialization of Human Feeling*. Berkeley, CA: University of California Press, 1983). This also includes an action element, the capacity to

move into action through will and hope (Brockner, J., 'Managing the Effects of Layoffs on Survivors', *California Management Review*, 1 (1992): 9–27.

9 This relationship between emotion and action has been described by Bruch, H. and Ghoshal, S. in *Building a Bias For Action*. Boston: Harvard Business School Press (in press); see also Ghoshal, S. and Bruch, H., 'Beyond Motivation to Volition: Unleashing the Power of the Human Will', *Sloan Management Review*, 44 (2003): 51–7.

10 This is what has been termed 'learned helplessness', which reflects an individual's subjective feeling that his or her destiny is being determined from outside. Seligman, M., *Learned Helplessness*. San Francisco: Freeman, 1975.

11 This relationship between motivation and individual traits including self-awareness has emerged as a strong relationship in a number of studies. See, for example, Deci, E.L., *Why We Do What We Do: Understanding Self-Motivation*. New York: Putnam, 1995 and Thomas, K.W., *Intrinsic Motivation at Work: Building Energy and Commitment*. San Francisco: Berrett-Koehler, 2000.

12 Uncovering what is invisible to the self, but apparent to others is seen as a key plank to motivated behaviour. See Janis, I.L. and Mann, L., *Decision Making: A Psychological Analysis of Conflict, Choice and Commitment*. New York: Free Press, 1977.

13 The term 'social capital' initially appeared in the context of community studies, highlighting the central importance of the networks of strong, cross-cutting personal relationships for the survival and functioning of city neighbourhoods. Since this early usage, this concept has been applied to elucidate a wide range of social phenomena (see Coleman, J.S., 'Social Capital in the Creation of Human Capital', *American Journal of Sociology*, 94 (1998): 95–120) but on economic performance of companies (see Baker, W., 'Market Networks and Corporate Behavior', *American Journal of Sociology*, 96 (1990): 589–625), geographic regions (Putnam, R.D., 'Bowling Alone: America's Declining Social Capital', *Journal of Democracy*, 6 (1995): 65–78) and nations (Fukuyama, F., *Trust: Social Virtues and the Creation of Prosperity*, Hamish Hamilton: London, 1995).

14 The impact of trust, trustworthiness and authenticity in the creation of strong relationships and hence, social capital has been explored by Fukuyama, F., *Trust: Social Virtues and the Creation of Prosperity*. London: Hamish and Hamilton, 1995 and Putnam, R.D., 'The Prosperous Community: Social Capital and Public Life', *American Prospect*, 13 (1993): 35–42.

15 This is the notion of structural and relational embeddedness, which concerns the properties of the social system and the network of relations as a

whole. Strong and weak network ties are described by Granovetter, M.S., 'Problems of Explanation in Economic Sociology, in Nohria, N. and Eccles, R. (eds), *Networks and Organizations: Structure, Form and Action*. Boston, MA: Harvard Business School Press, 1992.

16 The individual level concept of self-monitoring as a antecedent to the creation of social capital has been described by Mehra, A., Kilduff, M. and Brass, D.J., 'The Social Networks of High and Low Self-Monitors: Implications for Workplace Performance', *Administrative Science Quarterly*, 46 (2001): 121–46.

17 For a detailed description of the impact of strong and weak network ties see Burt, R.S., *Structural Holes: Social Structure of Competition*. Cambridge, MA: Harvard University Press, 1992.

18 However, these richer, tighter patterns of relationship networks are important where the meaning of information is uncertain and ambiguous or where the parties to the exchange differ in their prior knowledge. See, for example, Cohen, W.M. and Levinthal, D.A., 'Absorptive Capacity: A New Perspective on Learning and Innovation', *Administrative Science Quarterly*, 35 (1990): 28–152.

19 Weak network ties are described by, Granovetter, M.S., 'Problems of Explanation in Economic Sociology', in Nohria, N. and Eccles, R. (eds), *Networks and Organizations: Structure, Form and Action*. Boston, MA: Harvard Business School Press, 1992.

20 Burt, R.S., *Structural Holes: The Social Structure of Competition*. Cambridge, MA: Harvard University Press, 1992.

21 The link between individual emotional resilience and organizational resilience have been made by a number of scholars, see e.g. Tushman, M. and O'Reilly, C., 'Ambidextrous Organization: Managing Evolutionary and Revolutionary Change', *California Management Review*, 38 (1996): 8–30.

22 Personal autonomy is a crucial prerequisite to self-esteem and to learning. See e.g. Ryan, R.M. and Deci, E.L., 'Self Determination Theory and Facilitation of Intrinsic Motivation, Social Development, and Well Being', *American Psychologist*, 1 (2000), 69–78.

23 Kholb, D., *Experiential Learning*. Englewood Cliffs, NJ: Prentice Hall, 1984.

24 Bandura, A., 'Social Cognitive Theory of Self Regulation', *Organizational Behavior and Human Decision Processes*, 50 (1991): 248–87.

25 The feeling of personal mastery is key. People are more likely to work to their optimal performance if they believe they are capable of achieving the task. Alternatively, even if they are capable, if they believe they are not able to perform the task then this will significantly diminish their performance. See, for

example, Phillips, J.M. and Gully, S.M., 'Role of Goal Orientation, Ability, Need for Achievement, and Locus of Control in the Self-Efficacy and Goal-Setting Process', *Journal of Applied Psychology*, 82 (1997): 792–802.

26 The motivation Nina was demonstrating has been termed intrinsic motivation; it came from within her. Her feelings of intrinsic motivation were key to her believing she could fulfil her potential. For an overview of intrinsic motivation see, for example, Deci, E.L., *Why We Do What We Do: Understanding Self-Motivation*. New York: Putnam, 1995 and Thomas, K.W., *Intrinsic Motivation at Work: Building Energy and Commitment*. San Francisco: Berrett-Koehler, 2000.

27 Individuals' belief about their ability to make decisions, termed self-efficacy, has information giving as an important plank. Appelbaum, S.H. and Hare, A., 'Self-Efficacy as a Mediator of Goal Setting and Performance: Some Human Resource Implications', *Journal of Managerial Psychology*, 11 (1996): 33–47.

28 The framing of much of this description of self-awareness and autonomy comes from the Jungian perspective of self-development. For a useful overview of this, see Hollis, J., *The Eden Project: In Search of the Magical Other: A Jungian Perspective on Relationship*, Toronto: Inner City Books, 1998. For a description of the defence mechanisms described by Sigmund Freud see *The Future of an Illusion*. New York: W.W. Norton and Co., 1961. For an analysis of the 'swamplands' see Hollis, J., *Swamplands of the Soul: New Life in Dismal Places*. Toronto: Inner City Books, 1996.

29 The studies on bereavement show that these are fairly predictable stages from loss; denial and isolation, anger, bargaining and acceptance. See, for example, Kubler-Ross, E., *On Death and Dying*. New York: Collier Books, 1969.

30 My description of 'reflexivity' owes much to political philosopher Anthony Giddens' description of reflexivity in relationships which he describes in *The Transformation of Intimacy: Sexuality, Love and Eroticism in Modern Societies*. Stanford: Stanford University Press, 1992. His analysis of the modern relationship has many interesting and potentially insightful parallels of the modern relationship between the individual and the organization. Some of the threads in this work are pulled into his book *Modernity and Self-Identity*. Cambridge: Polity, 1991.

31 'Talking partners' are an enormously important part of the development of self-awareness and ultimately of autonomy. Their role is described in Theodore Zeldin's analysis of the topic: *Conversation: How Talk Can Change Your Life*. London: The Harvill Press, 1988.

32 This network of friends are what we earlier referred to as 'tight networks', Granovetter, M.S., 'Problems of Explanation in Economic Sociology, in Nohria, N. and Eccles, R. (eds), *Networks and Organizations: Structure, Form and Action*. Boston, MA: Harvard Business School Press, 1992.

33 I have described the importance of conversation and the combination of rational and emotional conversation in Gratton, L. and Ghoshal, S., 'Improving the Quality of Conversation', *Organizational Dynamics*: 31 (2003): 209–23.

34 Life stages have been an important way of looking at the unfolding of the model of self. This analysis of Nina's life stages is based on Levinson, D.J. in collaboration with Darrow, C.N., Klein, E.B., Levinson, M.H. and McKee, B., *The Seasons of a Man's Life*. New York: Knopf, 1978. The importance of having a concrete 'model' or 'vision' of the future has been described by Bandura, A., 'Human Agency in Social Cognitive Theory', *American Psychologist*, 9 (1989): 1175–84.

35 These possible courses of action are described by Pulley, M.L., *Losing Your Job: Reclaiming Your Soul*. San Francisco: Jossey Bass, 1997.

36 Weick, K., 'The Collapse of Sensemaking in Organizations: The Mann Gulch Disaster', *Administrative Science Quarterly*, 38 (1993): 628–52.

37 Maury Peiperl has described the paradoxes in 'Getting 360° Feedback Right', *Harvard Business Review*, 79 (2001): 142–7.

38 The developmental impact of positive feedback has been described by Appelbaum, S.H. and Hare, A., 'Self-Efficacy as a Mediator of Goal Setting and Performance: Some Human Resource Implications', *Journal of Managerial Psychology*, 11 (1996): 33–47. There is much evidence that the emotions associated with receiving negative feedback can reduce the capacity to move into action. For a review see Quy Nguyen Huy, 'Emotional Balancing of Organizational Continuity and Radical Change. The Contribution of Middle Managers', *Administrative Science Quarterly*, 4 (2002): 31–69.

39 For a more detailed description of the Myers Briggs Type Inventory, see Myers, I.B. and McCaulley, M.H., *Manual: A Guide to the Development and Use of the Myers-Briggs Type Indicator*. Palo Alto, CA: Consulting Psychologist Press, 1985 and Briggs Myers, I.S. and Myers, P.B., *Gifts Differing*. Palo Alto, CA: Consulting Psychologist Press, 1980. The foundation of the typology is Jung's work on personality types, Jung, C.G., 'Psychological Factors in Human Behavior, the Structure and Dynamics of the Psyche', *The Collected Works* (Bollingen Series XX). 20 vols. Trans. Hull, R.F.C. (ed.) Read, H., Fordham, M., Adler, G. and McGuire, W. Princeton: Princeton University Press, 1953–79.

40 For a description of the career anchors see Schein, E., *Career Dynamics: Matching Individual and Organizational Needs*. MA: Addison-Wesley, 1978 and 'Career Anchors Revisited: Implications for Career Development in the 21st Century', *Academy of Management Executive*. 10 (1996): 80–8.

41 The Socratic method of conversing and thinking involves location a common-sense statement and then searching for situations or contexts in which the statement would not be true. For a description of Socrates and his conversations see de Botton, A., *The Consolation of Philosophy*, London: Hamish Hamilton, 2000.

42 The word 'dehydrated' is taken from the poet David Whyte's exploration of the soul in the organization, Whyte, D., *The Heart Aroused*. Bantum Double-day Dell, 1994. Like Theodore Zeldin, he sees conversation as being key.

43 Zeldin, T., *Conversation: How Talk Can Change Your Life*. London: The Harvill Press, 1988.

44 I have made this point about reflection time and location as a prerequisite for 'good' conversation in Gratton, L. and Ghoshal, S., 'Improving the quality of conversation', *Organizational Dynamics*: 31 (2003): 209–23.

45 We return to this issue of the conversation that is an important part of the leadership philosophy of BP's CEO, John Browne. For a more detailed description see the case, *The Transformation of BP*, prepared by Michelle Rogan, Lynda Gratton and Sumantra Ghoshal, London Business School, 2001.

46 This issue of understanding choice and the consequences of action has been described by Argyris, C. in *Reasoning, Learning and Action: Individual and Organizational*. San Francisco: Jossey Bass, 1982.

47 The processs that support consumer insight are very similar to those that will be developed to create employee insight. For an overview of consumer insight, see e.g. Gilmore, J. and Pine, B.J., *Markets of One: Creating Customer-Unique Value through Mass Customization*. Boston: Harvard Business School Press, 1988.

48 For a description of the career anchors see Schein, E., *Career Dynamics: Matching Individual and Organizational Needs*. MA: Addison-Wesley, 1978.

49 The description of Tesco was drawn from interviews with members of the management team.

50 The strategic positioning of the firm has been described by CEO, David Reid, in, 'Taking Tesco Global', *McKinsey Quarterly*, No. 3, 2002.

51 I should note here that these data are specific to the population at Tesco. Other research has shown that while the drivers of commitment remain essentially similar, there is relative ranking change according to the demography of the workforce.

Chapter six

1 It has long been acknowledged that stretching and challenging job assignments are the primary mechanisms by which competencies are developed. For an overview of this, see Kolb, D.A., *Experiential Learning: Experience as the Source of Learning and Development*. Englewood Cliffs, NJ: Prentice Hall, 1984.

2 This type of restriction on the internal labour market has been demonstrated in many studies of career development in organizations. See for example, Gunz, H.P., *Career and Corporate Cultures: Managerial Mobility in Large Corporations*, Oxford: Basil Blackwell, 1989.

3 This description of BP is based on the case, *The Transformation of BP*, prepared by Michelle Rogan, Lynda Gratton and Sumantra Ghoshal, London Business School, 2001.

4 For a fuller description of how competency profiles can be created, see Boyatzis, R. *The Competent Manager: A Model For Effective Performance*. New York: John Wiley, 1982.

5 As organizations increasingly become 'virtual' and 'boundaryless', so the emphasis on development through short-term projects increases. For a deeper analysis of this see Arthur, M.B. and Rousseau, D.M., (eds), *The Boundaryless Career: A New Employment Principle for a New Organizational Era*. New York: Oxford University Press, 1996.

6 This case was developed through interviews with members of McKinsey. It was also informed by Bartlett, C., *McKinsey and Co.: Managing Knowledge and Learning*. Harvard Business School Case, 1996.

7 These insights came from a series of presentations by Rajat Gupta to alumni and students at London Business School during 2002.

8 The framing of jobs in this way was developed by Rosemary Stewart. See *Managers and their Jobs*. London: Macmillan, 1967; and *Choices for the Manager*. New York: Prentice Hall, 1982; and 'A Model for Understanding Managerial Jobs and Behavior. *Academy of Management Review*. 7 (1982): 7–13, and Fondas, N. and Stewart, R., 'Enactment in Managerial Jobs: A Role Analysis. *Journal of Management Studies*, 31 (1994): 84–103.

9 There has been a long history in psychology of research which has focused on self-determination and autonomy. For a review see Ryan, R.M. and Deci, E.L., 'Self Determination Theory and Facilitation of Intrinsic Motivation, Social Development, and Well Being', *American Psychologist*, 1 (2000): 69–78.

10 Empowerment experiments can be short lived particularly if the end goal is not clear.

11 The description of Sony is based on the cases *Sony-Regeneration (A and B)* prepared by Tomohiro Kida and Hidehiko Yamaguchi, under the supervision of Sumantra Ghoshal, London Business School. August 2002, LBS reference LBS-CS97-000-00.

12 Studies have shown that in relationship to job empowerment, role ambiguity has the strongest negative relationship to empowerment. Lack of clarity or overly flexible goals creates uncertainty and ambiguity, so making it more difficult for people to feel confident about the independent decisions they are called to make. Spreitzer, G.M., 'Social Structural Characteristics of Psychological Empowerment', *Academy of Management Journal*, 39 (1996): 460–83. The same study shows that higher levels of education are critical for enhancing empowerment, particularly in terms of providing skills and abilities individuals need to feel competent and able to develop mastery.

13 For a description of the importance of a vision in self-determination, see Quinn, R.E. and Spreitzer, G.M., 'The Road to Empowerment: Seven Questions Every Leader Should Consider', *Organizational Dynamics*, 26 (1999): 37–49.

14 Simons, R., 'Control in an Age of Empowerment', *Harvard Business Review*, 3 (1995): 80–8. This explores the levers of control: diagnostic control systems, belief systems, boundary systems and interactive control systems.

15 For a description of the importance of information in self-determination, see Lawler, E.E., *The Ultimate Advantage*. San Francisco: Jossey-Bass, 1992.

16 These four characteristics are described by Stewart, R., *Managers and their Jobs*, London: Macmillan, 1967 and *Choices for the Manager*. New York: Prentice Hall, 1982.

17 This description of training choice at Unisys was developed through interviews with a number of senior managers, technical associates and members of the training function.

18 This refers to the crucial partnership with Microsoft, where Gold Partner represents the highest level of partnering involvement. These are companies who have a proven commitment and expertise in one or more specialized areas.

19 Peter Drucker first used the term 'flotilla' in one of the early, seminal pieces on the possible implications of mass customization on manufacturing: 'The Emerging Theory of Manufacturing', *Harvard Business Review*, 68 (1990): 94–103.

20 Fitzgerald, C. and Garvey Berger, J. (eds), *Executive Coaching: Practices and Perspectives.* Palo Alto: Davies Black, 2002.

21 For an explanation of mentoring see Levinson *et al.*, *The Seasons of a Man's*

Life, Ballantine, 1986 and Scandura, T.A., 'Mentoring and Career Mobility: An Empirical Investigation', *Journal of Organizational Behavior,* 13 (1992): 169–74.

22 This case is drawn from interviews and public documentation, in particular Endlich, L., *Goldman Sachs: The Culture of Success.* New York: Knopf, 1999.

23 For an overview of the nature of tacit knowledge, see Polanyi, M., *The Tacit Dimension.* Garden City, NY: Doubleday Books, 1967.

24 Perception of the fairness of rewards have been described by Cooper, C.L., Dyck B. and Frolich, N., 'Improving the Effectiveness of Gain Sharing. The Role of Fairness and Participation', *Administrative Science Quarterly,* 37 (1992): 471–90.

25 The AstraZeneca case was created for interviews with members of the senior team, the consulting group advising the company and through the analysis of company documentation.

26 We will return to the concept of 'tinkering' and experimentation. For a description of some of the processes, see Brown, S.L. and Eisenhardt, K.M., *Competing on the Edge: Strategy as Structured Chaos.* Boston, MA: Harvard Business School Press, 1998.

27 This 'double loop' echoes the learning cycle that is at the centre of the development of the autonomous individual. See Argyris, C. and Schon, D., *Organizational Learning: A Theory of Action Perspective.* Reading, MA: Addison-Wesley, 1978.

28 This rapid learning curve has been predicated and observed in situations when people are able to exercise choice. See, for example, Deci, E.L., *Intrinsic Motivation,* New York: Plenum Press, 1975.

29 There is research which examines the impact of time and location choice on the individual's sense of meaning and their capacity to live in an emotionally balanced manner, see e.g. Clark, S.C., 'Work Culture and Work Life Balance', *Journal of Vocational Behavior,* 58 (2001): 348–65. In this study flexibility was seen to be associated with increased work satisfaction and increased family well-being.

30 The negative effect of lack of flexibility has been well documented, see e.g. Evans, P. and Bartolome, J.F., *Must Success Cost So Much?* London: Grant McKintyre, 1980 and Scase, R. and Goffee, R., *Reluctant Managers.* London: Routledge, 1989.

31 This information was taken through extensive interviews with managers and those people who are working flexibly at BT.

32 There is a growing body of evidence to suggest that the experiences of BT are mirrored in many other organizations. The Catalyst Studies reports that

80% of participants reported increases in morale for individuals working part-time or telecommuting; 46% reported productivity gains; 48% reported increased commitment (*A New Approach to Flexibility: Managing the Work/Time Equation,* New York: Catalyst, 2000).

33 The information for this description was based on interviews with senior managers and those engaged in time choice and from the case prepared for the Leading Edge Research Consortium at London Business School.

34 For a description of the HP culture, see Packard, D., *The HP Way: How Bill Hewlett and I Built Our Company.* New York: HarperCollins, 1996.

35 This notion of the 'terrain of sacrifice' is taken for mass customization of services and goods. For a detailed description of this see Pine, B.J., Pepper, D. and Rogers, M., 'Do You Want to Keep your Customers For Ever?', *Harvard Business Review,* 73 (1995): 103–14.

36 The emerging science of self-organizing systems can bring some interesting insights into the ways of thinking about the Democratic Enterprise. For an overview of some of the key issues see Axelrod, R. and Cohen, M.D., *Harnessing Complexity: Organizational Implications of the Scientific Frontier.* New York: Free Press, 1999 and Waldrop, M.M., *Complexity: The Emerging Science at the Edge of Order and Chaos.* New York: Touchstone, 1992.

37 For a description of the concept of 'tinkering' see Brown, S.L. and Eisenhardt, K.M., *Competing on the Edge: Strategy as Structured Chaos.* Boston, MA: Harvard Business School Press, 1998.

38 These are the key elements of self-organizing systems. Wheatley, M.J. and Kellner-Rogers, M., *A Simpler Way.* San Francisco: Berrett Koehler, 1996.

Chapter seven

1 Spreitzer, G.M., 'Social Structural Characteristics of Psychological Empowerment', *Academy of Management Journal,* 39 (1996): 483–505.

2 The personal 'dream' can be a powerful focus for action. The case for the volitional energy of the 'dream' is made by Bruch, H. and Ghoshal, S. in *Building a Bias for Action.* Boston, MA: Harvard Business School Press (in press).

3 The goal of the company can also be a powerful focus to unite people. See e.g. Morrison, E.W. and Phelps, C.C., Taking Charge at Work: Extrarole Efforts to Initiate Workplace Change', *Academy of Management Review,* 42 (1999): 403–19.

4 Relaxation of control in favour of autonomy requires trust and clarity of end-state, the general expectation that employees will exercise discretion in 'responsible' ways. Simons, R., 'Control in the Age of Empowerment', *Harvard Business Review*, 73 (1995): 80–8.

5 Packard, D., *The HP Way: How Bill Hewlett and I Built Our Company.* New York: HarperCollins, 1996.

6 For a more detailed description of the goal setting and monitoring at HP, see Gratton, L., Hope-Hailey,V., Stiles, P. and Truss, C., *Human Resource Management: Corporate Rhetoric and Human Reality*, Oxford: Oxford University Press, 1999 and Gratton, L., Hope-Hailey, V., Stiles, P., Truss, C. and Zaleska, J., *A Decade of Transformation at the Leading Edge*, Oxford: Oxford University Press (in press).

7 This quote comes from the 1994 HP Report for the Leading Edge Research Consortium at London Business School.

8 For a deeper insight into obligations and accountabilities, see Cleman, J.S., *Foundations of Social Theory.* Cambridge, MA: The Belknap Press of Harvard University Press, 1990; Fairclough, G., *Creative Compartments: A Design for Future Organization.* London: Adamantine Press, 1994; and Bourdieu, P., *Sociology in Question.* London: Sage Publications, 1993.

9 Rajat Gupta, presentation to the MBA class at London Business School, 2002.

10 This description of Jessica Spungin is taken from interviews with Sumantra Ghoshal which formed the basis of Chapter 3: Developing Focus: The story of Jessica Spungin, in Bruch, H. and Ghoshal, S. *Building a Bias for Action.* Boston, MA: Harvard Business School Press (in press).

11 Rousseau, D.M., *Psychological Contracts in Organizations.* Thousand Oaks, CA: Sage, 1995.

12 Anthony Giddens makes this point in the context of modern relationship, but the framing can be usefully brought to the relationship between the employee, their colleagues and the organization. *The Transformation of Intimacy: Sexuality, Love and Eroticism in Modern Societies.* Stanford: Stanford University Press, 1992.

13 The impact of performance management practices on the creation and support of a context of trust has been described by Judge, T.A. and Ferris, G.R., 'Social Context of Performance Evaluation Decisions', *Academy of Management Journal.* 36 (1993): 80–105 and by Cooper, C.L., Dyck, B. and Frolich, N., 'Improving the Effectiveness of Gain Sharing. The Role of Fairness and Participation', *Administrative Science Quarterly.* 37 (1992): 471–90.

14 Taylor, S.M., Tracey, K.B., Renard, M.K., Harrison, J.K. and Carroll,

S.J., 'Due Process in Performance Appraisal: A Quasi-Experiment in Proce-dural Justice', *Administrative Science Quarterly*, 40 (1995): 495–524.

15 The opportunity to have one's voice heard is crucial to the development of trust, as indeed is the opportunity to receive rich and meaningful informa-tion. Cropanzano, R., *Justice in the Workplace: Approaching Fairness in Human Resource Management*. Hillsdale, NJ: Lawrence Erlbaum, 1993.

16 The dignity of treatment form an important plank in the development of trust. See Bies, R.J. and Moag, J.S., 'Interactional Justice: Communication Criteria and Fairness', *Research in Negotiations in Organizations*, 1 (1986): 45–53.

17 For an overview of the impact of power on the development of trust, see Pfeffer, J., 'Understanding power in organizations', *Californian Management Review*, 35 (1992): 29–50.

18 The relationship between trust and obligations is explored by Powell who argues that concepts of trust often miss the extent to which co-operation is buttressed by sustained contact and obligations. Powell, W.W., 'Trust Based Form of Governance', in Kramer, R.M. and Tyler, T.R., (eds), *Trust in Orga-nizations: Frontiers of Theory and Research*. Thousand Oaks, CA: Sage, 1996.

19 The impact of power on an individual's sense of mastery has been described by Hardy, C. and Leiba-O'Sullivan, S., 'The Power Behind Empowerment: Implications for Research and Practice, *Human Relations*, 6 (1998): 451–83.

20 For an overview of the workings of the internal labour market, see Miner, A.S., 'Organizational Evolution and the Social Ecology of Jobs', in Cohen, M.D. and Sproull, R.S. (eds), *Organizational Learning*. Thousand Oaks, CA: Sage, 1991.

21 Barbara Townley, *Reframing Human Resource Management: Power, Ethics and the Subject at Work*. Thousand Oaks, CA: Sage, 1994.

Chapter eight

1 John Lloyd, *Company Law. The Business Financial Times Weekend Magazine*, 9 September 2000.

2 The quote is taken from *The Transformation of BP*, prepared by Michelle Rogan, Lynda Gratton and Sumantra Ghoshal, London Business School, 2001.

3 This information is drawn from interviews and public documentation, in particular Endlich, L., *Goldman Sachs: The Culture of Success*. New York: Knopf, 1999.

4 See *Sony: Regeneration (A and B),* cases prepared by Tomohiro Kida and Hidehiko Yamaguchi under the supervision of Sumantra Ghoshal, London Business School, 2002.

Chapter nine

1 In the democracy study HP and Kraft Foods were the most democratic companies in the study. HP has remained in the top three performing companies in the sector during the period of the study. With regard to ROCE and profit per employee, only Compaq outperformed HP in the period up to 1997 and only Fujitsu outperformed it from 1997 onwards. With regard to return on total assets, from the period of 1993 until 1999 HP had consistently the highest ROTA of its peer group. The financial data also show that for Kraft Foods between 1990 and 1992 the company was between 10% and 20% more successful than its competitors, between 1992 and 1995 it performed on par with its competitors and from 1995 to 1999 it exceeded the performance of its competitors. During this period of time ROE was between 10% and 25% higher; total return was between 3% and 12% higher, and profit per employee was between 14% and 27% higher.

2 For an overview of this research, see Cropanzano, R., *Justice in the Workplace: Approaching Fairness in Human Resource Management.* Hillsdale, NJ: Lawrence Erlbaum, 1993.

3 Cooper, C.L., Dyck B. and Frolich, N., 'Improving the Effectiveness of Gain Sharing. The Role of Fairness and Participation. *Administrative Science Quarterly,* 37 (1992): 471–90.

4 The importance of interactive justice to commitment and engagement has been described by Bies, R.J. and Moag, J.S., 'Interactional Justice: Communication Criteria and Fairness', *Research in Negotiations in Organizations,* 1 (1986): 45–53.

5 This point is made by Rousseau, D.M., 'The Idiosyncratic Deal: Flexibility versus Fairness?', *Organizational Dynamics,* 29 (2001): 260–306.

6 The idea of 'small wins' is seen as a central plank in the innovative, flexible company described by Brown, S.L. and Eisenhardt, K.M., *Competing on the Edge: Strategy as Structured Chaos.* Boston, MA: Harvard Business School Press, 1998.

7 March, J.G., 'Exploration and Exploitation in Organizational Learning', *Organizational Science,* 2 (1991): 71–81.

8 This is drawn from the metaphors of self-organizing systems. For a rich

description of the role of agents, see Axelrod, R. and Cohen, M.D., *Harnessing Complexity: Organizational Implications of the Scientific Frontier.* New York: Free Press, 1999.

9 The common platforms of IT and managerial practices are key to rapid integration. See Ghoshal, S. and Gratton, L., 'Integrating the Enterprise', *Sloan Management Review*, 44 (2002): 31–8.

Index